ACKNOWLEDGEMENT

My thanks are due to British Leyland Motor Corporation Ltd. for their unstinted co-operation and also for supplying data and illustrations.

I am also grateful to a considerable number of owners who have discussed their cars at length and many of whose suggestions have been included in this manual.

Kenneth Ball
Associate Member, Guild of Motoring Writers
Ditchling Sussex England.

[BRITISH LEYLAND]

Austin Morris 1800 1964-74 Autobook

By Kenneth Ball

Associate Member, Guild of Motoring Writers
and the Autopress Team of Technical Writers.

Austin 1800 Mk 1, 2, 3 1964-74
Austin 1800 S 1969-72
Morris 1800 Mk 1, 2, 3 1966-74
Morris 1800 S 1968-72
Wolseley 18/85 Mk 1, 2 1967-72
Wolseley 18/85 S 1969-72

Autobooks

Autopress Ltd. Golden Lane Brighton BN1 2QJ England

The AUTOBOOK series of Workshop Manuals is the largest in the world and covers the majority of British and Continental motor cars, as well as all major Japanese and Australian models. For a full list see the back of this manual.

CONTENTS

ISBN 0 85147 502 7

First Edition   1969
Second Edition, fully revised   1970
Reprinted   1971
Third Edition, fully revised   1971
Fourth Edition, fully revised   1973
Fifth Edition, fully revised   1974

790

Printed and bound in Brighton England for Autopress Ltd by G Beard & Son Ltd   B

INTRODUCTION

This do-it-yourself Workshop Manual has been specially written for the owner who wishes to maintain his car in first class condition and to carry out his own servicing and repairs. Considerable savings on garage charges can be made, and one can drive in safety and confidence knowing the work has been done properly.

Comprehensive step-by-step instructions and illustrations are given on all dismantling, overhauling and assembling operations. Certain assemblies require the use of expensive special tools, the purchase of which would be unjustified. In these cases information is included but the reader is recommended to hand the unit to the agent for attention.

Throughout the Manual hints and tips are included which will be found invaluable, and there is an easy to follow fault diagnosis at the end of each chapter.

Whilst every care has been taken to ensure correctness of information it is obviously not possible to guarantee complete freedom from errors or to accept liability arising from such errors or omissions.

Instructions may refer to the righthand or lefthand sides of the vehicle or the components. These are the same as the righthand or lefthand of an observer standing behind the car and looking forward.

CHAPTER 1

THE ENGINE

1:1 General description

Although the engine is combined with the transmission system, this chapter will deal with those operations which, apart from the removal of the complete unit from the car, concern the engine only.

The usual British Leyland features of engine design are again quite distinctive in all the models, and the following description will apply to Austin, Morris and Wolseley cars.

The engine is in unit construction with a four-speed manual gearbox or a Borg Warner automatic transmission. With the manual gearbox the transmission casing also forms the sump, the same oil being used to lubricate the engine and the transmission. With automatic transmission there are two separate lubricating systems. Power output from the engine to the manual gearbox is by gears. In the case of automatic transmission the crankshaft and torque converter are connected to the transmission by an inverted-tooth chain.

The engine capacity is 1798cc (109.75 cu in). Bore, stroke and compression ratios are given in **Technical Data**, together with full coverage of additional technical information. There are four cylinders, and a five-bearing crankshaft running in renewable bearing shells.

The pushrod-operated valves are set vertically in the detachable head. The camshaft runs in three plain white-metal bearing bushes and is chain-driven. A chain tensioner is fitted. These, and other internal parts may be seen in **FIG 1:1**. A camshaft gear drives the vertical oil pump and also drives a transverse shaft for the distributor.

On Mk 1 engines the connecting rod big-ends are split at an angle and the small-end is bushed for a floating gudgeon pin. Mk 2 connecting rods are split horizontally and the gudgeon pin is a press-fit in the small-end (see **FIG 1:15**). The big-ends are fitted with renewable bearing shells. Mk 1 pistons have three compression rings and one oil control ring, but the compression rings are reduced to two on Mk 2 engines.

The oil pump draws oil from a strainer in the sump and delivers it to a fullflow filter. From the filter, passages lead the oil to the main, big-end and camshaft bearings, and from one of the camshaft bearings to the rocker gear. From

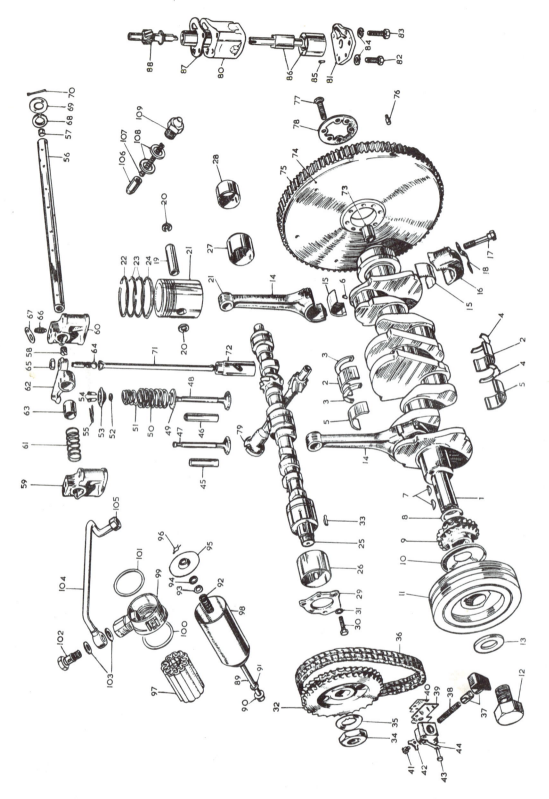

FIG 1:1   Internal components and external oil filter for 1800 Mk 1 engine. Parts are similar for Mk 2 and Mk 2S engines except for piston and connecting rod assembly

Key to Fig 1:1 1 Crankshaft 2 Crankshaft main bearing (Nos 1, 3 and 5) 3 Upper thrust washer 4 Lower thrust washer 5 Crankshaft main bearing (Nos 2 and 4) 6 Oil restrictor 7 Key 8 Gear packing washer(s) 9 Timing gear 10 Oil thrower (first type illustrated) 11 Pulley 12 Nut for crankshaft 13 Locking washer 14 Connecting rod 15 Big-end bearing 16 Big-end bearing cap 17 Setscrew 18 Tabwasher 19 Gudgeon pin 20 Circlip 21 Piston 22 Top compression ring 23 Second and third compression ring 24 Scraper ring 25 Camshaft 26 Front camshaft bearing liner 27 Centre camshaft bearing liner 28 Rear camshaft bearing liner 29 Locking plate 30 Screw 31 Shakeproof washer 32 Timing gear 33 Key 34 Nut 35 Locking washer 36 Timing chain 37 Slipper head and cylinder 38 Spring 39 Body backplate 40 Joint 41 Plug for body 42 Lockwasher 43 Bolt 44 Lockwasher 45 Exhaust valve guide 46 Inlet valve guide* 47 Exhaust valve* 48 Inlet valve* 49 Valve spring collar 50 Outer valve spring* 51 Inner valve spring* 52 Packing ring 53 Spring cap 54 Valve cotters* 55 Circlip for cotter* 56 Valve rocker shaft 57 Plain plug 58 Screwed plug 59 Bracket with tapped hole 60 Plain bracket 61 Spring 62 Valve rocker 63 Rocker bush 64 Adjusting screw 65 Locknut 66 Locking screw 67 Screw locating plate 68 Spring washer (D/C) 69 Washer 70 Splitpin 71 Pushrod 72 Tappet 73 Clutch shaft bush 74 Flywheel 75 Starter ring 76 Dowel for clutch 77 Bolt 78 Locking plate 79 Distributor drive spindle 80 Oil pump body 81 Cover 82 Short screw 83 Long screw 84 Spring washer 85 Dowel 86 Shaft with rotors 87 Joint 88 Driving spindle 89 Centre bolt 90 Washer 91 Sealing washer 92 Spring 93 Steel washer 94 Felt washer 95 Pressure plate 96 Circlip 97 Element 98 Container 99 Oil filter head assembly 100 Joint washer 101 Joint washer 102 Screw for banjo union 103 Washer 104 Oil pipe 105 Nut 106 Oil relief valve 107 Spring 108 Washer(s) 109 Cup nut *First type valve assembly

the rockers, oil drains down the pushrod holes to lubricate the bucket-type tappets. A relief valve near the pump restricts oil pressure to a safe maximum when the oil is cold and thick. A valve in the filter head allows oil to bypass a clogged filter element.

1:2 Routine maintenance

Engine lubrication:

If required, top-up with recommended oil to the 'MAX' mark on the dipstick. To change the oil every 6000 miles (10,000 km) or 6 months, remove drain plug from right-hand rear of casing (manual transmission). On cars with automatic transmission the engine drain plug is below the crankshaft pulley, between the engine oil cover and casing extension. Correct quantities of fresh oil required are given under 'Capacities' in **Technical Data**. Clean plug and refit, tightening to 40 to 50 lb ft (5.5 to 6.9 kg m). After refilling, run engine if filter has been renewed. Stop engine and leave for five minutes, then check dipstick.

Renewing filter element:

Do this every 6000 miles (10,000 km) or 6 months. The filter is low down near the starter. Parts are shown in **FIG 1:1**. Unscrew bolt 89, hold casing upright when released and tip out old oil. Throw away element 97. Clean inside casing with fuel, dry it and fit new element, after ensuring that felt washer 94 is between items 93 and 95. Joint washer 100 must be serviceable and not displaced. Fit casing and tighten bolt, checking that casing seats correctly on seal. **Start engine and check for leaks at once.** Check dipstick, and top-up.

Adjusting rocker clearance:

This operation is covered in **Section 1:4**.

1:3 Servicing cylinder head

This can be done with the engine in the car.

Removing:

1 Drain cooling system and remove top hose. Remove thermostat and housing (extreme left in **FIG 1:4**). Remove air cleaner and carburetter(s) as described in **Chapter 2**.
2 Release distributor suction pipe, brake vacuum hose, breather control valve (see **FIG 1:19**) and heater pipe (if fitted). Remove clamp securing exhaust pipe to manifold (Mk 1). Separate the manifold pipes from bracket and front exhaust pipe (Mk 2S).
3 Release manifold from head (six nuts and washers). Remove rocker cover (two nuts). Take care of washers, rubber seals and cork gasket. Unscrew (a turn at a time) the rocker bracket nuts and the cylinder head nuts shown in **FIG 1:4**. Take care of locating plate 67 in **FIG 1:1**. **Always drain cooling system if rocker assembly is to be removed, because four rocker bracket nuts also secure the head and all head fixings must be unscrewed evenly together to avoid distortion.**
4 Lift off rocker assembly. Withdraw pushrods, storing them in correct order. Remove sparking plugs. Disconnect heater hoses. Unscrew temperature transmitter from front end and release cable. Lever head free at one end and lift up squarely.

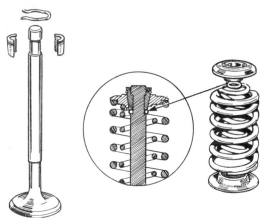

FIG 1:2 Valve parts, showing correct position of oil seal packing ring at bottom of cotter groove (centre)

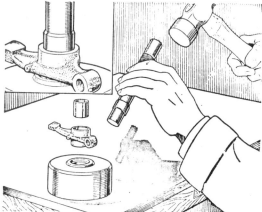

FIG 1:3 Removing and fitting rocker bushes with drift and anvil 18G.226

Decarbonizing:

Scrape carbon from chambers before removing valves. Refer to **FIG 1:1**. Remove clips 55, compress valve springs with suitable compressor and remove cotters 54, cap 53, seal 52, springs 50 and 51 and collar 49. Remove valves, storing them in correct order for reassembly.

Clean ports and valve heads and check seats, stems and guides 45 and 46. Correct clearance of stems in guides is given in **Technical Data**. To renew guides, drive downwards into combustion space. Use a hardened steel punch $\frac{9}{16}$ inch (14 mm) in diameter and 4 inches (102 mm) long. One end must be turned down for one inch (25 mm) to a diameter of $\frac{5}{16}$ inch (7.9 mm) to engage guide bore.

Press in new guides from top of head, inlets with larger chamfer at top and exhausts with counterbore at bottom. Inlet guides must project $\frac{3}{4}$ inch (19 mm) and exhaust guides $\frac{5}{8}$ inch (15.8 mm) above valve spring seat in head.

Deeply pitted valve faces must be reground at a garage, or the valve renewed. Badly worn or pitted head seats may be recut. If seats are too far gone, seat inserts may be fitted by a service station. Note that inserts cannot be fitted to engines with the prefix 18H.

To grind-in valves, smear a little fine or medium-grade grinding paste on the face, put a light spring under the head, fit the valve and use a suction-cup tool stuck to the valve head. Grind with a semi-rotating motion and let the valve rise by spring pressure occasionally. When both seatings are a smooth matt grey, clean off all traces of grinding paste from head and valves.

Check springs against free length given in **Technical Data** and renew if necessary. Always renew packing rings 52. **Do not fit old rings or oil sealing may be ineffective.** Soak new rings in engine oil to soften them. Refit valves in reverse order of dismantling, giving stems a light smear of oil. With springs compressed, push packing ring down to bottom of cotter groove as shown in **FIG 1:2**, fit cotters, release compressor and fit circlip. Press down on valve stem to check that all is well.

Although not a part of cylinder head servicing, decarbonizing must also include attention to the piston crowns. Remove head gasket and plug water holes with rag. Use blunt tool to scrape carbon from piston crowns and block face, but do not remove carbon ring at top of each bore. Leave a ring of carbon round outer edge of each piston. An old piston ring positioned on the crown will enable this to be done. Blow off all carbon dust and clean with a fuel-soaked rag.

Servicing rocker gear:

Remove grubscrew 66 and splitpins 70 (see **FIG 1:1**). Slide parts off shaft, taking care to store in correct order, or mark them if desired. Clean shaft bore by removing plug 58. Clean parts and check for wear. Shaft will wear on underside. Clearance of rocker bush on shaft must not exceed .002 inch (.051 mm). Reface rocker tip or renew rocker if tip is badly worn. Check adjusting screws 64 for wear of ball-end.

Renew rocker bushes by driving out old ones as shown top left in **FIG 1:3**. Oil holes may be drilled before or after fitting. If before, ensure correct positioning, with butt joint in bush at top and oil groove at bottom. Drive bush into place and burnish ream to size given in **Technical Data**. If oil holes are drilled after fitting bush, use a No. 47 drill (.0785 inch or 1.98 mm) for the top hole. Drill out the plug at the adjuster end of the rocker and continue the hole through the bush, using a .093 inch (2.36 mm) drill. Plug the outer end of the hole with a welded rivet. Ream as before.

Reassemble in reverse order, placing parts in their original positions. Use new splitpins, and oil running surfaces. Tighten locking grubscrew. Refit end plug in shaft.

Refitting head:

Cylinder block and head faces must be clean. Proceed as follows:

1 Fit new gasket. It is marked 'TOP' and 'FRONT'. Lower head into place. Refit vacuum pipe clip and heater clip and fit the seven external head nuts finger tight.
2 Check pushrods for wear of the ends and check straightness. Refit in correct positions. Oil the cups and then fit the rocker assembly. Nuts must be finger tight.
3 Tighten the 11 head nuts a turn at a time in sequence given in **FIG 1:4**. Torque must be 40 lb ft (5.5 kg m)

up to No. 18AMW/U/H95775, L94704. After this, use figure of 45 to 50 lb ft (6.2 to 6.9 kg m). Use higher torque figure only if studs protrude when a .125 inch (3.2 mm) thick washer is fitted. Finally tighten the four rocker bracket nuts to 25 lb ft (3.4 kg m).

4 Continue assembling in reverse order of dismantling. Switch on ignition and check fuel system for leaks. Run engine up to working temperature and check valve clearances as follows:

1 : 4 Checking valve rocker clearances

Correct clearance figures for various models are given in **Technical Data. Do not depart from these.** Method is shown in **FIG 1 : 5**, clearance being checked with feeler gauge at rocker tip while adjuster screw is turned after locknut is slackened. Press down on adjuster to disperse oil in pushrod cup.

Clearance must be checked with camshaft correctly positioned, so use the following sequence, starting with No. 1 at the water outlet end of the head:

Adjust No. 1 rocker with No. 8 valve fully open
Adjust No. 3 rocker with No. 6 valve fully open
Adjust No. 5 rocker with No. 4 valve fully open
Adjust No. 2 rocker with No. 7 valve fully open
Adjust No. 8 rocker with No. 1 valve fully open
Adjust No. 6 rocker with No. 3 valve fully open
Adjust No. 4 rocker with No. 5 valve fully open
Adjust No. 7 rocker with No. 2 valve fully open

Note that the numbers in each line add up to nine. This facilitates checking. To turn crankshaft, remove plugs and pull on fan belt or engage top gear and move car.

1 : 5 Servicing tappets

These are part 72 in **FIG 1 : 1**. They may be removed with the engine in situ. Remove carburetter(s) and rocker cover. Remove manifolds (see **Section 1 : 3**). Remove rocker assembly and pushrods as in same Section. Remove tappet covers from side of cylinder block and lift out tappets, keeping them in correct position for reassembling. Check for wear of barrel, inner cup and cam contact face. Lubricate when refitting. New tappets must be fitted by selective assembly so that they just fall in their guides when oiled.

Refit in reverse order, taking care that cover gaskets are sound. See **Technical Data** for torque on cover screws. Adjust rocker clearance as in **Section 1 : 4**.

1 : 6 The distributor driving spindle

This is part 79 in **FIG 1 : 1**. Remove it as follows:

1 Remove distributor (see **Chapter 3**). Remove screw and withdraw distributor housing. **Do not disturb distributor clamp plate.**

2 Drive spindle is threaded internally. Screw in a $\frac{5}{16}$ inch UNF bolt that is $3\frac{1}{2}$ inch (90 mm) long. With No. 1 piston halfway up bore, withdraw spindle. Pistons are numbered from fan end of engine.

3 Check spindle driving slot, gear teeth and spigot bearing for wear.

Refitting:

With No. 1 piston in same position, refit spindle. Turn crankshaft until the piston is at TDC on the compression stroke. The valves of No. 4 cylinder will then be just

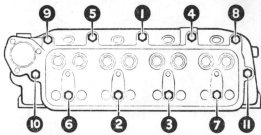

FIG 1 : 4   Correct sequence for slackening and tightening cylinder head nuts

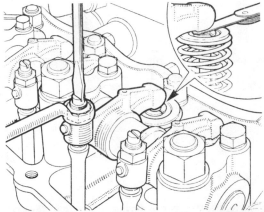

FIG 1 : 5   Adjusting valve rocker clearance. Inset shows feeler gauge between rocker tip and top of valve stem

'rocking', the exhaust just closing and the inlet just opening. With piston No. 1 at TDC, the groove on the crankshaft pulley will line up with the long pointer on the timing cover (see 2 in upper view of **FIG 1 : 6** for early engines). Position 1 is for later engines with the indicator above the pulley.

Withdraw spindle enough to clear the camshaft gear and turn it until the slot is just below the horizontal with the large offset uppermost. As spindle gear is re-engaged the slot turns anticlockwise until it is at approximately two o'clock. Remove bolt and refit distributor housing. Secure housing with correct bolt and washer, as bolt head must not protrude. Refit distributor. If clamp plate has been disturbed, refer to **Chapter 3** for details of ignition timing.

1 : 7 Servicing timing gear

It is possible to do this with the engine in situ. Refer to **FIG 1 : 1** for internal parts. Dismantle as follows:

1 Drain cooling system and remove radiator (see **Chapter 4**). Slacken generator bolts and remove belt. Flatten tab of lockwasher 13 and remove pulley nut 12 with a 'shock' spanner such as tool 18G.98A. Use a puller to withdraw the pulley.

2 Remove timing cover (9 bolts, plain and shakeproof washers).

3 Remove plug 41 from chain tensioner, insert $\frac{1}{8}$ inch (3.2 mm) Allen key and turn it clockwise to retract and lock slipper head 37. Remove tensioner (bolts 43), and backplate 39.

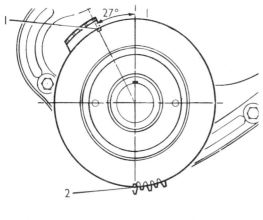

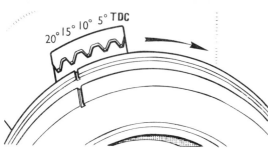

FIG 1:6 Relationship of timing groove to pulley keyway (top). Indicator above pulley (1). Indicator below pulley (2). Lower view shows later type of indicator with pulley groove indicating pistons 1 and 4 are at 15 deg. BTDC

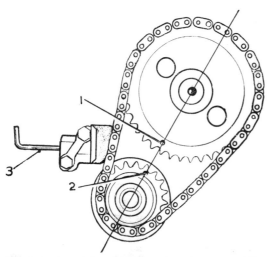

FIG 1:7 Set timing dimples 1 and 2 in line before removing or refitting chain and sprockets. Retract tensioner by turning Allen key 3 clockwise

4 Unlock and remove camshaft nut 34. Note locating tag on lockwasher. Using small levers, ease the camshaft sprocket 32 and crankshaft sprocket 9 simultaneously forward until clear. Take careful note of packing washer(s) 8. Check sprockets and chain for wear. It is best to renew both sprockets and chain if wear is considerable.

Servicing chain tensioner:

Dismantle by withdrawing slipper head and then inserting the Allen key, as used when removing tensioner. Turn key clockwise, holding key and plunger securely until cylinder and spring are released. Clean parts in fuel and use compressed air on oil holes in slipper and spigot.

Bore must not be more than .003 inch (.076 mm) oval near the mouth. Renew tensioner if wear is unacceptable. If satisfactory, a new slipper head and cylinder may be fitted in an existing body bore.

Reassemble by inserting spring in slipper bore and fitting cylinder to other end of spring. Compress until cylinder enters plunger bore with helical slot engaged with peg. Hold firmly and fit Allen key. Turn cylinder clockwise until end of cylinder is below peg, with spring held compressed. Remove key and insert assembly in body Fit backplate and joint and secure tensioner to block. Check that slipper head is free and does not bind on backplate. Release tensioner after chain is refitted as follows:

Reassembling timing gear:

1 If original sprockets are fitted, replace washers 8 on crankshaft. If sprockets are renewed, refit without chain and press a straightedge against the camshaft sprocket face so that its end lies adjacent to the crankshaft sprocket teeth. Measure gap between straightedge and crankshaft sprocket. Subtract .005 inch (.13 mm) from feeler gauge thickness and fit resultant thickness of packing washers to crankshaft.

2 Fit sprockets and chain with crankshaft keyway at TDC and camshaft keyway at about one o'clock looking from the front. With the two timing marks on the sprockets in the position shown in **FIG 1:7** at 1 and 2, press the crankshaft gear on to its key and turn the camshaft until the camshaft sprocket will engage its key. Push sprockets home and tighten and lock the camshaft sprocket. Make sure lockwasher tab engages in camshaft keyway.

3 On early engines, fit concave side of oil thrower 10 away from engine. Throwers are also stamped 'F' for front. Now release the chain tensioner by inserting the Allen key (see 3 in **FIG 1:7**) and turning it clockwise until the slipper head moves against the chain by spring pressure. **Do not turn anticlockwise, or use force.** Secure bolts with lockplate, refit bottom plug and lock with tabwasher.

Refitting timing cover:

Early type:

This must be used with the early-type oil thrower 10. Check oil seal for crankshaft and renew if leakage has been apparent. Press in a new seal with tools 18G.134 and 18G.134.BD. Fit a new gasket, grease lips of seal and then fit the cover. The oil seal must be centralized with tool 18G.3 before the cover screws are tightened evenly.

Later type:

Fit thrower with face marked 'F' away from engine. Fit a new oil seal as just described. Grease lips of seal and fit cover, centralizing it with tool 18G.1046. Taking care not to strain seal, refit cover screws and tighten evenly.

Refitting pulley:

A new cover may have the timing indicator on top as shown in the lower view of **FIG 1 : 6**. If an old pulley is being refitted and it is notched for the indicator shown at 2 in the upper view, obliterate the notch and cut a new one in the position shown at 1.

Oil pulley hub, refit the crankshaft, fit nut and lock-washer and tighten to 70 lb ft (9.6 kg m).

1 : 8 Removing power unit

The preceding operations may be carried out with the engine in the car. To work on the crankshaft, camshaft, oil pump, connecting rods and pistons it is necessary to remove the power unit by lifting upwards. Before tackling this it is advisable to read the earlier part of **Hints on Maintenance and Overhaul** at the end of this manual. This is essential in the interests of safety.

Removing (manual gearbox):

1 Drain engine and cooling systems. Scribe round hinge fixings and remove bonnet. Disconnect leads and remove battery, tray and support shelf.
2 Disconnect all fuel pipes, cables and wires that will prevent removal of unit. Remove starter solenoid from crossmember and disconnect cable from starter.
3 Disconnect radiator spill hose, heater hose (if fitted) and brake vacuum hose from servo. Remove adaptor and air cleaner complete (Mk 1). Release exhaust pipe from manifold (see **Section 1 : 3**). Remove horn(s) and bracket(s). Remove inlet and exhaust manifolds (Mk 2 and 2S).
4 Fit lifting brackets to rocker cover bolts and to second and fourth righthand cylinder head studs. Take weight of engine on rocker cover brackets. Remove engine damper top bolt and push damper out of way. Remove bolts from rear mounting rubber, from crossmember to body tube and from grille support. Withdraw crossmember. Release top of grille support and push aside for clearance. Release clutch slave cylinder and tie back out of the way (see **Chapter 5**).
5 Release exhaust pipe bracket from differential housing (Mk 1) and engine steady from transmission casing. With gearlever in neutral, remove six nuts and spring washers from gearchange cable housing. Pull housing steadily back to clear. Release speedometer drive from adaptor on front cover.
6 Remove righthand front engine mounting and nuts and washers securing lefthand mounting to front plate. **Mountings are forward of front plate and outside the body brackets.** Release upper tie rod (Mk 2S). Lift engine slightly and remove U-bolts from drive flanges and couplings. Leave couplings on drive shafts. Push drive flanges into their housings and pull couplings clear.

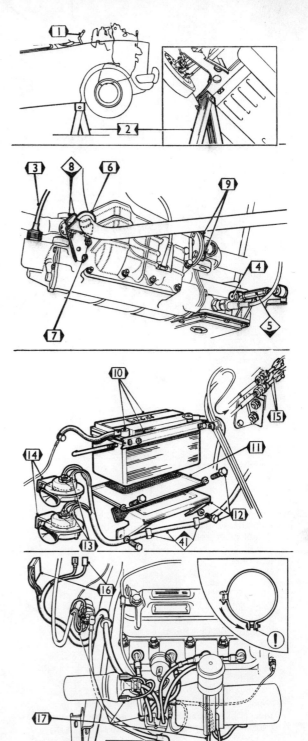

FIG 1 : 8 Removing and refitting engine and transmission unit (automatic transmission). Text refers to numbered sequences

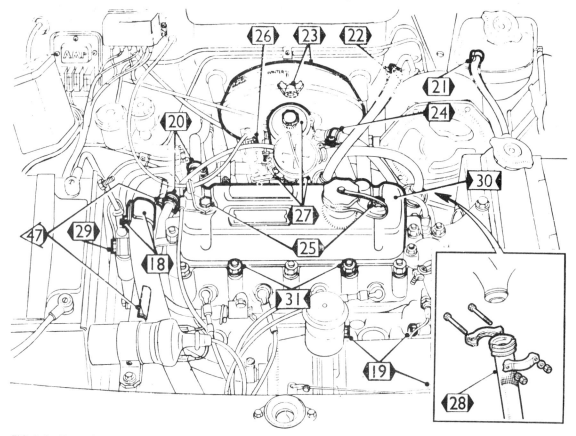

FIG 1 :9 Removing and refitting power unit when power steering gear is fitted (automatic transmission). Text refers to numbered sequences

7 Tie exhaust pipe back to Hydrolastic support bracket. Put wooden block under transmission and transfer lifting hooks to brackets on cylinder head studs. Check that all pipes and wires are disconnected, then lift the power unit, tilting it backwards to clear differential housing.

Removing (automatic transmission):

1 Mark hinges and remove bonnet (operation 1 in **FIG 1 :8**). Lift front, fit stands (2). Wheels must be free. Remove speedometer drive (3). Release tie-bar bolt (4). Set tie-bar to clear (5). Remove exhaust pipe U-bolt (6), release bracket (7) and slide it down pipe to clear (8). Remove eight self-locking nuts from drive shafts (9).

2 Remove battery, bar and tray (10 and 11). Remove support shelf (12). Remove cables (13) then horns and brackets (14). Remove clevis pins from selector and park cables and release cables from bracket (15).

3 Disconnect multi-connector and 'F' and 'D' leads (16). Disconnect starter solenoid leads (except battery lead), leads from coil, plug leads, distributor cap, leads from generator (power steering only) (17). Ensure that starter motor cover flange is facing down (!)

4 (Power steering cars only). Refer to **FIG 1 :9**. Remove hose clip (18). Remove generator fixings and place generator and pump assembly on righthand wing (19). Disconnect hoses and plug to prevent coolant loss (20 and 21). Detach servo hose (22) and remove air cleaner (23). Remove fuel pipe (24). Remove nuts and washers (25). Detach carburetter cable (26), remove carburetter and place it on righthand scuttle (27). Release exhaust pipe, plug end and tie back to cross tube (28). Release engine damper from cross-member and tip on one side to clear (29). Remove rocker cover and gasket (30).

5 (All cars). Refer to **FIG 1 :10**. Fit lifting brackets to second and fourth righthand cylinder head studs. Take weight of unit (31 and 32). Release support mounting (33), noting earth wires. Release support mounting (34), noting solenoid bracket on rear screw. Release support member (35). Release support channel (36), and move it to clear (37).

6 Remove lefthand front mounting (38 and 39), noting that lefthand mountings are on outside faces of engine front plate and brackets (!). Release rear lefthand mounting from engine front plate (40). Release forward harness from valance clips to clear (41). Lift unit until differential housing is against body (42).

7 Release drive shafts from differential shaft studs (or bolts), pushing studs back to clear if necessary (43). Pass control cable round righthand drive shaft (44). Lift unit, allowing it to tilt clear of righthand gusset plate. Keep unit square and converter housing close to valance, push back on chain to clear bonnet catch (when fitted) and lift away (45 !).

1:9 Separating engine from transmission

With manual gearbox:

1 If the camshaft is to be removed, take off the inlet and exhaust manifold and the mechanical fuel pump. Remove the pushrods and tappets (see **Section 1:5**). Remove the distributor and driving spindle (see **Section 1:6**). Remove timing cover, chain and sprockets (see **Section 1:7**).

2 Remove flywheel housing assembly (see **Chapter 6**). Remove clutch (see **Chapter 5**). Unlock screws 77 (see **FIG 1:1**) and remove flywheel. Remove bolts and spring washers and withdraw adaptor plate and joint washer from engine and transmission.

3 Withdraw fork rod retaining plate and laygear thrust springs (these were fitted intermittently before gearbox AA1850) to prevent loss. Remove 11 bolts and 6 nuts with spring washers securing crankcase and transmission case together. Lift engine from casing. Take care of joint washer and retain O-ring at oil suction port.

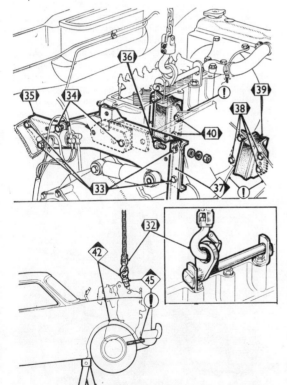

FIG 1:10 Removing and refitting engine and transmission unit (automatic transmission). Text refers to numbered sequences

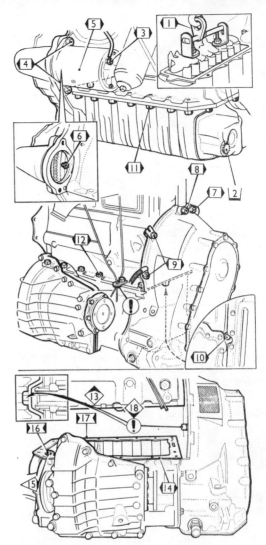

FIG 1:11 Separating engine from transmission (automatic transmission). Numbered sequences are referred to in text

With automatic transmission:

1 Refer to **FIG 1:11**. Fit lifting bar and brackets to rocker cover studs (1). Drain engine oil and replace plug (2). Drain transmission if it is to be split. Remove starter cable and motor (4 and 5). By turning starter ring gear, remove four bolts securing drive plate to converter (6).

2 Remove screw, nut, spring washer and wiring bracket (7). Remove damper bolt and flat washer (8). Remove wiring bracket and earth cable fixings (9). Remove screw and spring washer from below (10). Remove ten screws (11). One of these is between casing and converter.

3 Remove six screws (12). Note drain pipe bracket (!). Keep engine square and lift from transmission. Clear the drive plate from the converter. Take care of gasket (14) and oil suction sealing ring (15).

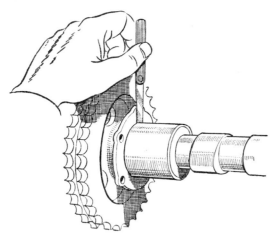

FIG 1:12 Using feeler gauges to check end float of camshaft

1:10 Servicing the camshaft

Follow operation 1 in the preceding Section.

On all Mk 1 units and early 18H units only:

Remove the transmission (see preceding section). Remove oil pump and drive (see **Section 1:13**). Release camshaft locating plate 29 (see **FIG 1:1**) and withdraw the camshaft.

On later 18H units:

Remove the camshaft locating plate. Let camshaft move up oil pump gear and use side clearance at rear bearing recess and intermediate bearing rib to withdraw camshaft. Refer to **FIG 1:1** for parts.

Checking:

After cleaning, check camshaft for wear against figures given in **Technical Data**. Clearance in bearing liners should be .001 to .002 inch (.0254 to .0508 mm). Inspect the pump and distributor drive gear for wear or broken teeth. Excessive wear or scoring of the cams calls for camshaft renewal.

Renewing bearing liners:

Because new liners must be line-reamed after fitting, this operation must be entrusted to a service station. These are parts 26, 27 and 28 in **FIG 1:1**.

Checking end float:

Before reassembling, check end float by assembling retaining plate and large sprocket on camshaft. Check clearance as shown in **FIG 1:12**. Correct figure is .003 to .007 inch (.076 to .178 mm). Renew plate if end float is excessive.

Reassembling:

This is simply a reversal of the dismantling procedure.

1:11 Servicing bores, pistons and connecting rods

First type (see FIG 1:1):

The big-ends are split at an angle and the gudgeon pins are full floating. Work on these parts is only possible after the engine has been separated from the transmission (see **Section 1:9**). The cylinder head must also be removed (see **Section 1:3**). Remove as follows:

1 Refer to **FIG 1:1**. Unlock and remove bolts 17. Note rod numbering at 'C' in **FIG 1:13**. Withdraw cap and release rod from crankshaft.
2 Remove carbon ring at top of cylinder bore and push piston and rod assembly upwards and away. Refit cap and make sure assembly is correctly marked for reassembly if it is not to be renewed. Mark pistons too, relative to position on rod and in bore.

Dismantling:

Prise the bearing shells 15 out of the cap and rod. Remove circlip 20 and push gudgeon pin 19 out from the other end. Remove rings 22, 23 and 24. Do this upwards and not down over the piston skirt. A narrow strip of thin sheet metal may be passed round under each ring while it is gently lifted upwards.

Cleaning and inspection:

After the parts have been cleaned, have the connecting rods checked for alignment, particularly if any pistons show heavy contact at the skirt and near the crown on the opposite side. Check bores, piston dimensions and running clearance against the figures given in **Technical Data**. If the pistons do not need renewal, clean the crowns and ring grooves free from carbon. Take care to remove no metal from the sides of the grooves. Check side clearance of rings as shown in top view of **FIG 1:14**. Check that gudgeon pin is a hand push fit in the piston and has no excessive clearance in the connecting rod small-end. The small-end bush is renewable.

Inspect the big-end bearing liners for break-up or excessive wear. The correct diametrical clearance of an

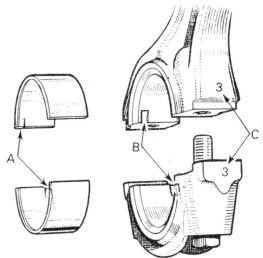

FIG 1:13 Mk 1 big-end assembly showing tags on liners (A), notches in rod and cap (B) and bore identification numbers (C)

assembled big-end is given in **Technical Data.** Wear may be corrected by fitting new bearing shells, but if the crankshaft journals are worn excessively oval it will be necessary to have them reground and undersize liners fitted. **Do not attempt to correct excessive clearance by filing the caps or rods.**

Refitting pistons to rods:

It is advisable to fit new rings at each overhaul, but the gap must be checked before fitting. Push ring about one inch (25.4 mm) down bore from top, using a piston to do so. Check with feeler gauges (lower view in **FIG 1:14**). Correct gap for all rings is .012 to .017 inch (.304 to .431 mm). Carefully file ring ends if necessary.

Refit rings from top. Second and third are tapered and marked 'TOP' or 'T' for correct way up. Fit piston to rod. Gudgeon pin must be hand push fit at room temperature of 20°C (68°F). Fit circlips, making sure they are firmly seated in their grooves. Piston must be fitted to rod the correct way round according to the original marks. Lubricate the pin.

Piston sizes and cylinder bores (all models):

Oversize pistons are available and are stamped on the crown with the actual oversize in an ellipse. A marking of +.020 inch (.508 mm) indicates a piston for a bore the same amount greater in diameter, and so on for other markings. Running clearance is allowed for in machining.

After checking pistons and bores for wear, if bores are satisfactory but new pistons or rings are to be fitted, remove the ridge at the top of each bore, if one has formed through wear. If bores are so worn that reboring is not possible, dry liners may be fitted by a service station. Bore of liner must be finished to 3.1595 to 3.1610 inch (80.251 to 80.289 mm).

When oversize pistons are fitted, stamp the oversize on the top face of the block near the appropriate bore.

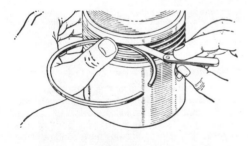

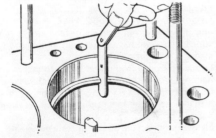

FIG 1:14 Using feeler gauges to check side play of piston ring in groove (top). Checking ring gap in bore (bottom)

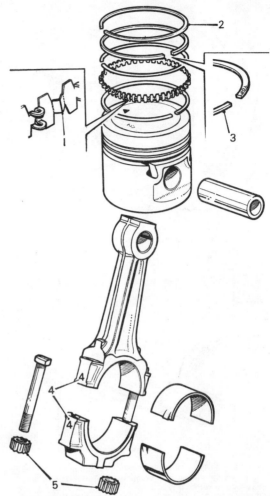

FIG 1:15 Piston and connecting rod assembly fitted to Mk 2 and Mk 2S engines. Gudgeon pin is press-fit in small-end

Key to Fig 1:15   1 Ends of expander ring must butt
2 Top compression ring   3 Second compression ring
4 Bore identification marks   5 12-sided nut

Servicing second type assembly (see FIG 1:15):

This type of assembly is fitted to 1800 Mk 2, 18/85 Mk 2 engines and 18/85 cars fitted with the 18H engine. Notice horizontally-split big-end and gudgeon pin without circlips.

These assemblies with the press-fit gudgeon pin are fully interchangeable with the earlier type having a fully floating gudgeon pin, **but only in complete sets.** Each assembly is removed as instructed for the earlier type. Do not forget to mark parts for correct reassembly if they will be refitted. Removing pistons from rods calls for the use of tool 18G.1150 and 18G.1150C, the method being shown in the top view of **FIG 1:16**. Proceed as follows:
1 Hold body 7 in a vice. Set nut 9 flush with end of screw 10, lubricate threads and push in screw until nut contacts thrust race 8. Fit adaptor 5 with cut-out for rings uppermost. Fit sleeve 6, groove end first.

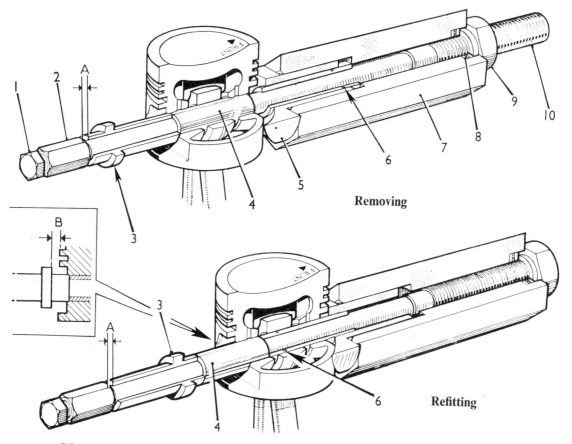

FIG 1 :16 Removing and refitting press-fit gudgeon pin with tools 18G.1150 and 18G.1150C

Key to Fig 1 :16 1 Lock screw   2 Stop nut   3 Remover/replacer bush with flange away from gudgeon pin (removing); with flange towards gudgeon pin (refitting)   4 Gudgeon pin   5 Adaptor   6 Sleeve with groove away from gudgeon pin (removing); with groove towards gudgeon pin (refitting)   7 Body   8 Thrust race   9 Large nut   10 Centre screw
End play of $\frac{1}{32}$ inch (.8 mm) at 'A'; distance from flange to piston .04 inch (1 mm) at 'B'

2 Fit piston correctly. **Word 'FRONT' or stamped arrow must face adaptor 5 as shown.** Fit remover/replacer bush 3 with flange away from gudgeon pin.

3 Screw on stop nut 2 until there is about $\frac{1}{32}$ inch (.8 mm) end play in the assembly and lock securely with screw 1. Check that bush and sleeve are correctly located in bore on both sides of piston. Curved face of adaptor must be clean and piston rings must lie over cut-away.

4 Tighten large nut 9 while holding screw 1 until gudgeon pin is withdrawn. Remove rings over crown of piston. Clean and inspect as advised for the earlier type with due allowance for difference in gudgeon pin fit (see **Technical Data**).

Follow the preceding instructions under 'Refitting pistons to rods' when dealing with the rings, but note difference in gap when in bore. Top and second ring gap is .012 to .022 inch (.30 to .60 mm). Gap of oil control rings (not expander) should be .015 to .045 inch (.38 to 1.14 mm).

Reassembling second type:

Fit bottom rail of oil control ring and position it below bottom groove. Fit expander in groove then move bottom rail up into groove. Fit top rail. Expander ends must butt and not overlap (see **FIG 1 :15**). Set gaps of rails and expander at 90 deg. to each other. Fit second (and thinner) ring with mark 'TOP' uppermost (3). Fit top ring.

Fit gudgeon pin as follows:

1 Refer to lower view in **FIG 1 :16**. Remove large nut and pull screw out of body a few inches. Fit piston support adaptor and oil screw threads thoroughly. Fit sleeve 6 with groove last.

2 Lubricate gudgeon pin and bores in piston and connecting rod with graphited oil such as Acheson's Colloids 'Oildag'. Fit rod and piston with marking 'FRONT' or arrow facing the adaptor as shown. Rod must fit on sleeve up to groove (see 6).

3 Fit gudgeon pin in piston up to connecting rod. Fit remover/replacer bush 3 with flange nearest gudgeon pin. Fit stop nut and adjust to give $\frac{1}{32}$ inch (.8 mm) play (see 'A' in illustration). Lock nut with screw.

4 **Curved face of adaptor must be clean.** Fit piston to adaptor with rings over adaptor cut-away. Screw large nut up to thrust race.

5 **Minimum load for acceptable fit of pin in rod is 12 lb ft (1.64 kg m).** Set torque wrench to this figure, hold lock screw and turn large nut with wrench to pull in gudgeon pin until flange or remover/replacer bush is .04 inch (1 mm) from piston skirt. **Do not let flange touch piston (see 'B').** If torque wrench does not break, fit is not acceptable. Renew faulty parts. Keep nut and screw well-lubricated.

6 Check that piston pivots freely and will slide sideways. If stiff, wash assembly in fuel or paraffin (kerosene), oil pin with Acheson's Colloids 'Oildag' and recheck. Persistent stiffness calls for dismantling and a check for dirt or damage. Check piston and rod for alignment.

Refitting (both types):

Assuming that the crankshaft journals are in good condition and within the wear limits (see **Section 1:12**), proceed to refit the piston and rod assemblies.

Oil rings with graphited oil and set compression ring gaps 90 deg. apart. Compress rings with tool 18G.55A or other suitable device. Fit assemblies into oiled bores, each in its original bore (if not renewed). Make sure piston and rod are the right way round. Check that big-end liners are correctly fitted, with tags 'A' in notches 'B' (see **FIG 1:13**). Top and bottom liners are interchangeable. See following section for undersizes.

Pull pistons down bores and refit big-end, tightening first-type nuts to 35 lb ft (4.8 kg m). 12-sided nuts must be tightened to 33 ± 2 lb ft ($4.5 \pm .3$ kg m) with threads oiled.

1:12 Servicing crankshaft, bearings and flywheel

With rods and pistons removed as in preceding Section, or with big-ends detached from journals, the crankshaft and main bearings may receive attention. The timing gear must be removed and also the front mounting plate. First check end float of crankshaft with dial gauge, by levering shaft backwards and forwards.

Remove self-locking nuts from main bearing caps, and two bolts securing front cap to front plate. Withdraw caps with tool 18G.42A as shown in **FIG 1:17**, or use an impulse extractor with sliding weight fitted to an adaptor screwed into the cap with a $\frac{3}{8}$ inch UNF thread. Mark caps and keep liners in correct positions for reassembly. Note thrust washers 3 and 4 on either side of centre bearing (see **FIG 1:1**). Lift out crankshaft.

Cleaning and inspection:

After parts are cleaned and all oilways cleared with compressed air and oil under pressure (this is essential if bearings have 'run'), check journals and liners for wear against figures given in **Technical Data**. If end float exceeds .002 to .003 inch (.051 to .076 mm) renew thrust washers. .003 inch (.076 mm) oversize washers are available.

Inspect journals for wear, scores and ovality. If unsatisfactory, main and big-end journals may be reground to four undersizes (see **Technical Data**). Undersize

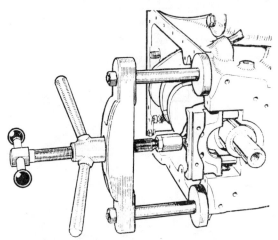

FIG 1:17 Withdrawing front main bearing cap with tool 18G.42A and adaptor 18G.42B. Alternatively, use an impulse extractor

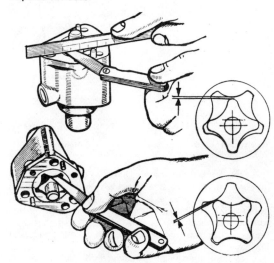

FIG 1:18 Using feeler gauges to check clearance between oil pump rotor faces and body face (top left). Checking lobe clearance of rotors (bottom)

liners are available to suit. Liners with surfaces that show scoring, pitting or breaking-up must be renewed.

Check fit of clutch shaft spigot bush 73 (see **FIG 1:1**). Extract worn bush with tool 18G.284 with adaptors D, H and L. Drive in a new bush with tool 18G.1037.

Refitting crankshaft:

Before fitting the shaft, make sure the transmission casing, oil pump and pick-up strainer are clean. This is essential if bearings have 'run', as particles of metal will circulate through the lubrication system.

Lubricate bearing surfaces liberally with oil. Fit upper thrust washers 3 (see **FIG 1:1**) with oil grooves facing outwards. The washers have no tabs. Fit upper main bearing liners, taking care to locate the tags in the notches correctly. There must be no dirt under the liners, or the bearings may be tight.

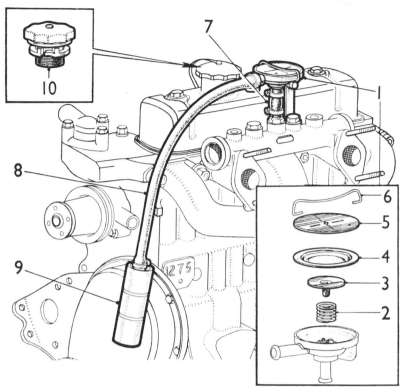

FIG 1:19 A typical crankcase emission valve control system

Key to Fig 1:19 1 Control valve 2 Valve spring 3 Metering valve 4 Diaphragm 5 Coverplate 6 Spring clip
7 Manifold connection 8 Breather hose 9 Oil separator 10 Filtered oil filler cap

Fit the crankshaft. Fit lower liners to caps with tags in notches. Fit lower thrust washers with tabs in grooves in centre cap and oil grooves facing out. Tighten main bearing nuts to 70 lb ft (9.7 kg m), checking crankshaft for free turning after each cap is fitted. If crankshaft becomes tight, remove cap and check for dirt or damage under liners.

Coat front main bearing sealing cork with oil before fitting. Clean the horizontal joint faces of the rear main cap and coat lightly with sealing compound. If cap has a recess, fit a sealing cork. Later-type caps without a recess must have an adaptor-plate-to-transmission case gasket with two inserts which are positioned on the centre of the crankcase-to-transmission joint line.

Flywheel:

Renew flywheel if starter teeth are excessively worn. Check friction face for clutch driven plate (manual transmission) and renew flywheel if face is cracked, deeply scored or pitted.

To fit a new starter ring, split the old one by starting a hacksaw cut and then splitting the ring with a cold chisel. Take care not to damage the flywheel register. Check that mating faces of ring and flywheel are clean and free from burrs. Heat ring evenly to 300 to 400°C (572 to 752°F), indicated by the scarlet strip turning a grey-brown. Alternatively, a polished section of the ring must turn a light blue. Fit ring to flywheel with chamfers on teeth facing

flywheel register. **Press or lightly tap into place without force.** Allow to cool naturally, when a permanent shrink fit will be established. Fit flywheel with '1/4' marks aligned. Lock setscrews on new lockwashers.

1:13 Overhauling the lubricating system

Changing engine/transmission oil (manual gearbox) and engine oil (automatic transmission) have been covered in **Section 1:2**, which also deals with renewal of the filter element. Note that when the manual transmission is drained, some oil is trapped in the primary drive case (see **Chapter 6**). If this oil is also drained, the casing must be primed before refitting the power unit to the car. Remove filler plug on top of primary drive cover and pour in $1\frac{1}{2}$ pints ($1\frac{3}{4}$ US pints or .8 litre) of oil.

Oil pressure:

If oil pressure warning light continues to glow with engine running at or above a fast idle, cause may be lack of oil or low pressure. Normally the running pressure should not drop below 70 lb/sq in (5.6 kg/sq cm) at ordinary road speeds and should be 15 lb/sq in (1.05 kg/sq cm) when engine is idling. A new engine with fresh oil may give higher readings at low engine speeds.

A sudden unusual drop in pressure demands an instant check. Examine the wiring connectors on the oil pressure transmitter, make sure they are clean and free of oil. See that the level in the sump is adequate and that the oil is not old and thin. Check that intake strainer and magnet are clean and not choked with sludge. A more serious cause of low pressure is excessive bearing clearances. Thin oil may be due to dilution caused by prolonged use of the choke and too much cold-running.

If the oil filter warning light comes on and continues to glow, with engine speeds at or above a fast-idle, fit a new filter element and change the oil within the next 300 miles or 500 km. A sticking transmitter will give a false reading, this should not be overlooked when tracing faults.

Pressure relief valve:

This is assembly 106, 107, 108 and 109 in **FIG 1 :1**. It is fitted in the rear righthand side of the cylinder block. Item 108 may be one copper washer or two fibre washers. Do not alter the arrangement. Check seating of valve 106. It may be ground in with tool 18G.69 but make sure every trace of compound is removed afterwards. Check free length of spring against correct length of 3 inch (76 mm). Renew if shorter.

Pick-up strainer (manual gearbox):

There are early and late types of strainer. When a new and later strainer and suction pipe are fitted to early engines, fit a new dipstick with 18 inch (457 mm) blade and a modified adaptor plate. **This second-type dipstick must not be used with the first-type strainer.**

Remove strainer by draining oil from transmission. Remove speedometer drive from transmission front cover (see **Chapter 6**). Withdraw front cover (10 nuts and spring washers). Remove locknut and washers from central stud and pull off strainer. Extract magnet and spring from recess in cover. Clean all parts and wipe magnet. **Do not use fluffy rag.** Renew sealing ring if faulty.

When reassembling in the reverse order, ensure that the locating lug on the strainer fits in the recess in the cover. Fit flat washer with fibre washer each side and tighten centre nut just enough to compress sealing ring. Line up speedometer drive tongue with slot in third motion shaft, fit joint washer and cover, lining up on dowels. Refit speedometer drive and refill transmission with oil.

Pickup strainer (automatic transmission):

To remove strainer, drain engine oil (see **Section 1 : 2**). Remove oil cover adjacent to drain plug (7 screws with spring washers). Pull out strainer and pickup tube complete with O-ring. Clean strainer with fuel and a brush. Do not use fluffy rag. When refitting, use a new O-ring and joint washer. Run engine and check for leaks.

Servicing oil pump:

Removing:

With engine separated from transmission (see **Section 1 : 9**), release pump (see **FIG 1 :1**). Early models with 18AMW units (3 nuts, spring and flat washers), later models (3 setscrews and flat washers). Allow to drain for ten minutes.

Dismantling:

Remove cover 81 (two screws). Withdraw rotors 86.

Inspection:

Clean all parts. Check for wear of shaft in body. Check rotors as in **FIG 1 :18**. Fit rotors, use straightedge and feelers as in top lefthand view. Clearance between face of rotors and underside of straightedge must not exceed .005 inch (.127 mm). With care, excessive clearance may be reduced by lapping face of body after removing dowels. Keep face square and flat.

Use feelers to check clearance between outer rotor and recess in body. Above .010 inch (.254 mm), renew rotors, body or pump assembly.

Fit rotors and check lobe clearance as in lower view. If in excess of .006 inch (.152 mm) renew rotors.

Reassembling:

Reverse dismantling operations. Oil all parts liberally. Fit outer rotor with chamfered end entering first. Check assembled pump for free turning. When refitting pump use a new joint washer 87 and tighten fixings to 14 lb ft (1.9 kg m).

1 :14 Reassembling power unit

As dismantling and reassembling instructions for details have been fully covered in each of the preceding sections, the reassembling of a stripped engine is a matter of working in the correct sequence.

Always fit new gaskets, which are available in kit form. Lubricate all running surfaces liberally.

Start by fitting the crankshaft, the pistons and connecting rods, followed by the camshaft. Fit the oil pump, and distributor driving spindle. Fit the timing gear and cover. With engine right way up, fit tappets. The pushrods, head and rocker gear may then be fitted.

Joining engine to transmission (manual gearbox):

Fit crankcase to transmission joint washer, oil suction O-ring and front and rear main bearing sealing corks. Lower engine into place and replace all fixings, tightening them finger tight only. Finally, tighten them a turn at a time to 25 lb ft (3.4 kg m).

Align layshaft cut-away with location in backplate, check that fork rod retaining plate is in position (see **Chapter 6**) and fit the laygear thrust springs. Oil lip of crankshaft oil seal with SAE.90.EP lubricant and refit the adaptor plate and joint washer.

Fit flywheel with '1/4' marks aligned. Tighten setscrews on new lockplates to a torque of 40 lb ft (5.5 kg m). Lock by turning up tabs.

Refit clutch (see **Chapter 5**). Refit flywheel housing (see **Chapter 6**).

Joining engine to transmission (automatic transmission):

Refer to lower view in **FIG 1 :11**. Fit oil suction sealing ring (16). Smear both sides of gasket with petroleum jelly and fit to casing (17). Lower engine until just clear of casing and engage converter spigot into crankshaft (18 !). Lower engine fully.

Reverse remainder of instructions for separating the parts. Leave transmission and crankcase screws finger tight. Fit converter housing to adaptor plate screws and tighten to 8 to 13 lb ft (1.1 to 1.8 kg m). Tighten crankcase screws a turn at a time to 25 lb ft (3.4 kg m).

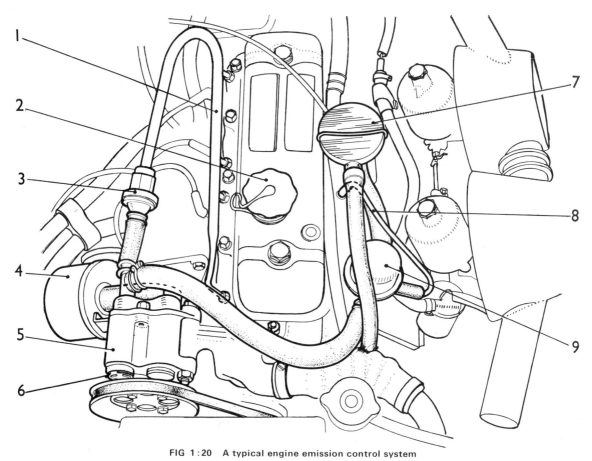

FIG 1:20 A typical engine emission control system

Key to Fig 1:20   1 Air manifold   2 Filtered oil filler cap   3 Check valve   4 Emission air cleaner   5 Air pump
6 Relief valve   7 Crankcase emission valve   8 Vacuum sensing tube   9 Gulp valve

1:15   Refitting power unit:

With manual gearbox:

Reverse the removal operations (see **Section 1:8**) but do not connect the engine steady until the engine mountings have been refitted so that they can take the weight of the unit.

Check the engine steady with its pickup on the casing and adjust if necessary until the holes line up. Fit bolt and tighten (see **Section 1:18** for Mk 2S).

Before refitting the cable housing, align the selector fork relay levers with gear shift in neutral. Insert levers, taking care not to displace relay levers (see **Chapter 6**).

Refill engine/transmission with fresh oil. Refill cooling system, start engine and check for oil and coolant leaks.

With automatic transmission:

Reverse dismantling sequences 1 to 45. Check selector operation (see **Chapter 6a**). On power steering cars, ensure that protection strips are correctly positioned on support mounting.

Adjust carburetter if necessary (see **Chapter 2**). Adjust engine steady to allow bolt to enter freely. Check engine

oil and coolant, start engine, check at once for oil or coolant leaks and check fluid level in automatic transmission (see **Chapter 6a**).

1:16   Checking valve timing

Timing cannot be checked with rocker clearance set for running. Open up clearance to .020 inch (.51 mm) on No. 1 inlet valve with engine cold. Turn crankshaft until valve is just about to open. Indicating notch in pulley rim should then be opposite correct pointer of indicator according to timing figures given in **Technical Data** (also see **FIG 1:6**). 16 deg. BTDC for the Mk 2S engines can be estimated with respect to the 15 deg. pointer. All the other timing positions should then be correct.

When satisfied, restore the inlet valve rocker clearance to the correct running figure.

1:17   The vertical damper

This telescopic hydraulic damper cannot be adjusted or replenished with fluid. If the damper is removed and held vertically in a vice, it may be tested by full compression and then release. The return should be even and controlled over the complete range. If not, renew the unit.

1:18 Mountings and tie-rods

Deterioration in the rubber mountings of the engine, exhaust system and the tie-rods (or steadies) may lead to judder, noise and vibration. Check these points and renew the rubbers if necessary. Note that the upper tie-rod fitted to the Mk 2S engine is mounted between an engine bracket and a mounting channel. It is not adjustable. When refitting the power unit, connect the upper tie-rod before the lower one is adjusted and connected.

1:19 Crankcase and exhaust emission control systems

Crankcase emission control:

The system is shown in **FIG 1:19.** Control valve 1 is connected between the inlet manifold and the crankcase. Separator 9 prevents entrained oil being pulled over. A small hole in filler cap 10 allows fresh air to enter crankcase. The control valve 1 varies the opening into the inlet manifold according to manifold depression or crankcase pressure. At low engine speeds and high manifold depression the valve is closed to prevent air from weakening the mixture strength.

Testing:

Run engine up to normal operating temperature. Run engine at idling speed and remove filler cap. An audible rise in engine speed means that the valve is functioning. If no speed rise, service valve.

Servicing:

Renew filler cap every 12,000 miles (20,000 km) or every 12 months. Filter incorporated in cap is not separately renewable.

Dismantle by removing clip 6 and lifting out the parts. Clean metal parts with fuel. **Do not use an abrasive.** If deposits are stubborn, immerse in boiling water before using fuel. Clean diaphragm with a detergent or methylated spirit. Renew worn or damaged parts.

When reassembling, check that metering valve 3 fits correctly in its guides. The diaphragm 4 must be correctly seated. Check valve after refitting.

Crankcase emission control through carburetter system:

Details of this system are given in **Chapter 2.**

Exhaust emission control:

Correct functioning depends on engine, ignition and carburetter tuning and it is essential that such tuning is carried out with proper test equipment. Always check exhaust emission readings after any tuning.

FIG 1:20 shows the layout of the system. Air under pressure from pump 5 is fed by manifold 1 into the exhaust port of each cylinder. Check valve 3 prevents blow-back. Air from the pump to gulp valve 9 is needed during deceleration and engine over-run. Relief valve 6 allows excess pump pressure to escape to atmosphere. See **Chapter 2** for details of carburation for engines with this control system.

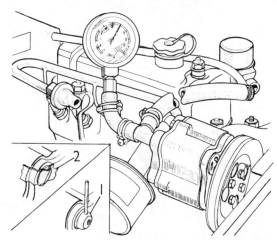

FIG 1:21 Pressure gauge connected for testing air pump of emission control system. Relief valve test fitment (1), duct made from tape (2)

Fault diagnosis:

1 **Backfiring in exhaust system.** Caused by leaks in exhaust, intake or hose systems (gulp valve 9 or vacuum sensing tube 8). Check for faulty gulp valve. May be high inlet manifold depression on over-run, so check carburetter limit valve (see **Chapter 2**).
2 **Hesitant acceleration after sudden throttle closure.** Caused by leaks in hoses or connections to gulp valve or vacuum sensing tube, or to a faulty gulp valve. May be a leak in intake system.
3 **Engine runs erratically at varying throttle openings.** See preceding checks (2) and check for restriction to air supply to adsorption canister.
4 **Erratic idling or stalling.** Check as in (2). Carburetter limit valve not seating.
5 **Burned or baked hose between pump and check valve.** May be no air from pump or faulty check valve 3.
6 **Noisy air pump.** May be incorrect belt tension, pulleys may be loose or misaligned and air pump may be faulty or seized.
7 **Excessive exhaust temperature.** Ignition timing may be incorrect. Air injector may be missing, air pump relief valve 6 may be inoperative or choke control may be partly open.
8 **Mixture must be enriched to get correct exhaust emission readings.** May be air leak into crankcase. On early cars the diaphragm of the crankcase control valve may be perforated or not properly seated. On later cars the crankcase breather hose or connections to carburetter may be leaking.

Servicing air pump:

Belt tension:

With moderate hand pressure belt should deflect a total of $\frac{1}{2}$ inch (13 mm) midway between longest belt run between pulleys. Tension by slackening pump mounting bolt and bolts of adjusting link below pump. Use hand pressure to move pump and tighten bolts to 10 lb ft (1.4 kg m).

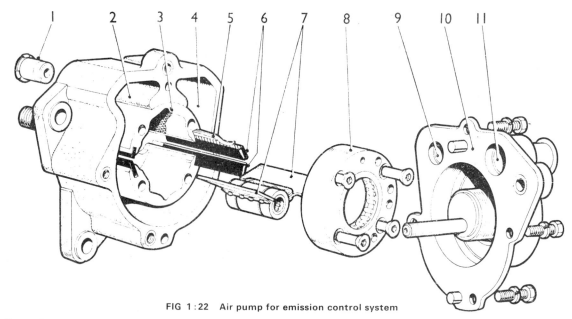

FIG 1:22 Air pump for emission control system

Key to Fig 1:22 1 Relief valve   2 Inlet chamber   3 Rotor   4 Outlet chamber   5 Spring   6 Carbons   7 Vane assemblies
8 Rotor bearing end plate   9 Outlet port   10 Port end cover   11 Inlet port

Testing:

1 Check belt tension. Connect tachometer (revolution indicator) to engine, by following instrument maker's instructions.

2 Connect pressure gauge (range to 10 lb/sq in) as in **FIG 1:21**. Note that hose to gulp valve is disconnected and securely plugged.

3 Run engine at 1000 rev/min. Gauge should read not less than 2.75 lb/sq in. If low reading, clean air filter 4, fit new element and retest. If no cure, blank off relief valve 6 and retest (see **FIG 1:20**). If correct reading, fit new relief valve. If still unsatisfactory, service air pump.

4 Stop engine and fit temporary air duct over relief valve using grommet IB.1735 and short piece of brake pipe (1) or make a duct from adhesive tape (2), as in **FIG 1:21. Never try to feel air flow by placing finger between valve and pulley.** Slowly increase engine speed until air flow from valve can be detected. Gauge should read 4.5 to 6.5 lb/sq in. A faulty valve must be renewed.

Servicing air pump:

1 Disconnect hoses and remove air cleaner. Slacken pump mounting and link bolts and slip belt off pulley. Release pump from mounting and link bolts.

2 Refer to **FIG 1:22** and remove cover 10. Remove rotor bearing end plate 8. Lift out vane assemblies 7. Remove carbon and spring assemblies 5 and 6.

3 Wipe all parts clean with non-fluffy cloth. Clean vane carrier and end plate bearings and repack with Esso 'Andok' 260 lubricant.

4 Inspect vane assemblies for contact with pump wall and for grooving in contact with carbons. Renew worn or damaged vanes.

5 Fit new carbons, using same springs if still serviceable. The deeper slots carry the carbons and springs. Fit carbons with chamfered edge on the inside.

6 Reassemble pump in reverse order. Use 'Locktite' under heads of rotor bearing end plate screws before tightening.

7 Fit pump but do not tighten mounting bolt. Fit, but do not tighten link bolt. Fit and tension belt. Connect hoses and fit air cleaner.

To renew the relief valve 1, remove pump and pulley. Pass a $\frac{1}{2}$ inch (13 mm) diameter soft metal drift through the pump discharge connection to register against the valve. Drift valve from pump.

Fit a new valve, using a new copper sealing washer. Drive it home with a tool made to the drawing in **FIG 1:23**. The sealing washer must be nipped but not compressed. Refit pump.

Servicing check valve:

This is part 3 in **FIG 1:20**. Test it by removing the hose and unscrewing the valve, holding the air manifold connection to prevent twisting. Blow through valve with the mouth. **Do not use air pressure.** Air should pass when blown from hose connection, but not from other end. If it passes when blown from the manifold connection, renew the valve.

Servicing air manifold and injectors:

These are part 1 in **FIG 1:20**. To test, disconnect from cylinder head connections. Slacken air supply hose clip at check valve 3. Turn manifold until injector connections are accessible. Tighten hose clip.

Run engine at idling speed and check flow of air from each manifold connection. If restricted from any connection, remove manifold and clear obstruction with air blast.

Let engine run at idle speed and check that exhaust gases blow from each injector. During this test, note that the injectors may be loose in the cylinder head, so be careful that they are not displaced.

To clear a blocked injector, crank engine until exhaust valve below particular injector is closed. Use a hand drill (**not a power tool**) and pass a $\frac{1}{8}$ inch (3.16 mm) drill through injector bore. **Take care that drill does not contact exhaust valve stem after passing through injector.** Insert air blast nozzle and clear carbon dust from port. Reconnect manifold.

Servicing gulp valve:

This is part 9 in **FIG 1:20**. To test, disconnect air hose from pump (see **FIG 1:24**). Use a T-piece to connect a vacuum gauge to the disconnected end. Run engine at idling speed.

Seal open end of T-piece with thumb and check that a zero reading is maintained for about 15 seconds. If a vacuum is registered, renew the gulp valve. Do not increase engine speed above an idle during this test.

With T-piece temporarily sealed, snap throttle rapidly from closed to open. Gauge should register a vacuum. Repeat several times, unsealing end of T-piece between each test to destroy the vacuum. If gauge does not register a vacuum, renew gulp valve.

Checking limit valve for inlet manifold depression:

Disconnect gulp valve sensing pipe from inlet manifold. Fit vacuum gauge to sensing pipe connection on inlet manifold. Connect tachometer (revolution indicator) to engine. Run engine up to operating temperature and then allow to idle. Increase engine speed to 3000 rev/min and close throttle suddenly. Gauge should immediately register 20.5 to 22 inches Hg. If reading falls outside these limits, renew carburetter throttle disc and limit valve assembly (see **Chapter 2**). Retune carburetter.

1:20 Fault diagnosis

(a) Engine will not start
1 Defective coil
2 Faulty distributor capacitor (condenser)
3 Dirty, pitted or incorrectly set contact breaker points
4 Ignition wires loose or insulation faulty
5 Water on sparking plug leads
6 Battery discharged, corroded terminals
7 Faulty or jammed starter
8 Sparking plug leads wrongly connected
9 Vapour lock in fuel pipes
10 Defective fuel pump
11 Overchoking or underchoking
12 Blocked petrol filter, sticking carburetter piston
13 Leaking valves
14 Sticking valves
15 Valve timing incorrect
16 Ignition timing incorrect

(b) Engine stalls
1 Check 1, 2, 3, 4, 5, 10, 11, 12, 13 and 14 in (a)
2 Sparking plugs defective or gaps incorrect
3 Retarded ignition
4 Mixture too weak
5 Water in fuel system
6 Petrol tank vent blocked
7 Incorrect valve clearance

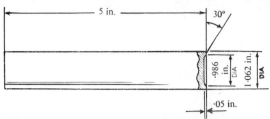

FIG 1:23 Tool for driving in relief valve on emission control air pump

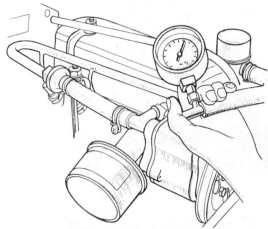

FIG 1:24 Vacuum gauge connected to test gulp valve on emission control system

(c) Engine idles badly
1 Check 2 and 7 in (b)
2 Air leak at manifold joints
3 Carburetter jet setting wrong
4 Air leak in carburetter
5 Over-rich mixture
6 Worn piston rings
7 Worn valve stems or guides
8 Weak exhaust valve springs

(d) Engine misfires
1 Check 1, 2, 3, 4, 5, 8, 10, 12, 13, 14, 15 and 16 in (a) and 2, 3, 4 and 7 in (b)
2 Weak or broken valve springs

(e) Engine overheats, see Chapter 4

(f) Compression low
1 Check 13 and 14 in (a); 6 and 7 in (c) and 2 in (d)
2 Worn piston ring grooves
3 Scored or worn cylinder bores

(g) Engine lacks power
1 Check 3, 10, 11, 12, 13, 14, 15 and 16 in (a); 2, 3, 4 and 7 in (b); 6 and 7 in (c) and 2 in (d). Also check (e) and (f)
2 Leaking joint washers
3 Fouled sparking plugs
4 Automatic advance not operating

(h) Burnt valves or seats

1 Check 13 and 14 in (a); 7 in (b) and 2 in (d). Also check (e)
2 Excessive carbon around valve seats and head

(i) Sticking valves

1 Check 2 in (d)
2 Bent valve stem
3 Scored valve stem or guide
4 Incorrect valve clearance

(j) Excessive cylinder wear

1 Check 11 in (a) and see Chapter 4
2 Lack of oil
3 Dirty oil
4 Piston rings gummed up or broken
5 Badly fitting piston rings
6 Connecting rod bent

(k) Excessive fuel consumption

1 Check 6 and 7 in (c) and check (j)
2 Ring gaps too wide
3 Oil return holes in piston choked with carbon
4 Scored cylinders
5 Oil level too high
6 External oil leaks
7 Ineffective valve stem oil seals

(l) Crankshaft and connecting rod bearing failure

1 Check 2 in (j)
2 Restricted oilways
3 Worn journals or crankpins
4 Loose bearing caps
5 Extremely low oil pressure
6 Bent connecting rod

(m) Internal water leakage, see Chapter 4

(n) Poor water circulation, see Chapter 4

(o) Corrosion, see Chapter 4

(p) High fuel consumption, see Chapter 2

(q) Faults in emission control system, see Section 1 :19

(r) Engine vibration

1 Loose generator bolts
2 Mounting rubbers loose or ineffective
3 Exhaust pipe mountings defective
4 Fan blades out of balance
5 Tie-rod steadies defective
6 Misfiring due to mixture, ignition or mechanical faults

CHAPTER 2

THE FUEL SYSTEM

2:1 General description

Mk 1, Mk 2 and Mk 3 cars have a single SU carburetter, type HS6. Twin carburetters of the same type are fitted to Mk 2S cars. An SU electric fuel pump (type AUF.209 or 215) is fitted to Mk 1 cars, but Mk 2, Mk 2S and Mk 3 cars have an SU mechanical pump, type AUF.704, that is driven by a cam on the engine camshaft.

Cars fitted with exhaust emission control systems have special carburetters of similar types but these require special tuning to give maximum pollution control. Later models also have crankcase emission control by hose connection to the carburetter body.

It must be stressed that sophisticated equipment is required when tuning carburetters fitted to vehicles with exhaust emission control systems, and exhaust gas analysis must be made to ensure that US legal requirements are met.

2:2 Routine maintenance

Every 3000 miles (5000 km) or 3 months, remove damper 7 and check oil level (see **FIG 2:6**). If required, top-up with engine oil to a level $\frac{1}{2}$ inch (13 mm) above the top of the hollow piston rod which takes the damper piston. Note, however, that on dust-proof carburetters with a transverse hole across the neck of chamber 9 and no vent hole in damper cap, level must be $\frac{1}{2}$ inch (13 mm) **below.**

To adjust idling speed, refer to **FIG 2:7** and turn screw 2.

Renew air cleaner element according to road conditions or at least every 12,000 miles (20,000 km) or 12 months. Unscrew wingnut, remove cover and element. Clean inner surfaces of casing, cover and intake tube and fit a new paper element. Set intake adjacent to exhaust manifold in cold climates, moving it away in warmer weather. Do not position intake between the two settings. Do not disturb element at any other time.

To clean filter gauze on electric pump, remove clamp 2 (see **FIG 2:1**). Remove inlet nozzle 4 and filter 6. Clean gauze with fuel and a brush.

To clean filter on mechanical pump, clean the outside, mark cover 1 for alignment and remove screws 2 (see **FIG 2:4**). Remove cover and filter 4. Clean with fuel and a brush. Remove sediment from chamber. Check seal 3, refit parts and tighten screws evenly.

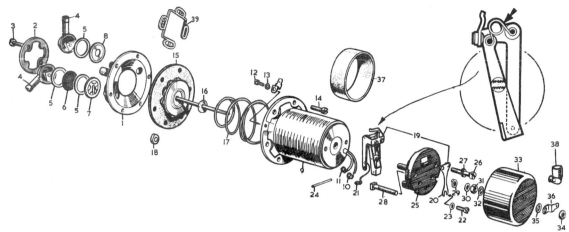

FIG 2:1 Components of electric fuel pump fitted to Mk I cars. Diaphragm assembly 15 may be centralized by rollers 18 or guide plate 39. Inset shows spring toggle for rockers

Key to Fig 2:1   1 Body   2 Clamp plate   3 Screw   4 Inlet/outlet nozzle   5 Sealing washer   6 Filter   7 Inlet valve
8 Outlet valve   9 Coil housing   10 5 B.A. terminal tag   11 2 B.A. terminal tag   12 Earth screw   13 Spring washer
14 Screw   15 Diaphragm assembly   16 Impact washer   17 Spring   18 Rollers (early pumps)   19 Rocker and blade
20 Blade   21 2 B.A. terminal tag   22 Screw for blade   23 Dished washer   24 Spindle for contact breaker   25 Pedestal
26 Pedestal screw   27 Spring washer   28 Screw for terminal   29 Spring washer   30 Lead washer for screw
31 Nut for screw   32 Spacer   33 End cover   34 Nut   35 Shakeproof washer   36 Lucar connector   37 Sealing band
38 Non-return valve   39 Armature guide plate

2:3 The fuel tank

Removing:

Drain tank. Remove rear bumper complete. Withdraw filler tube and disconnect outlet pipe. Pull connector from fuel gauge unit. Support tank, remove six nuts and washers from screws and studs and lower tank away. On later cars there are three setscrews on the wheel side.

Gauge unit:

To remove this, uncover the hole in the luggage compartment floor, remove gauge locking ring with tool 18G. 1001 and lift out unit and rubber ring. When refitting, use a new ring.

2:4 Servicing electric fuel pump

Before dismantling pump, if faulty, do a simple check. If pump is not working, disconnect fuel delivery pipe from pump. If pump then works, trouble is possibly a stuck needle in carburetter float chamber. If pump still does not operate, test electrical supply. If current is present, remove bakelite cover 33 (see **FIG 2:1**). Touch terminal with lead. If pump does not operate and contact points 19 are touching, dirt may be cause. Clean points by inserting piece of card between them, pinch points together and work card to and fro.

Removing:

Pump is secured to rear panel. Disconnect battery earth lead. Detach earth and supply leads from pump. Disconnect pipes and release pump (two bolts).

Dismantling:

Refer to **FIG 2:1**. Remove terminal parts and cover 33. Release contact blade 20 (screw 22). Separate housing 9 from body 1 (screws 14). On early pump with brass rollers 18, unscrew diaphragm 15 anticlockwise until spring 17 pushes diaphragm away from housing. Collect

11 brass rollers. On later pumps with guide plate 39, turn back diaphragm and prise ends of plate free. Unscrew diaphragm anticlockwise.

Remove washer 32, nut 31, lead washer 30 (cut it away) and spring washer 29 from terminal 28. Release pedestal 25 (screws 26), remove tag, tip pedestal and remove terminal. Rockers (part of 19) will come away with pedestal. Release rockers by pushing out pin 24.

Remove plate 2 to release nozzles, filters and valves. Clean all parts and check for cracks, damaged joint faces and faulty threads.

Check plastic valve assemblies 7 and 8 by sucking and blowing. Thin tongue on valve cage must not be bent and must allow a valve lift of about $\frac{1}{16}$ inch (1.6 mm). Fit a new body if valve recesses are heavily corroded and pitted. Check that coil housing vent tube is not blocked.

Clean filter 6 with fuel and a brush. Check leads and tag ends for continuity and security. Renew rocker and blade assembly 19 if contact points are burned and pitted. Check pedestal for cracks or damage to narrow ridge on which blade rests (see 7 in **FIG 2:2**). Renew diaphragm if deteriorated. Check that ball in valve 38 is free. Renew all gaskets and renew rollers 18 or guide plate 39 if worn.

Reassembling:

Refit rocker assembly to pedestal with pin 24. **This pin is hardened, so use a genuine spare part.** Set inner rocker against rear of contact points with central toggle spring above spindle carrying white rollers (see inset, top right in **FIG 2:1**). Rockers must swing freely. Set with pliers if necessary. Fit terminal screw in pedestal. Fit spring washer 29, terminal tag, a new lead washer 30 and nut 31 with coned face to lead washer. Tighten nut and fit sealing washer 32. Secure pedestal in place, putting spring washer 27 on lefthand screw between pedestal and earthing tag. When tightening, make sure tag does not turn or flexible lead may be strained. Do not overtighten. Do not fit contact blade.

Fitting diaphragm:

Fit spring in housing, large end first. Fit impact washer 16. Pass diaphragm rod through housing and screw end into trunnion in rocker assembly. Screw in until rocker will not 'throw over', but do not jam diaphragm in housing. **Do not put jointing on diaphragm.**

On pumps with brass rollers, hold diaphragm end uppermost and fit rollers. Fit contact blade and check lift 'A' in **FIG 2:2**. Bend stop finger behind pedestal for correction. Check gap at 'B', bending stop on rocker 3 if necessary. Note that early-type rocker assemblies may be obtained when servicing the pump. Remove contact blade.

On pumps with guide plate, turn back diaphragm and insert end lobes of plate (flat face to diaphragm) to enter recess between armature and housing. Insert remaining lobes, press centre lobes firmly home, followed by end lobes, to avoid distorting the connecting arms between lobes.

Push diaphragm firmly but steadily as shown in **FIG 2:3**. Unscrew diaphragm and try pushing until rocker just 'throws over'. Now turn diaphragm back by unscrewing it to nearest hole in edge and then a further four holes or two-thirds of a complete turn. On pumps with brass rollers, prevent them from falling out with a wedge behind the rocker assembly.

Assembling body:

Fit outlet valve 8 with tongue uppermost. Fit washer 5 and nozzle 4. Fit inlet valve 7 with tongue downwards. Fit washer, filter (dome side up), washer and nozzle. Align nozzles correctly and secure with plate 2.

Fit body to housing with lugs on housing at the bottom. Fit screws finger tight. Remove wedge behind rockers (brass rollers). Making sure rollers remain in place, tighten screws evenly in diametrical sequence. Do same for pumps with guide plate instead of rollers.

Fit contact blade and coil lead to pedestal. Adjust blade so that blade contacts are slightly offset above rocker points when closed. This gives a wipe contact when points open. To set contact gap, check that blade rests on ridge on pedestal with outer rocker back against housing face (see 7 in **FIG 2:2**). If it does not, swing blade to one side, set it downwards slightly and check. Check lift of contact blade above pedestal with contacts closed (see 'A' in **FIG 2:2**). Bend stop finger behind pedestal if necessary. Check gap at 'B', bending stop finger if necessary.

Park spare cable out of way of rockers and fit end cover. Test pump, then fit rubber sealing band over cover gap and seal with tape.

Testing:

If fuel delivery pipe is disconnected and turned into a glass jar, fuel should be delivered by pump free from air bubbles after a short time of operation. If not, suspect air leak on suction side of pump. If flow is normal at first and then diminishes rapidly and pump slows down, suspect blocked delivery pipe or clogged filter.

A pump that operates rapidly without much flow may have an air leak on the suction side or defective valves.

If pump does not operate and current is reaching terminal, remove cap. If contacts are touching, refit

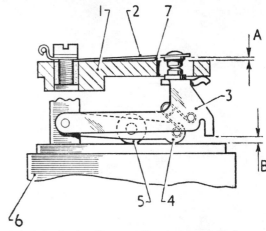

FIG 2:2   Rocker finger settings on electric fuel pump

Key to Fig 2:2   1 Pedestal   2 Contact blade
3 Outer rocker   4 Inner rocker   5 Trunnion
6 Coil housing   7 Ridge for blade
Dimension 'A' is .035 ± .005 inch (.90 ± .12 mm) and dimension
'B' is .070 ± .005 inch (1.8 ± .12 mm)

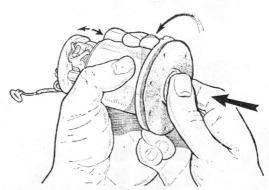

FIG 2:3   Pressing and unscrewing electric pump diaphragm until rocker just 'throws over'

terminal lead and short across contacts with bare wire. If pump makes a stroke, fault is in dirty or badly adjusted points.

If compressed air is used to clear blocked pipes, do not pass air through pump.

2:5 Servicing mechanical fuel pump

The pump is shown in **FIG 2:4**. It is fitted to Mk 2, Mk 2S and Mk 3 vehicles, and to the 18/85 with the 18H engine. The location is down on the rear lefthand side of the crankcase; a camshaft cam and short pushrod actuating rocker lever 14. Diaphragm 8 is pulled down and fuel is drawn from upper chamber past outer rim of combined valve 7. When pushrod retracts, spring 9 presses diaphragm upwards, forcing fuel out of central lips of valve 7 to outlet pipe in cover 1, the inlet rim of the valve being closed by the pressure. When needle valve in float chamber is closed, diaphragm stays down and rocker arm idles until pressure drops due to a further demand for fuel.

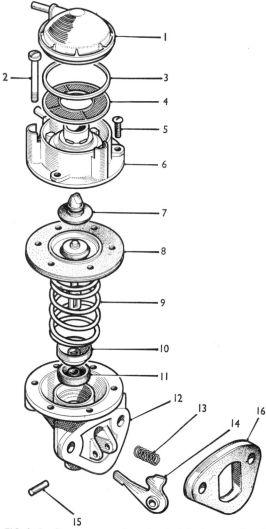

FIG 2:4 Components of mechanical fuel pump fitted to Mk 2 and 3 cars and the 18/85 with 18H engine. Rocker 14 is operated by pushrod from camshaft

Key to Fig 2:4   1 Outlet cover   2 Cover screws
3 Sealing ring   4 Filter   5 Body screws   6 Upper body
7 Combined inlet/outlet valve   8 Diaphragm/stirrup assembly
9 Diaphragm spring   10 Crankcase seal cup
11 Crankcase seal   12 Lower body
13 Rocker lever return spring   14 Rocker lever
15 Rocker lever pivot pin   16 Insulating block

Fault diagnosis:

To check fuel flow, disconnect delivery hose at carburetter and turn end into container. Remove negative lead from coil and operate starter. If flow from pump is in strong spurts, check float chamber needle valve. If flow starts well but falls off rapidly, check fuel tank vent for blockage. Also suspect blocked pump or tank filters. If air bubbles emerge, look for air leak on suction side of pump. If there is no flow, service pump if fuel is being delivered to it. **Do not pass compressed air through pump.**

Removing:

Disconnect battery. Remove air cleaner. Release hoses from pump. Release pump (two nuts and spring washers). Remove pump, block and washers. **Insulating block and two joint washers must be refitted.** Withdraw pushrod from block.

Dismantling:

1 Clean outside of pump. Mark cover and body flanges for alignment.
2 Remove cover 1, seal 3 and filter 4. Release upper body (screws 5). Remove valve 7. It is a push fit; take care of fine edge.
3 Hold rocker 14 up against spring pressure and tap out pin 15. Remove rocker and spring.
4 Lubricate stirrup at lower end of diaphragm rod to avoid damage to seal 11. Pull diaphragm and rod upwards. Remove seal only if renewal is necessary.
Clean all parts in fuel and check for wear, damage and for deterioration of valve edges and of diaphragm.

Reassembling:

Reverse order of dismantling. When fitting diaphragm, remove sharp edges from stirrup and oil lightly before passing it through seal. Turn stirrup slot for alignment with rocker. Fit valve in housing so that fine edge contacts its seating evenly. Press rocker so that diaphragm is flat when fitting short screws to join body halves. Leave screws slack. Fit filter, sealing ring and cover, then tighten all screws evenly.

Test dry pump by connecting vacuum gauge to outlet. Put extension on rocker lever and operate for three full strokes. Minimum vacuum reading should be 6 inches (150 mm) Hg and it must not drop more than 2 inches (50 mm) in 15 seconds.

Connect pressure gauge to dry pump, at outlet nozzle. Operate rocker lever through two full strokes. Minimum pressure must be 3 lb/sq in (.2 kg/sq cm) and must not drop more than $\frac{1}{2}$ lb/sq in (.04 kg/sq cm) in 15 seconds.

To test without gauges, hold finger over inlet nozzle and operate lever through three full strokes. On releasing finger, suction sound should be heard. With finger over outlet nozzle, depress lever fully. Pressure should hold up for 15 seconds.

2:6 Operation and tuning of SU carburetter

FIG 2:5 shows a typical HS6 carburetter exploded. There may be small variations in the control levers for twin installations. See **Section 2:10** for exhaust emission control installations. The section in **FIG 2:6** will be found useful in understanding the action.

The throttle valve is fitted in the bore to the right of the illustration. Piston 8 can rise and fall in suction chamber 9 according to the varying depression in the air intake system. It carries a tapered needle 8a that will thus rise and fall in jet 3. Being tapered, the needle provides a variable jet aperture according to its position in the jet. In this way a correct mixture of air and fuel is provided to suit all engine demands. Damper and oil well 7 prevent rapid fluctuations of the piston. Rich mixture for starting is provided by pulling the jet downwards to a smaller diameter of the needle. Adjusting nut 2 is used when tuning the carburetter. It sets the normal running position of the jet with respect to the needle.

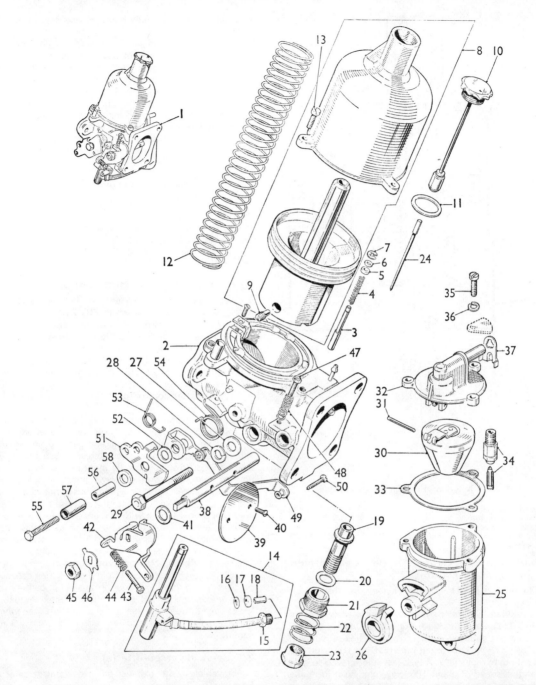

FIG 2:5 Components of standard SU carburetter, type HS6. Note later type of spring-loaded needle in FIG 2:13

Key to Fig 2:5   1 Carburetter assembly   2 Body   3 Piston lifting pin   4 Spring   5 Neoprene washer   6 Brass washer
7 Circlip   8 Chamber and piston assembly   9 Needle screw   10 Piston damper   11 Fibre washer   12 Piston spring
13 Screw   14 Jet assembly   15 Nut   16 Washer   17 Gland   18 Ferrule   19 Jet bearing   20 Brass washer
21 Jet locking nut   22 Jet locking spring   23 Jet adjusting screw   24 Needle   25 Float chamber   26 Adaptor
27 Plain washer   28 Spring washer   29 Float chamber to body bolt   30 Float   31 Float hinge pin   32 Float chamber lid
33 Sealing washer   34 Needle and seat   35 Screw   36 Spring washer   37 Baffle plate   38 Throttle spindle   39 Throttle disc
40 Screw   41 Brass washer   42 Throttle return lever   43 Cam stop screw   44 Spring   45 Nut   46 Tabwasher
47 Throttle adjusting screw   48 Spring   49 Pick-up lever and link   50 Screw   51 Cam lever   52 Washer
53 Cam lever spring   54 Pick-up lever spring   55 Pivot bolt   56 Pivot bolt tube   57 Outer tube   58 Distance washer

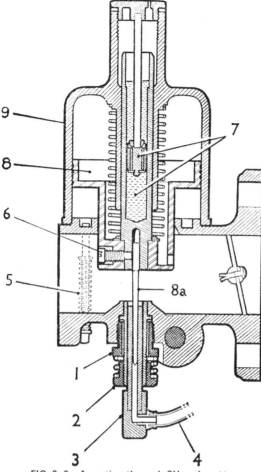

FIG 2 : 6   A section through SU carburetter

Key to Fig 2:6

2 Jet adjusting nut	1 Jet locking nut
5 Piston lifting pin	3 Jet head 4 Nylon feed pipe
7 Piston damper and oil well	6 Needle screw
9 Chamber	8 Piston 8a Needle

Tuning of single carburetter (vehicles without exhaust emission control) :

Check level in damper oil well (see **Section 2:2**). Proceed as follows:

1 Set idling to correct speed by turning screw 2 (see **FIG 2 : 7**). Close throttle and check that mixture control cable has about $\frac{1}{16}$ inch (2 mm) of free movement. Pull out choke knob about $\frac{5}{8}$ inch (16 mm) until linkage is about to move jet 7. Adjust fast-idle screw 3 to give engine speed of about 1000 rev/min. Push in choke knob and check that there is a small clearance between screw 3 and operating cam.

2 Warm-up engine to running temperature and switch off. Disconnect mixture control cable. Remove damper 10 and piston and chamber assembly 8 (see **FIG 2 : 5**). Turn throttle screw 2 until closed then open up by $1\frac{1}{2}$ turns (see **FIG 2 : 7**). Screw up nut 2 until jet 3 is flush with bridge in carburetter bore, or as high as possible (see **FIG 2 : 6**). Refit chamber and piston.

Check that piston falls freely. Screw down nut 2 by two full turns.

3 Start engine. Hold jet up against nut and turn nut slowly up to weaken, or down to enrich the mixture to get fastest engine speed consistent with smooth running. If necessary reduce engine speed at throttle screw. Check mixture with lifting pin 5. Pushing pin upwards to contact piston, raise piston about $\frac{1}{32}$ inch (1 mm). If engine speed increases and goes on doing so, mixture is too rich. If speed immediately decreases mixture is too weak. If speed momentarily increases very slightly, mixture is correct. Reconnect mixture control cable.

Tuning twin carburetters (vehicles without exhaust emission control) :

Idling :

Check level in damper oil wells (see **Section 2:2**). Slacken actuating levers 2 (see **FIG 2 : 8**). Turn throttle adjusting screws 2 (see **FIG 2 : 7**) equally to desired engine speed. Adjust throttle linkage.

Throttle linkage and mixture control :

There must always be clearance between lever and fork (see 2 and inset, top left in **FIG 2 : 8**). Set a gap of $\frac{3}{8}$ inch (9.5 mm) between intermediate throttle lever and spindle collar 1 (see inset, bottom right), by inserting a gauge. Press down on actuating levers until each one just contacts its fork and tighten bolt. Remove gauge. There should now be a gap of .012 inch (.3 mm) between levers and forks.

Set the mixture control (choke) as described for single carburetter.

Continue by following operation 2 in the tuning hints for the single carburetter, but note these variations. Disconnect linkage return spring and remove air cleaner. When opening the throttles by screw 2 (see **FIG 2 : 7**), do so by half a turn. Jet nuts must be moved by same amount each, and throttle screws turned equally when adjusting engine speed. To synchronize both carburetters, use a balancing device sold for the purpose or use a short length of rubber tubing with one end held to the ear and the other end held near the carburetter intakes, alternately in the same position for each one. Adjust throttle screws until intensity of hiss is the same on both intakes.

Use lifting pin to check mixture strength of righthand carburetter, then check the lefthand one. When satisfied, go back to the righthand one, because twin carburetters are interdependent. On completion, tighten actuating levers on throttle spindle interconnection, reconnect mixture control cables and refit air cleaner and linkage spring.

2 : 7 Servicing carburetter(s)

For vehicles with exhaust emission control, refer to **Section 2 : 12**.

Before dismantling, there are one or two operations that may be useful to know in the case of faulty performance.

1 If float chamber floods (see 25 in **FIG 2 : 5**), disconnect feed pipe, remove bolt 29 and lid 32. Push out pin 31, remove float 30 and unscrew needle and seat 34. Check for dirt or a worn needle and seat. Renew parts and check for flooding. If no cure, check float level. Do

this by holding lid and float assembly upside down. Insert a length of $\frac{3}{16}$ inch (5 mm) bar under float and across lid, parallel to float hinge pin. The face of float lever should just rest on bar with needle fully on its seat. Do not bend straight part of lever, but adjust by bending at the angle where the lever turns down to the pivot pin.

2 Difficulty in starting, or erratic running, may be due to a sticking piston. Remove chamber and piston and check for dirt. Piston rim must not actually touch inner walls of chamber. Oil piston rod before refitting, and top-up damper oil well. If sticking is due to bent or badly centred needle, refer to later instructions.

Removing single carburetter:

1 Remove air cleaner. Release mixture and throttle cables. Disconnect fuel pipe from float chamber.
2 Remove distributor vacuum pipe (see 8 in **FIG 2:7**). Release throttle return spring. On later models disconnect link at cam end (see top right in **FIG 2:9**).
3 Release carburetter from manifold and lift off, together with joint, distance piece and throttle bracket. Release throttle cable casing by squeezing lugs together (see top left in **FIG 2:9**). Red diaphragm locates on throttle bracket and black one on bulkhead.

Removing twin carburetters:

A similar operation to the preceding one, but remove breather hose from 'V' piece, unlock nipple from linkage and disconnect throttle cable stop (see 3 in **FIG 2:8**). Release cable stop bracket from inlet manifold.

Dismantling carburetter:

Refer to **FIG 2:5**. Mark flanges of chamber and body then remove chamber and piston 8. Spring 12 will be inside. Disconnect link 49 from jet (part of assembly

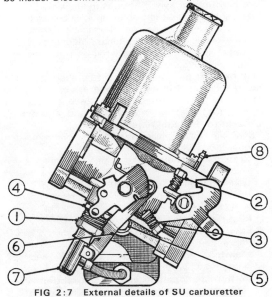

FIG 2:7 External details of SU carburetter

Key to Fig 2:7
2 Throttle adjusting screw   1 Jet adjusting nut
4 Jet locking nut   3 Fast-idle or choke screw
6 Jet link   7 Jet head   5 Float chamber securing bolt
   8 Vacuum ignition take-off

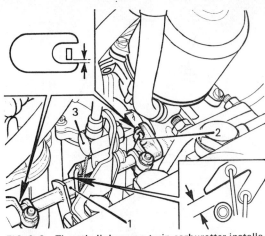

FIG 2:8 Throttle linkage on twin carburetter installation for Mk 2S cars

Key to Fig 2:8   1 Throttle spindle collar
2 Actuating lever   3 Throttle cable stop

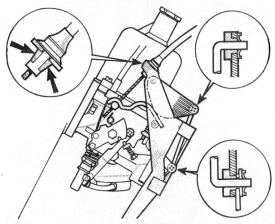

FIG 2:9 Cam operated progressive throttle lever assembly on later cars. Insets show throttle link and cable fittings

14). Disconnect nut 15 from float chamber and withdraw jet and nylon tube. Remove adjusting nut 23 and spring 22. Remove locknut 21 and washer 20. Remove float chamber 25 (bolt 29). Remove lid 32, push out pin 31, remove float 30 and unscrew needle assembly 34.

Inspection:

After cleaning, check parts for wear or damage. If spindle 38 and bushes in body 2 are excessively worn, air leaks will upset performance, so renew faulty parts. Check float for a puncture by immersing in warm water and looking for bubbles of expanding air. Clean interior of float chamber. Renew needle valve if shouldered or if chamber has been flooding. Clean piston and top chamber and check for damage, (do not use abrasives). On no account stretch spring 12. Spin piston in chamber to check that needle 24 is not bent. If a new needle is to be fitted, undo screw 9, remove old needle and fit new one with its shoulder flush with lower face of piston. Type of needle is stamped on shank.

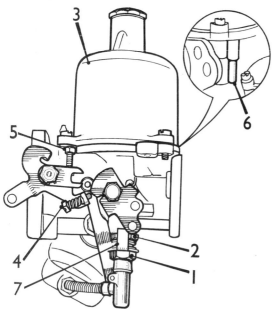

FIG 2:10 External details of SU carburetter for EECS applications

Key to Fig 2:10 1 Jet adjusting nut 2 Jet locking nut
3 Piston suction chamber 4 Fast-idle adjusting screw
5 Throttle adjusting screw 6 Piston lifting pin
7 Jet adjustment restrictor

Reassembling:

Do this in reverse order of dismantling. Lightly oil piston rod before inserting and check that piston moves freely. Do not forget piston spring. After a major overhaul it is advisable to re-centre the jet as follows. It may also prove to be a cure for a sticking piston..

1 Refer to **FIG 2:7**. Screw up adjusting nut 1 as far as possible. Lift piston with lifting pin (see 5 in **FIG 2:6**). When allowed to fall, piston should drop freely onto bridge with a soft metallic click. Repeat with nut screwed right down. If no click in either of these tests, re-centre jet.

2 Disconnect link from jet head 7. Disconnect nylon tube from base of float chamber. Pull jet downwards and away. Unscrew nut 1 and remove spring. Refit nut without spring and screw up as far as possible. Refit jet and nylon tube.

3 Slacken jet locking nut 4 until finger tight. Remove piston damper (7 in **FIG 2:6**). Use rod to press piston down onto bridge across lower part of intake bore. Tighten locknut.

4 Lift piston and check that it falls freely. Lower the adjusting nut and check again. If impact sounds differ, repeat centring operation. When satisfied, refit locking spring and damper and top-up damper oil well (see **Section 2:2**).

2:8 Controls and cables

Removing cables:

Release mixture (choke) cable from trunnion on carburetter lever. Release locknut behind cable bracket and pull cable clear. Release throttle cable from carburetter lever. Press in retainers (see top left in **FIG 2:9**) to release cable from bracket and bulkhead. Inside car, release clip retaining cable to pedal lever, disengage inner cable and pull cable from rocker cover bracket (RHD).

Removing accelerator pedal:

To remove accelerator pedal, disengage inner cable and return spring. Release lever bracket from bulkhead. To remove floor pedal, release pedal link spring. Release pedal from floor.

Progressive throttle assembly:

This is shown in **FIG 2:9**. When connecting the throttle link to the cam, always use new Starlock washers. Adjust throttle cable at trunnion on inner cable so that the cam lever just touches the cam face.

2:9 Crankcase breather system

In this system, as fitted to later vehicles with exhaust emission control, the engine breather is connected by hoses to the carburetter(s). Intake depression draws fumes through an oil separator incorporated in the engine outlet connection. Fresh air into the crankcase is drawn in through a combined oil filler cap and filter.

Service the system by renewing the filler cap every 12,000 miles (20,000 km) or 12 months. If system fails, check hoses for leaks or obstruction. Loss of crankcase depression is a sign of failure, as observed by vacuum gauge.

2:10 Fuel system and exhaust emission control (EECS)

Carburetters fitted to vehicles with this system of exhaust control are balanced to give best performance with maximum pollution control. **Do not attempt to alter carburetter specifications in any way.**

It must be emphasised that tuning must be carried out with the engine emission control equipment connected and operating. If the required settings cannot be obtained, the carburetter(s) must be serviced as instructed and tuning again carried out.

An exhaust gas analyser must be used to check the results of tuning and operatives must be familiar with the United States Clean Air Act and be satisfied that their methods and equipment conform to the legal requirements.

Briefly, the following are the tests and readings needed in connection with the fuel system.

1 **Crankcase vacuum.** The engine is cranked and a vacuum gauge connected. With crankcase ventilation system operating, gauge should read 6 to 10 inches Hg. With ventilation system blocked, reading should be 8 to 15 inches Hg.

2 **Idling speed.** 800 rev/min by tachometer.

3 **Fuel mixture.** Exhaust analyser reading 3% CO (maximum).

4 **Manifold vacuum.** Engine idling efficiency 12 inches Hg on vacuum gauge with engine fully run-in.

5 **Carburetter opening and closing action.** Initial rich, leaning off at throttle closure, using exhaust gas analyser and vacuum gauge.

6 **Fuel mixture at 6000 rev/min.** Leaning off following peak when test speed is reached, using exhaust gas analyser.

2:11 Basic tuning of carburetter(s) (EECS)

Tuning conditions:

Tachometer (revolution indicator) must be connected. Engine must be run for the five minutes after thermostat opens (indicated by a sudden rise in header tank temperature (see **Chapter 4**). Preferably work in a surrounding temperature of 16 to 27°C (60 to 80°F). Set engine speed at 2500 rev/min and run for one minute without load. Carry out tuning quickly. If operations take longer than three minutes, run engine up to 2500 rev/min for one minute and then resume tuning. Repeat whenever three minutes is exceeded.

Tuning single carburetter:

Follow the instructions early in **Section 2:6**, but note differences between **FIG 2:10** and **2:7**. These concern numbering of parts and the presence of jet adjustment restrictor 7 in **FIG 2:10**. **This restrictor must not be removed or repositioned.** If tuning is unsatisfactory within limits of restrictor, service carburetter as in **Section 2:12**.

Note also, that when topping-up the piston damper with engine oil, the level must be $\frac{1}{2}$ inch (13 mm) **below** top of hollow piston rod on dust-proofed carburetters with a transverse hole across neck of piston chamber and no vent hole in damper cap. Parts may be identified in **FIG 2:5**.

In addition to the original instructions, note the following:

1. Tachometer must read 800 rev/min. Ignore other speed recommendations.
2. Select setting where maximum speed is recorded on tachometer consistent with smooth running.
3. There is no need to check mixture strength with piston lifting pin.
4. When tuning is completed, check mixture control as in original operation 1, but set fast-idle speed to 1100 to 1200 rev/min.

Tuning twin carburetters:

Follow instructions for single carburetter to point where damper oil level has been checked. Refer to **FIGS 2:11** and **2:12**. Do the following:

1. Use tachometer to check that idling speed is 800 rev/min. If it is not, stop engine and remove air cleaners. Slacken bolts 10 and 11 (see **FIG 2:12**).
2. Start engine and adjust both throttle screws 5 (see **FIG 2:11**) to give correct idling speed.
3. Use approved carburetter balancing device to obtain equal performance from both carburetters, adjusting throttle screws as required and keeping idling speed correct. If balance is unsatisfactory, check intake system for air leaks. If still unsatisfactory, service carburetters (see **Section 2:12**).
4. If correctly balanced, but idling is still erratic, do the following:
5. Turn adjusting nuts 1 to obtain maximum speed on tachometer with smooth running. Adjust throttle screws 5 equally to give correct idling speed. If idling speed and smooth running cannot be obtained, service carburetter as in **Section 2:12**.

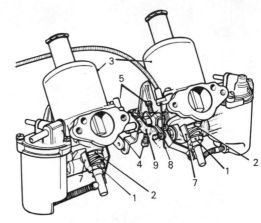

FIG 2:11 A twin carburetter installation on cars with EECS

Key to Fig 2:11
2 Jet locking nuts
4 Fast-idle adjusting screws
7 Jet adjustment restrictors
9 Jet lever
1 Jet adjusting nuts
3 Piston/suction chambers
5 Throttle adjusting screws
8 Mixture control cable

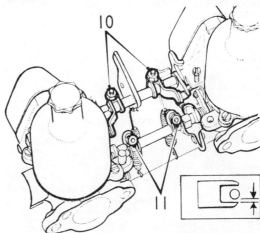

FIG 2:12 Throttle interconnection clamps 10 and jet interconnection clamps 11 on carburetters for EECS installations. Inset shows relative positions of link pin and fork

6. Set levers 10 so that link pin is .012 inch (.3 mm) from lower edge of fork (see inset, lower right in **FIG 2:12**). Tighten bolts, giving $\frac{1}{32}$ inch (1 mm) end float to interconnecting rod.
7. With both jet levers 9 (see **FIG 2:11**) at lowest position, set clamp bolts 11 so that jets move simultaneously. Run engine at 1500 rev/min and check carburetters, using a balancing device. If not balanced, reset levers, re-balance at idling speed, then recheck at 1500 rev/min.
8. Mixture control cable 8 must have about $\frac{1}{16}$ inch (2 mm) free play before starting to move jet levers 9. Pull choke knob until linkage is about to move jets. Using balancing device for equal adjustment, turn fast-idle screws 4 to give speed of 1100 to 1200 rev/min. Refit air cleaners.

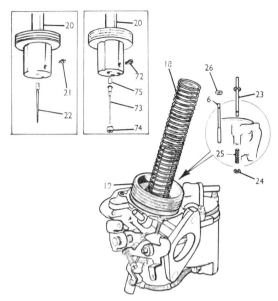

FIG 2:13 Piston details on carburetters for EECS installations. Insets (top left) show fixed and spring-loaded needles. Inset on right shows both types of piston lifting pin

Key to Fig 2:13 18 Spring 19 Piston 20 Piston rod
21 Needle screw 22 Fixed needle 6 and 23 Piston lifting pin
24 and 26 Circlip 25 Spring 72 Needle screw
73 Spring-loaded needle 74 Needle support guide
75 Needle spring

2:12 Servicing carburetters (EECS)

Dismantling:

Clean carburetters, mark chamber 3 and remove damper and chamber (see **FIG 2:10**). Lift chamber squarely, collect spring 18 and remove piston 19 (see **FIG 2:13**). Tip out damper oil. If fixed needle is to be be removed undo screw 21 (see lefthand inset). If needle is of spring-loaded type shown in righthand inset, remove screw 72 and withdraw needle 73, guide 74 and spring 75. Do not bend needle. Inset (top right) shows the two types of piston lifting pin. Continue as follows:

1 Refer to **FIG 2:14** at 'A'. Remove screw 27 from link 28 and jet 26, relieving tension of spring 29 after screw is slackened. Release tube 32 from float chamber and withdraw jet.
2 Bend small tag on restrictor 7 to clear nut 1. Remove nut, restrictor and spring 37. Remove jet locking nut 2 and withdraw jet bearing 38. Lockwasher 39 is fitted only to fixed-needle types.
3 Refer to **FIG 2:14** at 'B'. Unscrew bolt 42 and detach lever 9 with associated parts.
4 Refer to **FIG 2:14** at 'C'. Release float chamber by unscrewing bolt 50. Mark lid 53 and remove. Detach float (pin 57). Extract needle 58 and seating 59.
5 Refer to **FIG 2:14** at 'D'. Close throttle and mark relative positions at 60. **Do not mark throttle disc 61 in region of limit valve 63.** Remove screws 64 and disc. Mark position, then remove lever 68.

Clean and inspect all parts, rejecting those worn or damaged. Note any relevant points in **Section 2:7**.

Reassembling fixed needle type:

Reverse the order of dismantling, also doing the following:

1 When spindle is in place, holes for disc screws must have countersinks facing outwards. Centralize disc in bore by opening and shutting throttle. Fit screws finger tight. Check that disc closes properly and that there is clearance between lever and body in closed position, then tighten screws and open the split ends a little.
2 Do not overtighten float needle seating. Check that spring-loaded plunger in end of needle operates freely. Fit needle with cone entering first. Check float position as in **Section 2:7**.
3 Piston and chamber must be perfectly clean. **Do not use abrasives.** Check action of piston by refitting damper and washer. Refer to **FIG 2:15** and temporarily plug transfer holes 78 on the outside. Fit piston. Fit a large washer to the face of the chamber, using a nut and screw in one of the chamber fixing holes. This will act as a stop. Invert assembly so that piston falls from top of chamber to the bottom. Time taken should be 5 to 7 seconds. If times are longer, check for dirt or damage. If still unsatisfactory, renew assembly.
4 Refer to **FIG 2:15**. Fixed needle (left) must have shoulder 22 flush with face of piston 20. Spin piston in chamber to check that needle is not bent. Fit piston, spring and chamber. Refit jet bearing, locking washer and nut, but do not tighten. Centralize jet as follows:

Centralizing jet (fixed needle type):

Loosely secure nylon tube in float chamber base without gland or washer (see 'A' in **FIG 2:14**). Introduce jet without spring, restrictor or adjusting nut. With inlet flange downwards, insert piston loading tool in top of chamber and screw fully home (see **FIG 2:16**). Unscrew tool until stamped arrow points towards inlet flange. **Do not disturb during centring.**

With piston fully down and jet hard against jet bearing, slowly tighten jet locking nut. Check that jet moves freely. If it does not, repeat process. Remove jet loading tool.

Finish assembling by withdrawing jet and fitting all parts shown in **FIG 2:14** at 'A'. When nylon tube is assembled, its end should project not less than $\frac{3}{16}$ inch (5 mm) beyond gland. Overtightening of gland nut in float chamber may cause leaks.

Reassembling spring-loaded needle type:

Repeat operations 1, 2 and 3 in preceding instructions. Continue as follows:

1 Refit jet bearing and tighten locking nut (see 'A' in **FIG 2:14**). Jet centring is not required with spring-loaded needle. Fit spring and adjusting nut, screwing nut on as far as possible.
2 Insert jet and attach nylon tube to float chamber as in preceding instructions. Refit spring to needle, locating it in groove in needle support (see inset top right in **FIG 2:15**). Note that needles are supplied with shouldered spring seats. **Do not try to alter position of seat or convert a fixed-type needle for spring-loaded use.** Raised 'pip' in needle guide ensure a centralized needle. **Do not remove or reposition this 'pip'.**

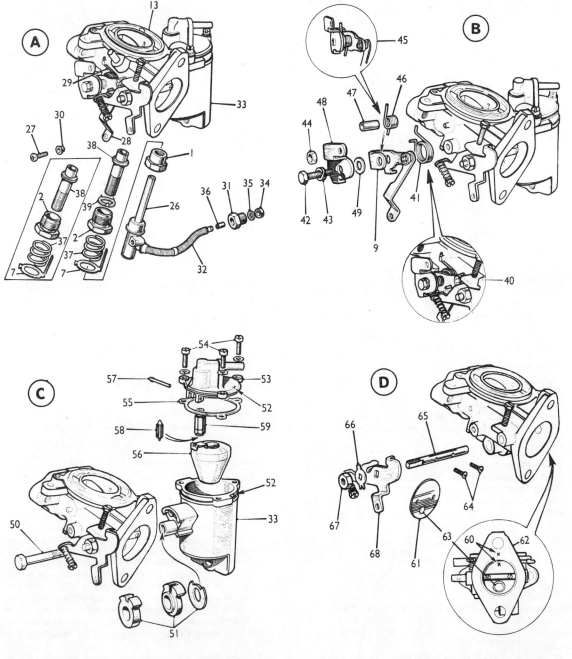

FIG 2:14 Details of jet assembly (A), mixture control (B), float assembly (C) and throttle assembly (D) on carburetters for EECS

Key to Fig 2:14   For 'A':   1 Jet adjusting nut   2 Jet locking nut   7 Restrictor   13 Body   26 Jet
27 Link screw   28 Link   29 Pick-up lever spring   30 Bush   31 Sleeve nut   32 Nylon tube   33 Float chamber   34 Gland
35 Washer   36 Ferrule   37 Spring   38 Jet bearing
For 'B':   9 Lever and link   40 and 41 Lever return spring   42 Pivot bolt   43 Spring washer   44 Spacer
45 and 46 Cam lever spring   47 Tube   48 Cam lever   49 Skid washer
For 'C':   33 Float chamber   50 Bolt   51 Flexible mounting   52 Location mark   53 Lid   54 Screws
55 Gasket   56 Float   57 Float pivot pin   58 Needle   59 Needle seating
For 'D':   60 Location marks   61 Throttle disc   62 Flange   63 Limit valve   64 Disc screws   65 Throttle spindle
66 Tabwasher   67 Spindle nut   68 Throttle lever arm

1800 Mk 2

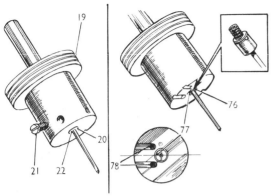

FIG 2:15 Assembling needle to piston. Fixed needle type (left) and spring-loaded type (right)

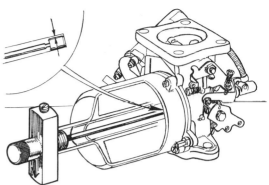

FIG 2:16 Piston loading tool in use when centralizing needle and jet on fixed-needle carburetters for EECS installations

3 Fit needle and guide assembly into piston with lower edge of guide flush with face of piston (see 76). Position guide so that etched mark at 77 is midway between transfer holes 78, as shown. Some needle guides may have a machined flat. Position this so that the guide locking screw tightens on the flat. If this is not done, screw will project.

4 Fit a new locking screw. This is shorter than screw used with fixed needles. Fit piston, spring and chambers.

Final assembling—all types:

Refit damper. Refit parts shown at 'B' in **FIG 2:14**. Double-coil spring washer or spacer must fit over projecting end of tube on pivot bolt. Fit ferrule 30 in end of jet link (see 'A' in **FIG 2:14**). Relieve pull of return spring and fit link to jet with screw 27, supporting moulded head of jet while tightening.

Without removing top chamber, screw in the jet adjusting nut until top of jet is flush with bridge across bore in carburetter body. Turn adjusting nut down by 12 flats for basic position before tuning. Refit carburetter(s) and tune them according to the instructions in the next Section.

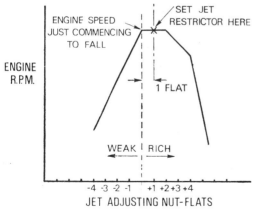

FIG 2:17 Graph showing principle of jet adjustment when tuning EECS carburetter, using exhaust gas analyser for checking

2:13 Complete tuning of carburetter(s), (EECS)

These instructions are for tuning new carburetters or those that have been serviced as in the preceding Section. Tune with the exhaust emission control equipment connected and operating.

Initial setting:

Disconnect mixture control (choke) cable. Set fast-idle screw 4 well clear of cam (see **FIG 2:10**). Unscrew throttle screw 5 until just clear of stop with throttles closed, then screw it one full turn open. **Do not alter setting of jet adjusting nut 1.**

Tuning conditions:

Follow those given in **Section 2:11** but also connect an exhaust gas analyser.

Tuning procedure (single carburetter):

Again, follow the instructions in **Section 2:11** concerning the damper oil level. Then do the following:

1 Turn throttle adjusting screw to give idling speed of 800 rev/min. During adjustments, before readings are taken from the tachometer and the exhaust gas analyser, gently tap the neck of the suction chamber with something non-metallic like a screwdriver handle.

2 Turn jet up to weaken and down to strengthen the mixture. Do this until the fastest speed is given by the tachometer. Turn nut upwards very slowly, to weaken the mixture until engine speed just starts to fall, then turn nut one flat down to strengthen mixture. The diagram in **FIG 2:17** shows the principle behind the adjustments. Check and adjust idling speed to 800 rev/min.

3 Check that exhaust gas analyser reads 3% CO. If outside this reading, turn adjusting nut the minimum to bring reading just within limit. If turning by more than two flats is required, check the test equipment for correct calibration.

4 Refer to **FIG 2:10** and hold adjusting nut 1 to stop it turning while restrictor 7 is turned until the long vertical tag touches the carburetter body on the lefthand side when viewed from the end with the air cleaner flange. Now bend the small restrictor tag downwards on a

flat of the nut to lock the restrictor in place. It will now turn with the nut. Paint over the small tag and the flat of the nut to identify the locking position.

5 Reconnect mixture control cable 8 with about $\frac{1}{16}$ inch (2 mm) of free play. Pull out mixture (choke) control knob until linkage is about to move jet and adjust fast-idle screw to give a speed of 1100 to 1200 rev/min on the tachometer.

Tuning twin carburetters:

Follow the instructions under the same heading in **Section 2:11**, but carry out adjustments to the jets as instructed in the preceding operations on the single carburetter. Use the balancing device and exhaust gas analyser to achieve the desired settings. When satisfied, and after the restrictors and adjusting nuts have been painted for identification, follow instructions 6, 7 and 8 (twin carburetters) in **Section 2:11** to complete the tuning.

2:14 Fault diagnosis

(a) Leakage or insufficient fuel delivered

1 Air vent in fuel tank restricted
2 Fuel pipes blocked
3 Air leaks at pipe connections
4 Pump filter blocked
5 Pump gaskets faulty
6 Pump diaphragm defective
7 Pump valves sticking or seating badly
8 Fuel vaporizing in pipelines due to heat

(b) Excessive fuel consumption

1 Carburetter(s) need adjusting
2 Fuel leakage
3 Sticking mixture control
4 Dirty air cleaner
5 Excessive engine temperature
6 Brakes binding
7 Tyres under-inflated
8 Idling speed too high
9 Car overloaded

(c) Idling speed too high

1 Rich fuel mixture
2 Carburetter controls sticking
3 Slow-running screws incorrectly adjusted
4 Worn throttle butterfly valve

(d) Poor idling

1 Distributor vacuum pipe detached or leaking
2 Leaks in EECS hoses
3 Faulty gulp or limit valves (EECS)
4 Worn throttle spindle and bushes
5 Sticking carburetter piston

(e) Difficult starting

1 Check (d)
2 Mixture control disconnected
3 Fast-idle setting incorrect
4 Defective fuel pump
5 Defective float chamber parts
6 Jet setting incorrect
7 Air leaks in intake system
8 Check ignition and engine condition

(f) Noisy electric fuel pump

1 Loose mountings
2 Air leaks on suction side or at diaphragm
3 Obstruction in fuel pipe
4 Clogged pump filter

(g) No fuel delivery

1 Float needle stuck
2 Vent in fuel tank blocked
3 Electrical connections to pump faulty
4 Pump contact points dirty (electric)
5 Pipeline obstructed
6 Pump diaphragm stiff or defective
7 Inlet valve in pump not closing
8 Air leak on suction side of pump
9 Operating mechanism broken or defective (mechanical)
10 Pump filter completely clogged

(h) Difficulties with EECS installation

1 See 'Fault Diagnosis' in **Chapter 1, Section 1:19**

NOTES

CHAPTER 3

THE IGNITION SYSTEM

3:1 General description

The distributor is the Lucas 25D4, incorporating centrifugal and vacuum unit timing control. The rotor turns anticlockwise. Fine adjustments to the ignition timing can be made by turning nut 2 (see **FIG 3:1**).

The centrifugal device is shown as parts 11, 12, 13 and 14 in **FIG 3:2**. Weights 13 fly outwards as engine speed rises, altering the relative positions of contact breaker cams 11 with respect to driving shaft 14, and thus give advanced ignition. Vacuum unit 16 is connected by pipe to the engine intake system. Depression in the system operates on a diaphragm in the vacuum unit and this alters the position of the contact breaker with respect to the cams. As suction varies with engine load, at small throttle openings with no load on the engine the high vacuum in the inlet manifold causes the vacuum unit to advance the ignition. When hill-climbing on large throttle openings, the much reduced vacuum causes the unit to retard the ignition. Thus, the centrifugal and vacuum units are complementary and give automatic control over the ignition timing.

3:2 Routine maintenance

Every 6000 miles (10,000 km) or every 6 months, carry out the following maintenance operations:

Lubrication:

Refer to **FIG 3:1**. Lift off rotor and add a few drops of oil to the recess in the spindle (see righthand arrow). **Do not remove the screw.** Smear cams lightly with grease or oil. Introduce a few drops of oil into gap between cams and baseplate to lubricate the centrifugal mechanism (top arrow). **Do not let oil get onto the contact points.** Put one drop of oil on moving contact pivot.

Contact breaker adjustment:

Remove sparking plugs and turn crankshaft by means of fan belt (not the fan). When contact points 6 are fully open, check gap with feeler gauges. Correct gap is .014 to .016 inch (.35 to .40 mm), but do not adjust unless gap is a long way out. With points still fully open, slacken screw 4, insert a screwdriver blade in notches 5 and adjust until satisfied. Tighten screw. Clean or renew points if faulty (see **Section 3:5**).

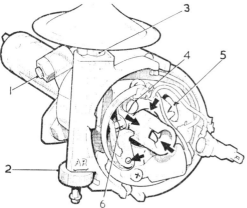

FIG 3:1 Arrows indicate lubrication points for contact breaker and centrifugal mechanisms. A screwdriver is used in notches 5 when adjusting gap of contact points, after slackening screw 4

Key to Fig 3:1
1 Pinch bolt for clamp plate
2 Micrometer adjusting nut
3 Graduations
4 Fixed plate screw
5 Notches
6 Contact points

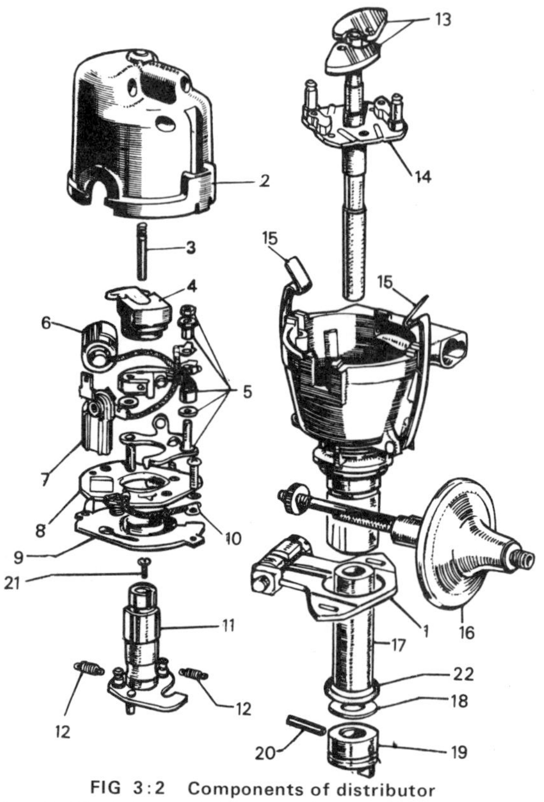

FIG 3:2   Components of distributor

Key to Fig 3:2
1 Clamping plate
2 Moulded cap
3 Brush and spring
4 Rotor arm
5 Contacts (set)
6 Capacitor
7 Terminal and lead (low-tension)
8 Moving contact breaker plate
9 Contact breaker baseplate
10 Earth lead
11 Cam
12 Automatic advance springs
13 Weight assembly
14 Shaft and action plate
15 Cap retaining clips
16 Vacuum unit
17 Bush
18 Thrust washer
19 Driving dog
20 Parallel pin
21 Cam screw
22 'O' ring oil seal

Distributor cap:

Clean all surfaces and check for cracks or 'tracking' (see **Section 3:5**). Check high-tension leads (see **Section 3:5**).

Advance mechanism:

Turn rotor anticlockwise and release. It should return to original position without sticking. Check action of moving plate 8 with a screwdriver (see **FIG 3:2**). A better check is to cut a window in an old but serviceable distributor cap and watch the action under running conditions. Alteration in degree of intake vacuum should lead to movement of plate by vacuum unit.

Sparking plugs:

Clean and adjust these as advised in **Section 3:6**. Renew them every 12,000 miles (20,000 km) or 12 months.

3:3 Ignition faults

Difficult starting and uneven running may be due to ignition faults, but it is essential to be quite sure that carburation or mechanical faults in the engine are not also to blame. If the sparking plugs have been well-used and might be suspect, it is false economy to put off buying new ones, particularly as a new set is relatively cheap.

If the ignition system fails completely, remove the high-tension coil lead from the distributor cap, operate the starter and hold the metal end of the lead about $\frac{1}{4}$ inch (6 mm) from a good earthing point on the engine. Keep fingers well away from exposed metal end to avoid shocks. A strong regular spark will indicate that the coil and contact breaker are working and the fault may lie in the rotor, leads, or sparking plugs. However, complete failure is most likely to be traced to carbon brush in cap (see arrow in **FIG 3:5**). When pressed in, the brush should spring out again. It should make contact with the brass segment, on the rotor (look for a bright rubbing mark).

A defective cap may cause uneven firing. Check as advised in **Section 3:5**. Check that contact breaker moving point is free on its pivot (apply one drop of oil only, see **FIG 3:1**). Check that contact breaker spring is not broken. Check capacitor (condenser) by substitution. Excessive wear of drive shaft may give uneven firing due to erratic movement of cams.

Checking low-tension circuit:

The contact points must be clean and set to the correct gap (see **Section 3:2**). Turn crankshaft to check that they open and close properly.

Disconnect cable from 'CB' terminal on coil (see **FIG 3:3**), and from terminal on distributor. Connect test lamp between terminals. Lamp should light when contacts close and go out when they open if circuit is in order. If lamp does not light, points are dirty or there is a break or loose connection in low-tension wiring. If test indicates a fault, switch on ignition and turn crankshaft until contact points are fully open. Refer to **FIG 3:3** and check with a 0 to 20 voltmeter as follows:

1 In all tests, reading on meter should be about 12 volts. **Check battery to control box terminal 'B'.** With voltmeter between terminal 'B' and earth, no reading indicates faulty cable or loose connection.

2 **Control box.** Voltmeter between earth and auxiliary 'B' terminal on box. No reading indicates a broken or loose connection.

3 **Control box auxiliary terminal 'B' and terminal '3' on ignition switch.** With voltmeter between terminal '3' and earth, no reading indicates faulty cable or loose connection.

4 **Ignition switch.** Voltmeter between ignition switch terminal '2' and earth. Turn key to 'Ignition'. No reading indicates faulty switch.

5 **Ignition switch to fusebox terminal 'A3'.** Connect meter between 'A3' and earth. No reading indicates faulty cable or loose connection.

6 **Fusebox terminal 'A3' to ignition coil terminal 'SW'.** Meter between terminal 'SW' and earth. No reading indicates faulty cable or loose connection.

7 **Ignition coil.** Disconnect cable from 'CB' terminal on coil. Connect meter between terminal and earth. No reading indicates fault in primary winding of coil. Fit new coil. If correct reading, replace cable.

8 **Coil to distributor.** Disconnect cable from low-tension terminal on side of distributor. Connect meter between end of cable and earth. No reading indicates faulty cable or loose connection.

9 **Contact breaker and capacitor.** Connect meter across contact points. No reading indicates fault in capacitor.

Faulty capacitor (condenser):

The best check is by substitution. Disconnect original capacitor and connect new one between low-tension terminal on side of distributor and earth. If test shows need for new capacitor, secure it in place with the screw (see 6 in **FIG 3:2**). Note correct capacity in **Technical Data**.

3:4 Timing the ignition

FIG 3:4 shows the crankshaft pulley notch and timing indicator on early engines. The indicator that is above the pulley is shown in **FIG 1:6** in the Engine chapter. On very early engines without the 15 deg. pointer it should be possible to estimate the position for a timing of 14 deg. BTDC. Proceed to set the timing on Mk 1 engines as follows:

1 Take out sparking plugs and remove rocker cover so that valves can be seen. Turn micrometer adjusting nut on distributor to central position (see 2 in **FIG 3:1**). Remove distributor cap. Set contact breaker gap (see **Section 3:2**).

2 Turn crankshaft pulley by fan belt (not the fan). Alternatively, engage top gear and move car or lift front wheel and pull it by hand. Set No. 1 piston (nearest fan) at top of compression stroke so that No. 4 inlet valve is just opening and companion exhaust valve is just closing. At this point, rotor arm in distributor should be pointing to No. 1 segment in cap (trace through sparking plug lead), and the groove in the crankshaft pulley should be opposite the long pointer of the timing indicator (see **FIGS 3:4** and **1:6**). Turn crankshaft backwards to take up drive backlash and then forward to bring notch nearly into line with correct pointer according to timing of 14 deg. BTDC.

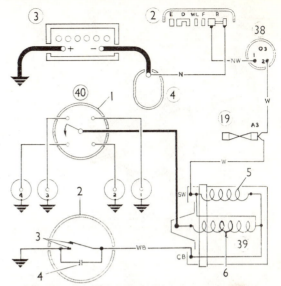

FIG 3:3 Circuit diagram of the ignition system

Key to Fig 3:3   (2) Control box   (3) Battery
(4) Starter solenoid   (19) Fuse unit
(38) Ignition and starter switch   (39) Ignition coil
(40) Distributor   1 Distributor cap   2 Contact breaker
moving plate   3 Contact breaker points   4 Capacitor
5 Primary winding   6 Secondary winding

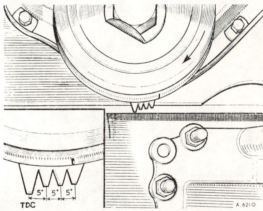

FIG 3:4 Timing indicator and crankshaft pulley notch. (Mk 1). See FIG 1:6 for indicator on models 18H(Mk 2).

3 Slacken clamp bolt and securing bolts of plate 1 (see **FIG 3:2**). Turn distributor body until points are just breaking, then tighten the three bolts in the clamp plate. Tighten clamp bolt first. Correct torque on clamp bolt is 2.5 lb ft (.35 kg m). Alternatively, connect battery and bulb across the points. Bulb will light up when points just break as distributor body is turned.

4 For fine tuning, turn micrometer nut 2 (see **FIG 3:1**) towards 'R' if points open before desired setting, or towards 'A' if after. 55 clicks of nut or one graduation on the scale is equal to about 5 deg. of crankshaft movement.

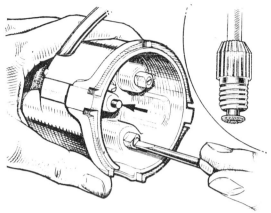

FIG 3:5 Arrow points to carbon brush in distributor cap. On early models, plug leads are secured by screws, as indicated

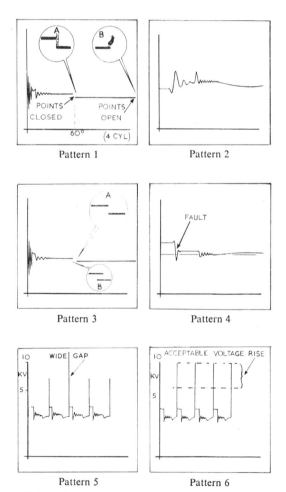

Pattern 1

Pattern 2

Pattern 3

Pattern 4

Pattern 5

Pattern 6

FIG 3:6 Scope patterns when electronic tuning equipment is used for checking ignition system (EECS)

Mk 2 and 3 models (static timing):

Although the distributor is the same type the serial numbers differ in relation to the compression ratio of the engine. This also has some effect on the ignition settings. Refer to **Technical Data** for the correct settings which are allied to their respective distributor serial numbers.

Timing by stroboscope lamp:

This is the more accurate method and it should be used on all Mk 2, Mk 2S and Mk 3 engines and 18/85 vehicles with 18H engines. Connect lamp according to maker's instructions and run the engine, keeping the speed below 600 rev/min so that the centrifugal mechanism in the distributor does not operate.

Notch on crankshaft pulley should be halfway between the 10 and 15 deg. pointers (see **FIGS 3:4** and **1:6**). The correct timing is 12 to $12\frac{1}{2}$ deg. BTDC at 600 rev/min. If engine is slowly speeded up, notch should move away from pointer in opposite direction to crankshaft rotation which will indicate that the centrifugal device is working.

If the ignition timing on Mk 1 engines is to be carried out with a stroboscopic lamp, the correct position is 16 deg. BTDC at 600 rev/min.

3:5 Overhauling distributor

Removing:

Turn crankshaft until pistons 1 and 4 are at TDC with the rotor arm pointing to No. 1 segment in the cap and the contact points just breaking. Disconnect lead from side terminal on distributor and suction pipe from vacuum unit. Remove the cap. Release clamp plate 1 from crankcase (see **FIG 3:2**). **Do not slacken clamp bolt.** Withdraw distributor. Note position of driving slot in shaft to be seen in housing in crankcase. If shaft position is wrong, perhaps after an engine or camshaft overhaul, refer to **Chapter 1, Section 1:6** in the Engine chapter for method of resetting.

Dismantling distributor:

1 Remove contact assembly 5 (one nut and one screw). Parts are shown in **FIG 3:2**. Remove capacitor 6 (one screw). Remove baseplate 9 and earth lead (two screws into body). When lifting plate, disconnect flexible link that is part of the vacuum unit.

2 Before removing cam spindle 11, note relative positions of rotor slot above cams and offset driving dog 19 so that timing will not be 180 deg. out on reassembly. Release springs 12, remove screw 21 and lift off cam spindle 11.

3 At this stage, check end float of shaft 14 and wear in bush 17. Tap out parallel pin 20, remove dog 19 and washer 18. Pull shaft 14 from body.

Clean all parts and check for wear or damage. If an O-ring is fitted to shank of body, check for deterioration. Check condition of springs 12, weights 13 and the pivot pins.

If bush 17 is worn, press it out. Prepare a new bush by soaking in SAE.30 or 40 engine oil for 24 hours or for two hours if oil is heated to 100°C (212°F). Allow oil to cool before removing bush. Insert new bush into lower end of shank with its smaller diameter entering first. Press fully home until lower end is flush and upper end protrudes slightly into body interior. Drill oil hole through bush from drain hole in shank.

If new bush has been fitted, oil the shaft and run it in a lathe for fifteen minutes, remove shaft and re-lubricate it. **Do not use a reamer to enlarge the bore of the bush or it will lose its self-lubricating qualities.**

Check condition of contact points. It is possible to clean up the faces by polishing on a fine carborundum stone, keeping them square and flat. They must then be cleaned with a cloth moistened in fuel. It is best to fit a new contact set if there is any doubt about their condition.

Clean the distributor cap and check that carbon brush 3 is free to move. It is readily pulled out if renewal is required. Check cap for cracks and 'tracking'. The latter may be seen as black tracks between electrodes and adjacent metal parts. If new plug leads are needed, remove electrode screws as shown in **FIG 3:5** (early type). The later type of lead is pushed in. Cut new leads to length of old ones, renewing them one at a time to avoid confusion. Secure with the screw, or on later types, fit the terminal clips in the cable ends, push fully into the cap and fit the sealing sleeve. If leads have screwed fittings like those shown in the inset, spread the bare wire over a washer, the washer abutting the insulation of the cable. Correct firing order is 1, 3, 4, 2.

Reassembling:

Do this in the reverse order, lubricating the shaft and fitting the driving dog with a new parallel pin. Oil the bore of the cam spindle and fit it, making sure the rotor slot is correctly aligned with the offset driving dog. Put a trace of oil on the moving parts of the centrifugal advance mechanism. When engaging the cam driving pins with the weights, make sure they are in their original positions. Seen from above, the small offset segment of the driving dog must be on the right and the rotor arm slot at six o'clock. Tighten cam screw securely.

Turn manual adjuster nut to halfway position. If clamp bolt has been slackened, tighten it before tightening the two bolts securing the distributor to the crankcase. Check the timing as described in **Section 3:4**.

3:6 Sparking plugs

Clean and adjust sparking plugs regularly. Remove plugs by loosening them a turn or two and blowing away any dirt in the recesses. Use a box spanner and avoid tilting it or the porcelain insulator may be broken.

Inspect deposits on firing end of plug for an indication of running conditions. If powdery and brown to greyish tan in colour with only slight wear of the electrodes, the deposits are due to normal driving with mixed periods of slow- and high-speed driving.

If deposits are white or yellowish they indicate long periods of constant-speed driving or much low-speed driving.

Black, wet deposits are due to oil entering the combustion chamber past worn pistons or down valve stems. Do not confuse with wetness caused by prolonged attempts to start with the choke out.

Dry, black fluffy deposits are due to running with a rich mixture, or to defective ignition or excessive idling.

Overheating leads to a white, blistered look about the electrodes and these may also be badly eroded. Cause may be poor cooling, ignition problems or sustained high speed with heavy loads.

Have plugs cleaned on an air-blast machine and tested under pressure. Electrodes may be cleaned up with a fine file until the edges are bright. Set the gap to .025 inch (.64 mm). Do this by bending the outer electrode. **Never try to bend the centre electrode.**

Clean threads with a wire brush and refit plugs, using new gaskets if the old ones are less than half the original thickness. Tighten to a torque of 30 lb ft (4.1 kg m). Use Champion N5's for Mk 1 engines and type N9Y for Mk 2 and 2S engines.

3:7 Checking ignition system (EECS)

This is carried out using electronic test equipment. Scope patterns are given in **FIG 3:6**.

Cranking to start engine. Scope trace should indicate a minimum coil output of 17 KV.

Engine idling. See pattern 1 (inset 'A'). Dwell meter and scope should indicate a dwell angle of 57 to 63 deg. Check timing with timing light.

Engine at fast idle: Dwell meter should show no more than 2 deg. variation. Ignition circuit polarity test, see inverted trace in pattern 2. Check cam lobe accuracy for maximum variation of 3 deg. (see pattern 3). Inset 'A' is correct, inset 'B' shows overlap indicating cam error. Check of plugs, leads, cap and rotor should give a standard scope pattern. Check of coil windings and capacitor should give pattern 4 (lack of oscillations indicates fault). Condition of breaker points should give pattern 1 at 'B'. Plug firing voltage, see pattern 5; voltage at 6 to 9 KV.

Accelerate and decelerate. Sparking plugs under load, scope trace as pattern 6 (acceptable voltage rise 6 to 10 KV).

At 6000 rev/min. Timing light and advance meter should indicate a crankshaft movement of 42 deg. ±1 deg. with vacuum pipe disconnected. Maximum coil output when testing coil, capacitor and ignition primary should give a standard pattern on the scope with a minimum reserve 2/3 rds more than requirement. Scope trace will be a standard pattern when testing secondary circuit insulation (high-tension leads, cap and rotor).

3:8 Fault diagnosis

(a) Engine will not fire

1 Battery discharged
2 Distributor contact points dirty, pitted or wrongly adjusted
3 Distributor cap dirty, cracked or 'tracking'
4 Carbon brush inside distributor cap not touching rotor
5 Faulty cable or loose connection in low-tension circuit
6 Distributor rotor arm cracked
7 Faulty coil
8 Broken contact breaker spring
9 Contact points stuck open

(b) Engine misfires

1 Check 2, 3, 5 and 7 in (a)
2 Weak contact breaker spring
3 High-tension plug and coil leads cracked or perished
4 Sparking plug(s) loose
5 Sparking plug insulation cracked
6 Sparking plug gap incorrectly set
7 Ignition timing too far advanced

NOTES

CHAPTER 4

THE COOLING SYSTEM

4:1 General description

The system incorporates a belt-driven pump and fan, a thermostat and a radiator with associated expansion tank. The pump impeller circulates coolant from the bottom tank of the radiator through the cylinder block to the cylinder head. If the coolant is cold, a thermostat in the head closes the outlet to the radiator. Coolant is then bypassed and recirculated through the engine until it is hot enough to open the thermostat valve and pass to the top of the radiator core. It is cooled as it flows down through the finned core.

The system is pressurized to approximately 13 lb/sq in (.91 kg/sq cm) by a relief valve in the expansion tank cap (see 21 in **FIG 4:3**). Any overflow from expanding coolant passes into the expansion tank. When it cools, a partial vacuum causes the excess coolant to be drawn back into the radiator.

There is no need for regular topping-up but the coolant level should be checked occasionally to ensure that there has been no leakage.

4:2 Routine maintenance

Coolant level:

Every 3000 miles (5000 km) or three months, check level of coolant in radiator. Leave system to cool and remove radiator cap 1 (see **FIG 4:1**). **There is a serious risk of scalding if pressure is suddenly released when the system is hot.** If required, add coolant to bring level to top of filler neck. Add anti-freeze solution if anti-freeze is in the system, otherwise dilution with plain water may lead to frost damage.

Remove expansion tank pressure relief cap 6 very slowly, taking great care if system is hot. If depth of coolant is under $2\frac{1}{2}$ inch (65 mm), top-up as required. Note that radiator cap is plain.

Fan belt adjustment:

Check belt tension every 6000 miles (10,000 km) or 6 months. **FIG 4:2** shows the adjustment points. Owners of vehicles with an orthodox generator will find that the principle is the same.

Use moderate hand pressure to deflect the belt midway between pulleys on the longest run. Total deflection should be about $\frac{1}{2}$ inch (12 mm). If adjustment is required, slacken mounting bolts 1 and link bolts 1 and 2. Lift generator by hand. In the case of alternator illustrated, lift by hand pressure on bracket 3. Tighten mounting and link bolts and check tension. Do not over-tension, or belt and bearings will be overloaded.

Check condition of belt and renew if cracked or frayed. To renew a belt, push generator towards engine and lift belt off pulleys. Pass belt between fan and cowling until in front of fan. Withdraw belt between a fan blade and

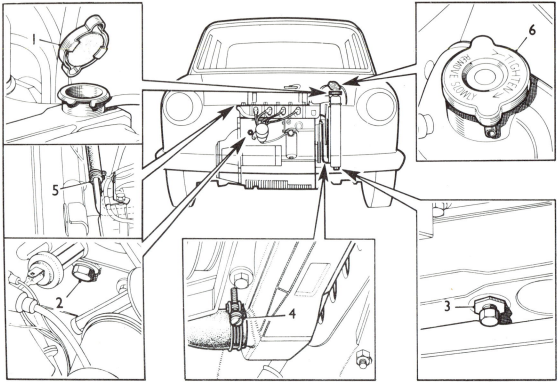

FIG 4:1 Location of filler caps and drainage points on Mk 2 vehicles. Positions are the same on other models but there may be taps instead of plugs

Key to Fig 4:1   1 Radiator filler cap   2 Cylinder block drain plug   3 Radiator drain plug   4 Clip for bottom hose
5 Heater return hose   6 Expansion tank filler cap

clearance at righthand top of cowling. Refer to **Technical Data** for type of belt with reference to generator, alternator or power steering embodiments. An alternator cannot be fitted if power steering is incorporated.

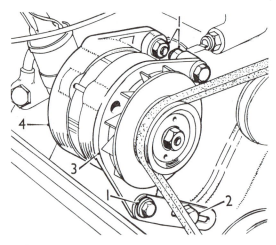

FIG 4:2 To adjust tension of fan belt, slacken bolts 1 and 2 and position alternator 4 by pressing on bracket 3. Method is similar when a generator is fitted instead

Lubrication:

Early water pumps have a screwed plug for lubrication purposes (see arrow in lefthand view of **FIG 4:4**). Every 12,000 miles (20,000 km) or 12 months, remove this plug and introduce a small quantity of grease. Do this sparingly or grease may pass the bearings and contaminate the carbon seal. There is no provision for lubrication on later pumps.

4:3 Draining and refilling system

Draining:

The heater core and expansion tank are not drained with the cooling system. If vehicle is to be left without coolant, leave a warning notice to that effect.

Refer to **FIG 4:1**, remove filler cap 1 (note warning in **Section 4:2**) and then remove drain plug 2 from front of engine and plug 3 from base of radiator. Some engines may be fitted with taps instead. If there is no plug in the base of the radiator, release bottom hose at 4. Collect the coolant in a clean container if it contains antifreeze and can be used again.

Flushing:

This is a good plan after a vehicle has covered a considerable mileage, or when coolant water contains unusual salts that lead to corrosion. Insert a hose in the filler neck and let water run through the system and out

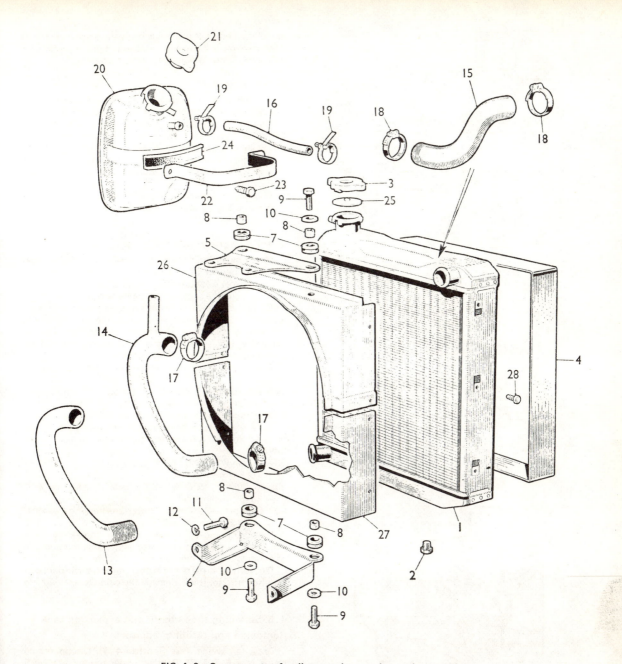

FIG 4:3 Components of radiator and expansion tank assembly

Key to Fig 4:3   1 Radiator   2 Drain plug   3 Filler cap   4 Radiator cowl rubber surround*   5 Top radiator support bracket
6 Bottom radiator support bracket*   7 Bracket grommet   8 Bracket distance piece   9 Screw   10 Plain washer
11 Bottom bracket screw   12 Spring washer   13 Radiator to pump hose   14 Radiator to pump hose (heater fitted)
15 Radiator to cylinder head hose   16 Radiator to expansion tank hose   17 Hose to pump clip   18 Hose to cylinder head clip
19 Hose to expansion tank clip   20 Expansion tank*   21 Expansion tank cap   22 Tank clamp   23 Screw   24 Clamp seating
25 Filler cap seal   26 Top cowl   27 Bottom cowl   28 Cowl to radiator screw   *1st type illustrated

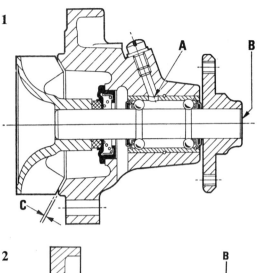

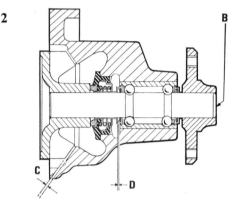

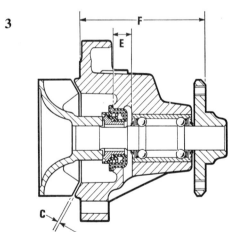

FIG 4:4 A cross-section through the three successive water pumps

Key to Fig 4:4   1 First type with grease plug and locating wire   2 Second type with sealed bearing, thrower and locating wire   3 Third type with sealed bearing and pressure balanced seal   A Coincidence of lubricating holes   B Hub face flush with spindle end   C .020 to .030 inch (.51 to .76 mm) clearance   D .042 to .062 inch (1.1 to 1.6 mm) clearance   E .527 to .537 inch (13.39 to 13.64 mm)   F 3.244 to 3.264 inch (82.4 to 82.9 mm)

at the drain holes. If radiator is badly furred, remove it and flush through in the reverse direction. Remove thermostat if flushing is being done by machine pressure.

Refilling system:

Refit plugs or close taps. Check all hose connections. Check level in expansion tank (see **Section 4:2**). Fill system to top of radiator filler neck and refit cap. If a heater is fitted, set control to 'HOT' and disconnect heater outlet hose 5 at the return pipe. Holding the pipe at its original level, fill the system until coolant flows from the hose and the return pipe. Reconnect pipe, fill to top of filler neck and refit cap.

Run engine briskly for about 30 seconds, remove cap slowly and top-up to the correct level once more.

4:4 Frost precautions

If a heater is fitted, antifreeze must be used because heater core cannot be drained. Use antifreeze to Specifications BS.3151 or 3152.

After using the same antifreeze for two years, drain and flush the system, check hoses for deterioration and leaks and refill with antifreeze solution. At the same time add .25 pint ($\frac{1}{3}$ US pint or .15 litre) of neat antifreeze to the expansion tank. If a heater is fitted, follow the refilling instructions in the preceding Section.

The recommended quantities of antifreeze are as follows:

25% solution: $2\frac{1}{4}$ pints ($2\frac{1}{2}$ US pints, 1.3 litres).
33$\frac{1}{3}$% solution: 3 pints ($3\frac{1}{2}$ US pints, 1.7 litres)
50% solution: $4\frac{1}{2}$ pints (5 US pints, 2.4 litres)

These are for systems without heater. Add $\frac{1}{4}$ pint ($\frac{1}{2}$ US pint, .15 litres) if a heater is fitted. Protection given is as follows:

25% solution: —13°C or 9°F (starts freezing). —26°C or —15°F (frozen solid).
33$\frac{1}{3}$ solution: —19°C or —2°F (starts freezing). —36°C —33°F (frozen solid)
50% solution: —36°C or —33°F (starts freezing). —48°C or —53°F (frozen solid).

When topping-up radiator system containing antifreeze, always use an antifreeze solution as the addition of water will cause dilution.

Do not put antifreeze solution in the windscreen washer bottle. It will damage the paintwork.

4:5 Servicing the radiator and expansion tank

Removing and refilling radiator:

Drain the system (see **Section 4:3**). Disconnect all hoses (see **FIG 4:3**). Remove upper support bracket 5 and the bolts securing lower bracket 6. Remove screws and lift off upper half of cowling 26. Lift out the radiator.

Refit in the reverse order. Refill as advised in **Section 4:3**.

Removing and refitting expansion tank:

This tank is mounted on the engine bulkhead. Refer to **FIG 4:3**. Disconnect spill hose 16 from radiator top tank and from the clip on the cowling 26. Remove clamp 22 and lift away tank 20.

After refitting, refill as advised in **Section 4:3**.

4:6 Servicing coolant pump

Removing:

Remove radiator (see preceding Section). Remove fan belt (see **Section 4:2**). Remove fan and pulley (4 set-screws). Release pump from cylinder block and remove joint washer.

In most cases it will be more expedient to renew the pump on an exchange basis rather than trying to get individual components.

Dismantling:

Three successive types pf pump have been fitted since the introduction of the 1800 models. These are shown in cross-section in **FIG 4:4**. Apart from their physical differences the component seals and bearings also differ, however, as a unit they are interchangeable within the different marks.

Use a puller to withdraw the fan hub from the spindle and, if it is applicable, take out the bearing locating wire 5. Support the pump and press out the bearing complete with spindle, impeller and seal. Use the puller again to withdraw the impeller from the spindle. Remove the seal.

Renew all obviously worn parts including suspect ones. Renew the seals whatever the condition. The bearing and spindle cannot be separated and are renewed as an assembly.

Reassembling:

Assemble in the reverse order of dismantling noting the following, relative to the different types:

1st type: Align the lubricating holes of the pump body and bearing and the locating wire groove. Spindle end must be flush with hub (B).

2nd type: Align the locating wire groove and ensure the bearing to thrower clearance (D) is correct. Spindle end must be flush with hub (B).

3rd type: The bearing must be accurately positioned to maintain the dimension (E) and the hub mounted to obtain dimension (F), from the pump mounting face to the outer face of the hub.

All types: Fit the seal lubricated with silicone grease and press the impeller onto the spindle to give clearance (C).

In all instances the hub and the impeller must be a good press-fit in the spindle.

Refitting:

Simply reverse the removal sequence, using a new joint washer. Adjust fan belt tension as advised in **Section 4:2**. Refill system as in **Section 4:3**.

4:7 Thermostat and temperature gauge

Removing thermostat:

Partially drain cooling system and disconnect top hose to radiator. Hose is connected to thermostat cover on cylinder head. Remove cover (3 nuts) and lift off. The two front studs hold the radiator support bracket. Remove joint washer and thermostat.

Inspecting thermostat:

Renew thermostat if valve is permanently open or if damage is obvious. Check action of thermostat if valve is closed. Immerse in water and use a thermometer. Do not let thermostat or thermometer touch bottom or sides of container. Heat water and watch for valve to open. It should do this at temperature stamped on thermostat flange. If valve does not open, renew thermostat.

Refitting:

Reverse removal procedure, fitting a new joint washer. Refill cooling system (see **Section 4:3**).

Temperature gauge:

This is connected by a cable in the ignition circuit and a bi-metal voltage stabilizer to a thermal transmitter secured by a gland nut into the cylinder head. Check electrical connections and component parts in the event of failure.

4:8 Fault diagnosis

(a) Internal water leakage

1 Cracked cylinder wall
2 Loose cylinder head nuts
3 Cracked or distorted cylinder head
4 Faulty head gasket

(b) Poor circulation

1 Radiator core blocked
2 Engine water passages restricted
3 Low water level
4 Loose fan belt
5 Defective thermostat
6 Perished or collapsed radiator hoses

(c) Corrosion

1 Impurities in water
2 Not enough draining and flushing

(d) Overheating

1 Check (b)
2 Sludge in crankcase
3 Faulty ignition timing
4 Low oil level in sump
5 Tight engine
6 Choked exhaust system
7 Binding brakes
8 Slipping clutch
9 Incorrect valve timing
10 Retarded ignition
11 Mixture too weak

NOTES

CHAPTER 5

THE CLUTCH

5:1 General description

The clutch fitted to vehicles with manual transmission is of the single dry-plate type with diaphragm spring (see **FIGS 5:2** and **5:3**). The driven plate 2 (see **FIG 5:2**) has a splined hub that is mounted on the shaft carrying the first gear in the train of three primary drive gears in the flywheel housing (see **Chapter 6**). Friction rings are riveted to both sides of this plate. The hub carries damper springs to absorb driving shocks and torsional vibration.

The plate is sandwiched between the flywheel face and pressure plate 10 (see **FIG 5:3**). A dished diaphragm spring 9 is mounted in cover 1 which is bolted to the flywheel. The driven plate, being nipped by spring pressure between the faces, transmits drive from the flywheel to the shaft and primary gears. To disengage the clutch, a release bearing 7 is operated by hydraulic mechanism connected to the clutch pedal. Pressure of the release bearing dishes the spring in the opposite direction. The pivoting action caused by annular rings 8 means that the outer rim of the spring lifts pressure plate 10, relieving the clamping effect on the driven plate, which is then no longer taking the drive from the flywheel.

5:2 Routine maintenance

The clutch operating mechanism is self-adjusting. The only maintenance needed is attention to the fluid level in the clutch master cylinder reservoir seen in **FIG 5:1**. This is mounted on the engine bulkhead.

Every 3000 miles (5000 km) or three months, clean all round the cap, unscrew it and check the level of fluid inside. There is a level mark on the outside (see 1 in the illustration). Check that hole 3 is clear.

If required, top-up with Castrol Girling Brake Fluid Amber or a fluid conforming to specification SAE.J.1703a (grade 1). **Do not use any substitutes and never put mineral oil in the system or complete failure will result.**

If frequent topping-up is required, check for leaks and rectify.

Be very careful to avoid dropping the fluid on the paintwork, as it has a solvent effect. Be as clean as possible when dealing with the fluid and the internal surfaces of the hydraulic equipment.

5:3 Servicing the clutch

Removing:

Remove the power unit as described in **Chapter 1, Section 1:8** of the Engine chapter. Remove the primary drive cover and flywheel housing (see **Chapter 6**).

Note the clutch plate centralizing tool 18G.1027 shown in the bottom righthand corner of **FIG 5:2**. This is used to ensure that the hub of the plate is always central with the

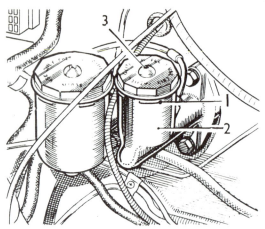

FIG 5:1 Location of clutch master cylinder 2 on engine bulkhead. Correct fluid level indicated at 1 and vent hole in cap at 3

spigot bush in the crankshaft. A temporary one can be turned out of hardwood. The larger diameter fits the splined bore of the hub and the shouldered end fits in the bush in the crankshaft. This bush supports the inner end of the primary gear shaft that carries the driven plate.

Insert the centralizing tool and unscrew the cover-to-flywheel bolts 5 a turn at a time until spring pressure is released. Lift off cover assembly 1 and driven plate 2 in FIG 5:2.

Remove release bearing 3 by turning retainers 4 through 90 deg.

Servicing clutch:

Do not dismantle the cover assembly. Any wear or clutch problems are best cured by fitting a new assembly, available on an Exchange basis. This also applies to the driven plate. Do not try to rivet on new facings.

Condition of driven plate:

Examine the facings for colour. A high polish is not detrimental. If the grain of the material can be seen, the facings are probably serviceable. Facings that are very dark, with the grain obliterated, have been subjected to oil contamination that has been burned by heat generated. **It is most important that neither grease nor oil should contact the facings so do not handle with greasy fingers.** If the presence of oil has been due to leakage, the cause must be traced and rectified.

Check the fit of the hub splines and the condition of the damper springs. Slackness in the splines may cause backlash and juddering.

Check wear of facings. Reduction in thickness is about .001 inch (.02 mm) for every 1000 miles (1500 km) of normal use. Set plate on a mandrel and check runout with a dial gauge. It must not exceed .015 inch (.38 mm).

Checking release bearing and flywheel:

Look for excessive wear, ridging or grooving of release plate 6 and graphite face of release bearing 7 (see FIG 5:3). Alignment of the face with respect to the trunnions must be within .005 inch (.12 mm). Renew the release bearing as an assembly.

Check friction contact face of flywheel for scoring, cracking or pitting. If clutch persists in fierceness or juddering, cause may be flywheel runout. Use a dial gauge to check this. Reading should not vary by more than .003 inch (.07 mm) at any point on the contact face.

Refitting:

Fit the driven plate with large end of hub towards flywheel. Centralize plate by using tool 18G.1027, a homemade mandrel, or a spare clutch shaft. Fit the cover assembly over the flywheel dowels and start the bolts. Screw them in by diametrical selection, tightening a turn at a time to keep the cover square. Finally tighten to 25 to 30 lb ft (3.4 to 4.1 kg m), and then remove the centralizer. There should now be no difficulty in inserting the clutch shaft.

Refit the flywheel housing and primary drive cover (see **Chapter 6**). Refit power unit (see **Chapter 1**).

5:4 The hydraulic system

The master cylinder shown in **FIG 5:4** is bolted to the engine bulkhead so that pushrod 9 can be coupled to the clutch pedal. Pressure on the pedal and pushrod forces plunger 8 down the bore, pushing fluid along pipe 18, through a flexible hose to slave cylinder (see **FIG 5:6**). The slave cylinder piston 3 is forced outwards, causing pushrod 6, which is connected to the clutch release bearing fork, to have the effect of pressing on the release bearing and disengaging the clutch.

The initial movement of plunger 8 in the master cylinder, closes valve assembly 1, 2, 3 and 4. When the pedal is released, this valve is slightly retracted so that fluid is free to flow from the reservoir into the cylinder bore if any has been lost by leakage.

5:5 Servicing the master cylinder
Removing:

Drain fluid from reservoir by attaching a rubber tube to bleed screw 11 (see **FIG 5:6**). Open screw by a turn and depress clutch pedal, catching fluid in a container. With pedal down, tighten screw and let pedal rise unassisted. Repeat until reservoir is empty.

Remove pin 11 from pushrod and clutch pedal lever (see **FIG 5:4**). Clean area round pipe 18 and disconnect from master cylinder. Fit plugs in outlet port and end of pipe to keep out dirt.

Unscrew bolt 16 and nut 17 and lift cylinder away.

Dismantling:

Remove dust cover 13. Remove circlip 10 and pushrod assembly 9. Withdraw plunger assembly 5, 6, 7 and 8. Lift leaf of thimble 6 and withdraw from plunger (see **FIG 5:5**). Remove seal 7. Compress spring 5 so that valve stem 3 can move sideways and then out of the keyhole slot in the thimble. Separate the components of the valve.

Inspection:

Clean all the parts in Girling Cleaning Fluid or industrial methylated spirit. Examine cylinder bore for scoring or corrosion. Bore must be smooth and polished. Renew cylinder if it is not. Check that port from reservoir into cylinder bore is clear.

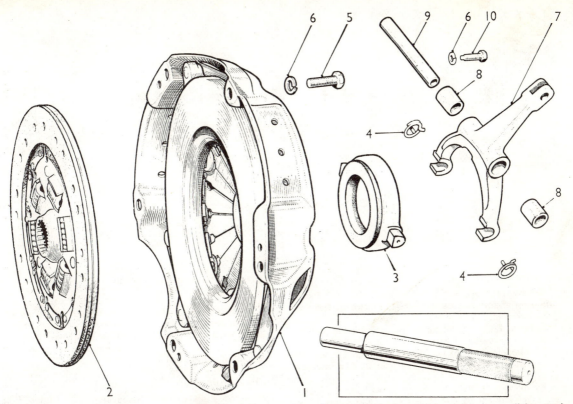

FIG 5:2 Components of clutch and release mechanism. Inset (lower right) shows driven plate centralizing tool 18G.1027

Key to Fig 5:2   1 Cover assembly with straps, diaphragm spring, release plate and pressure plate   2 Driven plate assembly
3 Release bearing assembly   4 Bearing retainers   5 Clutch to flywheel screw   6 Spring washers   7 Clutch withdrawal lever
8 Withdrawal lever bushes   9 Fulcrum shaft   10 Fulcrum shaft screw

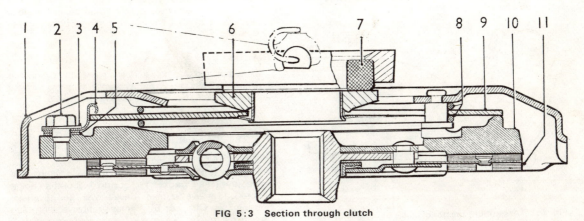

FIG 5:3   Section through clutch

Key to Fig 5:3   1 Cover   2 Strap bolt   3 Washer   4 Clip   5 Pressure plate strap   6 Release plate   7 Release bearing
8 Annular rings   9 Diaphragm spring   10 Pressure plate   11 Driven plate

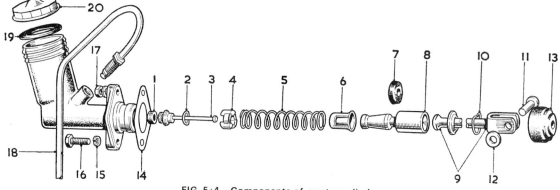

FIG 5:4 Components of master cylinder

Key to Fig 5:4   1 Valve seal   2 Valve stem curved washer   3 Valve stem   4 Valve spacer   5 Spring   6 Thimble   7 Plunger seal   8 Plunger   9 Pushrod   10 Pushrod circlip   11 Pedal to master cylinder clevis pin   12 Plain washer   13 Dust cover   14 Packing   15 Spring washer   16 Screw   17 Stud nut   18 Master to slave cylinder pipe   19 Filler cap gasket   20 Filler cap

Reassembling:

Renew all seals, which are available in kit form. **Observe absolute cleanliness at all times.** Dip the parts in correct fluid and assemble wet.

Refer to **FIG 5:5**. Fit valve seal so that flat side is seated on valve head. Fit curved washer with domed side against underside of head as in inset (top right). Hold it in place with the spacer. Legs of spacer must face towards seal.

Fit spring 5 centrally on spacer (see **FIG 5:4**). Insert thimble 6 into spring, compress spring and engage valve stem in hole in thimble. Fit a new seal 7, using the fingers only. The flat face goes against the large shoulder of the plunger. Insert small end of plunger in thimble until leaf engages behind small shoulder of plunger (see lower arrow in **FIG 5:5**). Press leaf fully home.

Insert plunger assembly into bore, taking care not to trap or turn back the lip of the seal as it enters. Fit pushrod and retaining washer and secure with circlip. Smear inside of dust cover with Girling Rubber Grease and fit to pushrod. Pack cover with the same grease and fit to cylinder.

Refit cylinder in reverse order to removal. Bleed the system as advised in **Section 5:8**.

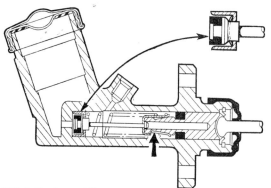

FIG 5:5 Assembling master cylinder plunger thimble and valve. Arrow points to leaf on thimble, inset shows correct assembly of valve seal, curved washer and spacer

5:6 Servicing slave cylinder

Removing:

Drain the system as described in the preceding Section. Release feed pipe from cylinder and release cylinder 13 from flywheel housing (see **FIG 5:6**). When cylinder is withdrawn, pushrod 6 will remain behind, being attached to clutch withdrawal fork.

Dismantling:

Remove dust cover 5. Remove end cap 4 after lifting crimped retainers. With gentle air pressure, blow out the piston 3, seal 2 and spring 1. Drape cloth over cylinder mouth to catch parts. Discard seal and dust cover.

Cleaning and reassembling:

Clean all the parts in methylated spirit and allow to dry. Wet all internal parts with genuine fluid and assemble wet.

Fit seal with flat face against shoulder of piston. Use the fingers to avoid damage. Fit spring with small end on stem. Insert assembly into cylinder, taking great care not to trap or turn back the lip of the seal.

If end cap is serviceable, refit it and crimp the slots. Smear inside of dust cover with Girling Rubber Grease and refit.

Refitting:

Enter pushrod into hole in dust cover and fit cylinder to housing. Fit bolts and spring washers. Refit pressure hose and bleed the system as described in **Section 5:8**.

5:7 The clutch withdrawal lever

Removing:

The lever is part 7 in **FIG 5:2**. To remove it, remove the power unit (see **Chapter 1, Section 1:8** of the Engine chapter). Remove primary drive cover and flywheel housing (see **Chapter 6**). Remove rubber sealing plug from housing. Remove screw 10 and withdraw shaft 9 by screwing a $\frac{5}{16}$ inch UNF bolt into the tapped end. Renew worn shaft and bushes 8.

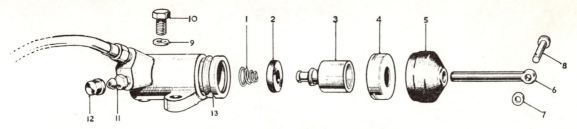

FIG 5:6 Components of the slave cylinder

Key to Fig 5:6 1 Spring 2 Piston seal 3 Piston 4 Piston stop end cap 5 Dust cover 6 Pushrod 7 Plain washer
8 Clevis pin 9 Spring washer 10 Cylinder to housing screw 11 Bleed screw 12 Bleed screw cover 13 Cylinder

Refitting:

Reverse the removal procedure. Note that from Engine Nos. 18AMW/U/H11020 and L2754, the height of the clutch cover assembly was increased (see part 1 in **FIG 5:2**). To maintain clearances the release bearing, withdrawal lever and flywheel housing were also modified.

When refitting a new clutch cover, the latest modified release bearing, withdrawal lever, slave cylinder pushrod and flywheel housing must be fitted to engines with numbers before those which follow:

Clutch withdrawal lever and release bearing—H25030 and L20548 and intermittently between H24647 and L25025.

Flywheel housing and slave cylinder pushrod—H29739 and L20568.

5:8 Bleeding the clutch system

This is necessary if reservoir has become empty or if any part of the hydraulic pipe system has been disconnected or cylinders serviced. Proceed as follows:

1 Attach a tube to the slave cylinder bleed screw (see 11 in **FIG 5:6**). Open screw about three-quarters of a turn. Immerse open end of tube in a glass jar containing a small quantity of clean fluid of the recommended grade.

2 Fill reservoir with correct fluid (see **Section 5:2**). **Ensure that level does not fall too low during the operation.**

3 Use rapid full strokes of the clutch pedal until fluid emerging from end of tube is free from air bubbles. On a downward stroke of the pedal, tighten the bleed screw. Remove tube and refit dust cap. Check fluid 'evel in reservoir.

5:9 Fault diagnosis

(a) Drag or spin

1 Oil or grease on driven plate
2 Leaking master cylinder, slave cylinder or piping
3 Driven plate hub binding on splines
4 Distorted driven plate
5 Broken driven plate facings
6 Air in the clutch hydraulic system

(b) Fierceness or snatch

1 Check 1, 2, 4 and 5 in (a)
2 Worn clutch facings

(c) Slip

1 Check 1 in (a) and 2 in (b)
2 Weak diaphragm spring
3 Seized piston in master or slave cylinder

(d) Judder

1 Check 1 and 4 in (a)
2 Pressure plate or flywheel face running out of true
3 Contact area of driven plate linings unevenly distributed
4 Faulty rubber mountings on power unit
5 Driven plate and shaft splines excessively worn
6 Damper springs broken

(e) Tick or knock

1 Check 5 and 6 in (d)
2 Worn release bearing
3 Faulty drive pinion on starter
4 Loose parts in clutch cover

NOTES

CHAPTER 6

SYNCHROMESH TRANSMISSION

6:1 General description

This transmission, with synchromesh engagement of all forward gears, is housed beneath the engine to form the power unit. Also integral with the unit is the pair of final drive gears, the differential assembly and the two output shafts that are coupled by drive shafts and universal joints to the front wheels. This assembly is carried in a housing bolted to the gearbox casing.

The drive from the crankshaft and flywheel down to the input or first motion shaft of the gearbox can be seen in **FIG 6:1**. There is a gear on clutch shaft 12 that drives an idler gear 14 which in turn drives a gear on the input or first motion shaft 29. The layout of the gearbox is shown in **FIG 6:2** where it can be seen that the inner end of the input or first motion shaft now becomes part 5. The inner gear on this shaft meshes with the largest gear on laygear 35. The four forward gears are in constant mesh with counterparts on the output or third motion shaft 29. Through the action of selector forks 10 and 14 and couplings 15, cones are applied that speed up or slow down pairs of dogs so that they will eventually engage without clash. The drive is then from the laygear to either

of the three gears on the third motion shaft and finally through the dogs to synchronizer hub 25. As the hubs are splined to the shaft, the drive is completed to final drive pinion 26. Top gear is obtained by engagement of dogs on shaft 5 with the first/second synchronizer operated by fork 10.

Reverse gear is obtained by sliding an additional gear assembly (on a separate shaft) into mesh with a laygear and gear 18 on the third motion shaft.

The assembly is shown in **FIG 6:5**.

The arrangement of the final drive and differential assembly can be seen in **FIG 6:6**. Gear 13 meshes with pinion 26 in **FIG 6:2**.

The selection of gears is obtained through cables linked between levers in the gearbox and a gearlever control box under the floor (see **FIG 6:10**).

6:2 Routine maintenance

As the transmission unit shares its lubrication source with that of the engine, refer to **Chapter 1, Section 1:2** in the Engine chapter for the correct routine of checking oil level and draining and refilling.

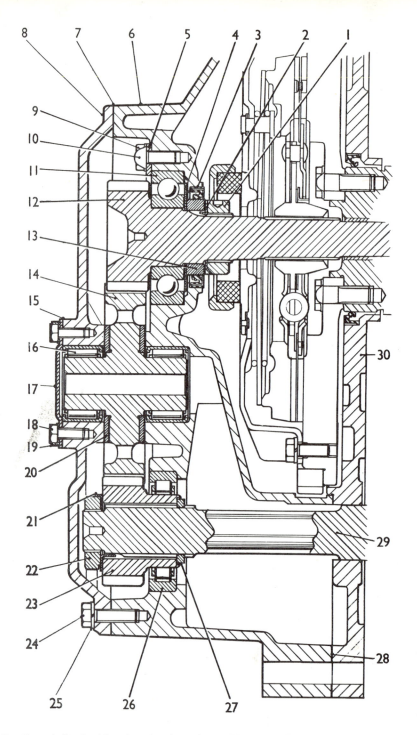

FIG 6:1 Section through flywheel housing showing primary drive gears. The clutch and flywheel are top right

Key to Fig 6:1 1 Clutch shaft nut   2 Tabwasher   3 Oil seal   4 Oil flinger   5 Bearing retainer   6 Flywheel housing
7 Joint washer   8 Primary drive cover   9 Retainer bolts   10 Lockwasher   11 Clutch shaft bearing   12 Clutch shaft
13 Distance piece   14 Idler gear   15 Joint washer   16 Needle roller bearings   17 Cap   18 Cap bolts   19 Lockwasher
20 Idler gear thrust washers   21 Tabwasher   22 First motion shaft nut   23 Drive gear   24 Cover bolt   25 Spring washer
26 Roller bearing   27 Collar   28 Joint washer   29 First motion shaft   30 Adaptor plate

6:3 Servicing flywheel housing and primary drive gears

Removing:

Remove the power unit from the car as described in **Chapter 1, Section 1:8** of the Engine chapter. Proceed as follows:

1 Refer to **FIG 6:1**. Remove bolts 24 and withdraw cover assembly 8 and joint washer 7. Oil will drain from the casing. Withdraw idler gear 14 with thrust washers 20.
2 Move both top selectors to the right to engage two gears simultaneously. Unlock washer 21, remove nut 22 and pull off drive gear 23.
3 Remove starter motor. Withdraw housing 6 and joint 28 (7 nuts, housing to transmission casing studs, one of these from inside casing; 4 bolts and nuts from housing to adaptor plate 30). More oil will drain out when housing is removed.

Dismantling:

1 Unlock and remove bolts 9. Remove bearing retainer 5. Press out bearing 11 and extract oil seal 3 if renewal is required.
2 Unlock and remove clutch shaft nut 1, using a peg spanner or tool 18G.1023A (see **FIG 6:11**). Remove oil flinger 4 and distance piece 13. Press the shaft from bearing if necessary.
3 Press bearing 26 out of housing after removing location plate. Unlock and remove bolts 18 and remove cap 17 with joint 15. Extract needle roller bearings 16 if required. **Do not remove bearings or oil seal unless they are to be renewed.**

Inspection:

After cleaning, check for worn, cracked or broken gear teeth. Check bearings for roughness when unlubricated. Renew clutch shaft if driven plate splines are worn. Also check fit of clutch shaft spigot in bush in end of crankshaft. Renew oil seal if oil has been leaking into the clutch housing. The running surface of spacer 13 must be perfectly smooth if the oil seal is to function properly. Clean off old joint material.

Reassembling:

Do this in the reverse order of dismantling. Note the following:

1 Fit new joint washers. When refitting the clutch shaft, fit tool 18G.1051 over the locknut to protect the oil seal (see **FIG 6:11**).
2 Check that collar 27 is seated in its groove before tightening nut 22 to correct torque, then return gear selectors to neutral positions.
3 Tighten flywheel housing and primary drive cover nuts and bolts finger tight at first, then tighten down a turn at a time by diagonal selection to get even pressure on the joints.
4 Before fitting cap 17, set up a dial gauge and check end float of idler gear, especially if a new gear and thrust washers have been fitted. Register the gauge on the idler hub and check that end float is .008 to .010 inch (.20 to .25 mm). If necessary, adjust by fitting

alternative washers available in four .002 inch (.05 mm) steps between .128 to .129 inch (3.25 to 3.28 mm) and .134 to .135 inch (3.40 to 3.53 mm).

When reassembly is completed, remove filler plug from top of primary drive cover and pour in $1\frac{1}{2}$ pints ($1\frac{3}{4}$ US pints or .8 litres) of oil. **Do this before refitting power unit in car.**

6:4 Dismantling gearbox

After removing power unit (see **Chapter 1, Section 1:8**), flywheel housing assembly (**Section 6:3**) and clutch (see **Chapter 5, Section 5:3**), proceed as follows:

1 Remove the flywheel. Remove adaptor plate 30 (see **FIGS 6:1** and **6:3**). Withdraw fork rod retaining plate and laygear thrust springs (intermittent fitting prior to gearbox AA.1850) to prevent loss.
2 Release transmission case from engine crankcase (11 bolts and six nuts). Collect the O-ring round the oil suction port.
3 Withdraw the differential shafts 22 (see **FIG 6:6**). Mark them for correct refitting. Remove differential assembly from casing (see **Section 6:6**).
4 Withdraw transmission front cover. Check end float of laygear at the front end (see small thrust washer 32 in **FIG 6:2**). If excessive, oversize washers are available. Tap out layshaft from front end and withdraw laygear 35 and thrust washers 32 and 37. If third motion shaft is to be dismantled, unlock and slacken retaining nut 28 (lefthand thread).
5 Refer to **FIG 6:2** and remove circlip 1 and distance piece 2. Tap first motion shaft 5 outwards to remove from casing. If bearing 6 needs renewing, remove it from shaft.
6 Drive out reverse fork rod from front of box (see 1 in **FIG 6:4**). Retrieve ball 9, spring 8 and plate 7 from the box. Unlock and remove reverse shaft bolt (lower lefthand one in bearing retainer). Drive out shaft and remove gear and fork 2.
7 Drive out two remaining selector rods 3 and 6, retrieving the balls and springs. Unlock and remove bolts and nut from bearing retainer 31 (see **FIG 6:2**). Keeping forks out of the way, drive third motion shaft assembly forward until bearing housing 20 is clear. Use tools 18G.1045 (or 18G.1028 prior to engine No. 18AMW/U/H301). These are shown in **FIG 6:11**. Take the weight of the assembly, remove the third/fourth synchronizer assembly (see fork 10), turn retainer 31 to clear front cover aperture and remove assembly.

Inspection:

Clean all parts and check bearings for roughness and play when dry. Check gear teeth and fit of gears on third motion shaft. Check all splines for wear. Check fit of third motion shaft spigot and needle roller bearing in bore of first motion shaft. Check layshaft for wear at bearing tracks and check laygear for wear and condition of gear teeth. Renew forks if side play is excessive. Renew parts if synchronizing has been ineffective. This is mainly due to wear of synchronizing cones and baulk rings 16. Check synchronizer springs and end float of gears according to figures given in **Technical Data**. If baulk rings do not engage before they contact edge of gear, renew hub and baulk rings. Check casings for cracks and damage.

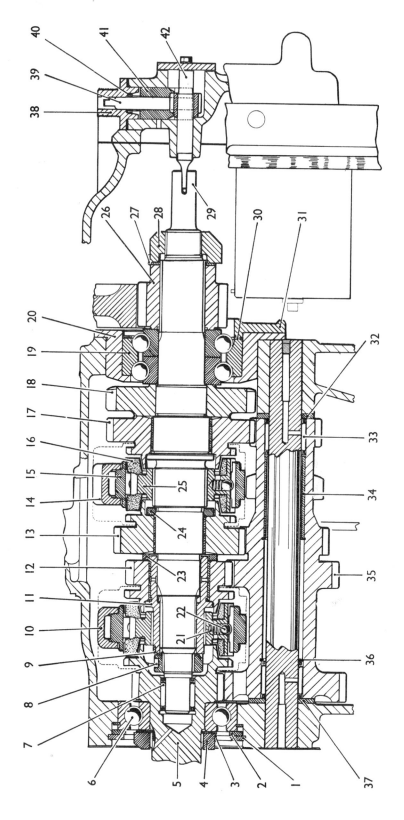

FIG 6 : 2 Section through gearbox showing third motion shaft (top) and laygear (bottom)

Key to Fig 6 : 2 1 Circlip 2 Distance piece 3 Lockwasher 4 Nut 5 First motion shaft 6 Ballbearing 7 Needle roller bearing 8 Nut 9 Nut lockwasher
10 Third/fourth-speed fork 11 Mainshaft sleeve 12 Third-speed gear 13 Second-speed gear 14 First/second-speed fork 15 Sliding coupling 16 Baulk ring
17 First-speed gear 18 Reverse mainshaft gear 19 Ballbearing (special) 20 Bearing housing 21 Synchronizer spring 22 Synchronizer ball 23 Interlocking thrust washer
24 Second-speed gear thrust washer 25 Synchronizer hub 26 Final drive pinion 27 Lockwasher 28 Nut 29 Third motion shaft 30 Bearing shim*
31 Retainer for bearing 32 Small thrust washer 33 Needle roller bearing 34 Distance tube 35 Laygear 36 Spring ring 37 Large thrust washer
38 Screwed speedometer pinion bush 39 Speedometer pinion bush 40 Oil seal 41 Plain speedometer pinion bush 42 Wheel speedometer spindle
*Up to Engine No. 18AMW/U/H99312, L97831, and 18WB/SbU/H1114

64

Dismantling third motion shaft:

Hold assembly at final drive gear end, using soft jaws in the vice. Do the following:

1 Unlock and remove nut 8, using peg spanner 18G.1024 (see **FIG 6:11**). Withdraw sleeve 11, third-speed gear 12 and interlocking washer 23. Withdraw second-speed gear 13 and thrust washer 24. Withdraw first/second-speed synchronizer (see 15 and 25). Turn the shaft and hold assembly carefully to avoid damage to splines and bearings.

2 Unlock and unscrew nut 28 (lefthand thread), using tool 18G.1022. Withdraw pinion 26.

3 Press shaft through bearing assembly by supporting underneath face of first-speed gear 17. Do not support on cone face or dog teeth. Remove retainer 31 and shims 30 to extract bearing if due for renewal.

4 Withdraw reverse and first-speed gears 18 and 17. Dismantle synchronizer assemblies by removing the baulk rings 16. Wrap assembly in cloth and push hub 25 from coupling 15 to release three sets of balls and springs 21 and 22. Note that sliding couplings are etched 36 deg. on outside diameter. Third/fourth coupling is larger on outside diameter. Later couplings have detent grooves in three teeth at 120 deg.

5 Check all parts as advised under 'Inspection'. Check that threads of shaft and retaining nuts are in good condition.

Dismantling laygear:

The needle rollers 33 and distance tube 34 are readily extracted. There is no need to remove the spring rings 36. Check parts as advised under 'Inspection'.

6:5 Reassembling gearbox

Reassembling laygear:

Lubricate and fit needle roller bearings. Do not forget tube 34 (see **FIG 6:2**). Push bearings home against spring rings.

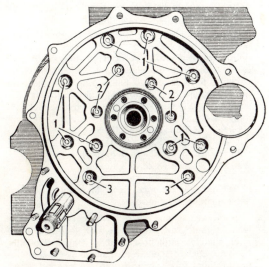

FIG 6:3 Location of adaptor plate bolts. Bolts (1) are $\frac{3}{8}$ inch UNF, bolts (2) are $\frac{5}{16}$ inch UNF and bolts (3) are $\frac{5}{16}$ inch UNC

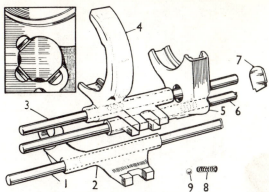

FIG 6:4 Gear selector forks and rods. Inset shows end view of rods with locating plate fitted

Key to Fig 6:4   1 Reverse fork rod   2 Reverse fork
3 1st/2nd fork rod   4 1st/2nd fork   5 3rd/4th fork
6 3rd/4th fork rod   7 Locating plate   8 Spring
9 Locating ball

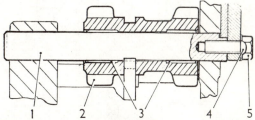

FIG 6:5 Reverse gear assembly showing shaft location

Key to Fig 6:5   1 Reverse shaft   2 Reverse wheel
3 Bushes   4 Lockwasher (tabwasher, early units)
5 Screw

Reassembling third motion shaft:

Lubricate all parts. Smear inside bore of first-speed gear 17 with Duckham's Moly Disulphide Grease (max. size 5 microns). Proceed as follows:

1 Assemble synchronizer assemblies, taking care to align the cut-outs. Fit balls and springs in hub, press them down and slide hub into coupling.

2 Fit first-speed gear 17 followed by reverse gear 18 with its bearing face towards first-speed gear. If removed, press bearing 19 into housing. On early assemblies, shims are required between bearing and retainer to provide the necessary nip of .001 to .002 inch (.025 to .05 mm). Always check this if a new housing is fitted. However, if a new retainer is fitted to a new housing, no shims are needed on the early-type assemblies. For shimming, measure depth of bearing face from face of housing. Fit shims according to following table:

Depth of bearing	Shim thickness
.183 to .184 inch (4.65 to 4.67 mm)	None
.185 to .186 inch (4.70 to 4.72 mm)	.002 inch (.05 mm)
.187 to .188 inch (4.75 to 4.77 mm)	.004 inch (.10 mm)
.189 to .190 inch (4.80 to 4.82 mm)	.006 inch (.15 mm)
.191 to .192 inch (4.85 to 4.87 mm)	.008 inch (.20 mm)

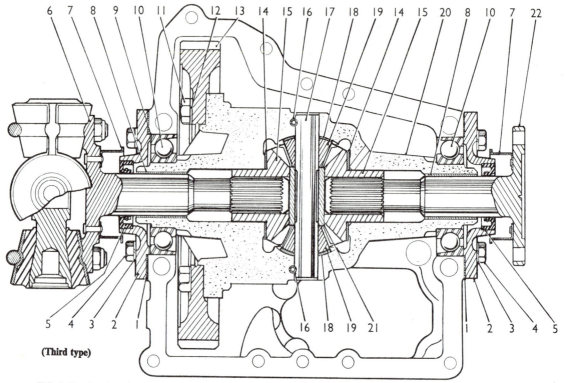

FIG 6:6 Section through differential assembly (third type). Wheel 13 is driven by pinion 26 in FIG 6:2

Key to Fig 6:6   1 Joint washer   2 End cover   3 Spring washer   4 End cover to transmission case setscrew
5 Oil seal   6 Differential shaft (flexible coupling type)   7 Dust cover   8 Bush   9 Ballbearing to end cover shim
10 Ballbearing   11 Final drive wheel to differential case bolt   12 Lockwasher   13 Final drive wheel   14 Washer for differential gear
15 Differential gear   16 Roll pin   17 Pinion centre   18 Washer for differential pinion   19 Differential pinion   20 Differential case
21 Distance piece   22 Differential shaft (flange type)

3 Fit lockwasher 27 and nut 28 (lefthand thread). Hold shaft in vice at drive gear end. Fit first/second synchronizer 15, 16 and 25. Engage hub on splines, fitting the assembly either way round. Fit thrust washer 24 and gear 13. Fit sleeve 11, gear 12 and washer 23, engaging the washer and sleeve. Fit third/fourth synchronizer either way round. Fit lockwasher 9 and tighten nut 8 to 40 lb ft (5.5 kg m) minimum. Lock nut with washer.

4 Check end float of gears according to figures in **Technical Data**. Renew parts if end float is excessive.

Final assembly:

1 Fit springs and balls to selector forks (see **FIG 6:4**). Hold in place with ½ inch lengths of round bar or use tool 18G.1029 (see **FIG 6:11**). Position first/second and third/fourth forks in bottom of casing.

2 Pass the third motion shaft assembly through front cover aperture. Turn bearing housing to enter retainer. Hold forks clear and gently drift bearing housing into casing. Secure the retainer with bolts and nut, turning up tabs of lockwashers. Make sure that tab nearest to final drive gear will not foul.

3 Position forks as in **FIG 6:4** and push third/fourth rod, followed by first/second rod through forks from rear

of box. Do not forget to collect the short pieces of rod used to keep the balls and springs in place.

4 Fit needle roller bearing 7 (see **FIG 6:2**). Press bearing 6 squarely into place, fit distance piece and secure with circlip 1. If a new bearing has been fitted to shaft, select a distance piece that will just not allow the circlip to fit in its groove. Select a distance piece the next thickness down, from the following table. This should give a clearance not exceeding .004 inch (.10 mm):

.117 to .118 inch (2.97 to 3.00 mm)
.121 to .122 inch (3.07 to 3.10 mm)
.125 to .126 inch (3.17 to 3.20 mm)
.129 to .130 inch (3.28 to 3.30 mm)
.133 to .134 inch (3.38 to 3.40 mm)

Remove test distance piece, fit selected one and engage circlip in its groove.

5 Position reverse gear and fork with gear engaged and lead on teeth towards rear of box (see **FIG 6:5**). Push shaft through box, locating it against bearing housing. Lock setscrew 5 after securing. Push reverse rod 1 through fork 2 (see **FIG 6:4**). Fit locating plate 7. Retrieve short rod used to keep ball and spring in place. Set gear in neutral.

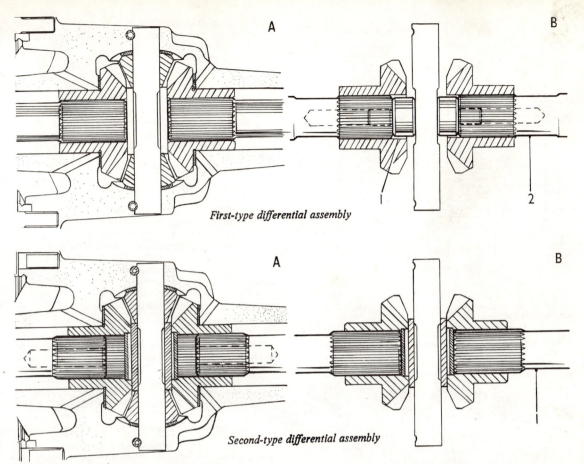

First-type differential assembly

Second-type **differential assembly**

FIG 6:7 Earlier plunging (sliding) differential shafts at 'A' may be modified to fixed shafts suitable for plunging drive shafts as at 'B'

Key to Fig 6:7
First type: **A** Plunging differential shafts and fixed-length drive shafts. Up to 18AMW/U/H54626, L42211
             B Modified for plunging drive shafts   **1** Distance piece   **2** Second-type differential shaft
Second type: **A** Plunging differential shafts with foam-filled drilling, Welch-plugged gear, and fixed-length drive shafts. Between
             18AMW/U/H54627 to 89667, L42212 to 42273
             B Modified for plunging drive shafts.   **1** First-type differential shaft

6 Fit laygear and thrust washers (small washer at front end). Fit shaft from rear with cut-away end to the rear. After passing shaft through large thrust washer and laygear, select a small thrust washer that will give the correct end float of .002 to .003 inch (.05 to .08 mm). Washers are available in the following thicknesses:
.123 to .125 inch (3.12 to 3.17 mm)
.1265 to .1285 inch (3.21 to 3.26 mm)
.130 to .132 inch (3.30 to 3.35 mm)
.133 to .135 inch (3.38 to 3.43 mm)

7 Fit front cover assembly complete. Fit differential assembly and shafts (see **Section 6:6**). Fit a new joint washer to face of transmission casing. Make sure oil suction O-ring is in place. See that the front and rear main bearing sealing corks are in place.

8 Lower engine into place, do up fixings finger tight and then tighten evenly, a turn at a time. Align layshaft cut-away with its location in backplate, check that fork rod retaining plate is still in position and fit the laygear thrust springs. Smear lip of crankshaft seal with SAE.90.EP oil and refit adaptor plate on a new joint washer. Refer to **FIG 6:3** for position of bolts and tighten to torque given in **Technical Data**. If red rubber seals are fitted, lubricate them with Bentone grease for ease of assembly.

9 Align '1/4' mark on crankshaft and flywheel, fit bolts and tighten to 40 lb ft (5.5 kg m). Turn up tabs of new lockwashers. Refit clutch assembly (see **Chapter 5**). Fit flywheel housing (see **Section 6:3**). Refit power unit (see **Chapter 1**).

6:6 Servicing differential assembly

Note that the differential housing and gearbox are a matched pair and cannot be renewed separately. This also applies to the final drive gear and pinion.

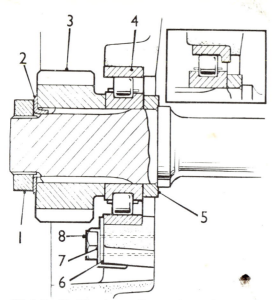

FIG 6:8 Modifications to first motion shaft bearing. Alternative bearing (top right)

Key to Fig 6:8 1 Nut 2 Lockwasher 3 Drive gear
4 Roller bearing   5 Retaining ring   6 Location plate
7 Lockwasher   8 Setscrew

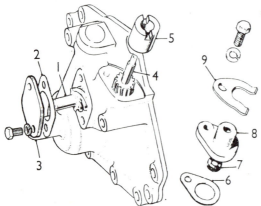

FIG 6:9 Speedometer drive components

Key to Fig 6:9   1 Drive wheel   2 Joint washer
3 End plate 4 Pinion 5 Pinion bush 6 Joint washer
7 Oil seal   8 Screwed bush   9 Spring plate

Removing:

1 Refer to **FIG 6:6**. Remove power unit from vehicle (see **Chapter 1**). Withdraw shafts 22. Remove end covers 2. Note oil return holes and number of shims 9. Mark parts for correct refitting.

2 Release differential cover from casing (10 nuts). Withdraw cover and differential assembly.

Dismantling:

1 Withdraw bearing outer rings and use a puller to remove bearings. Note stamped identification marks on outer faces of bearings.

2 Release drive wheel 13 from case 20 (8 bolts). Mark wheel and case for correct refitting. Drive out rollpins 16 and pinion centre pin 17.

3 Remove pinions 19, gears 15 and washers 14 and 18.

Inspection:

After cleaning, check bearings for roughness when dry. Check gear teeth for wear, cracks or chipping. Check fit of drive shaft splines. Check condition of thrust washers and mating surfaces. Check pinion pin and bores of pinions for wear. Check condition of bushes 8.

Servicing differential shafts:

Differential shafts 22 may be either fixed or plunging (sliding), the later fixed type being used with plunging (sliding) drive shafts (see **Chapter** 7).

If the sliding type of drive shafts are being fitted then the differential shafts must be modified to the fixed state. This is desirable when renewing parts. **FIG 6:7** shows first and second-type assemblies, the lefthand views being those of the earlier type with plunging differential shafts and fixed drive shafts. To modify these to the desirable condition of fixed differential shafts and plunging drive shafts, refer to the righthand views.

Reassembling:

Refit all parts in their original positions, working in the reverse order to dismantling. When fitting the differential gear thrust washers 14 and 18, set the slightly chamfered bores against faces of gears. If necessary, lever out defective oil seals 5 and press in new ones. Service the differential shafts as advised in the preceding notes.

Refitting differential assembly:

Place assembly in transmission casing with a slight bias towards the flywheel. Refit differential casing and new joint washer. Tighten nuts just enough to hold bearings and yet allow them to move when the righthand end cover is fitted. Fit righthand cover on a new joint washer. Line up oil holes and tighten fixings evenly and diagonally so that the cover remains square. Differential assembly will be displaced away from flywheel. Note, however, that some assemblies may have shims fitted at the flywheel end. In this case fit assembly with bias towards final drive wheel and shim it at the flywheel end.

Setting bearing preload (first method):

Fit lefthand cover with joint washer. Tighten bolts just enough to nip bearing outer race. **Do not overtighten or cover will be distorted.** Use feelers to measure gap between cover flange and differential housing and transmission casing. Check at several points. Variations show that cover bolts have not been tightened evenly. Adjust accordingly but be careful not to distort flange. If there is no gap, add shims until clearance is measurable.

Compressed joint washer measures .008 inch (.20 mm). Required preload on bearings is .003 to .005 inch (.08 to .13 mm). Gap required is therefore .011 to .013 inch (.28 to .33 mm). Make adjustments by altering shims between bearing and register on inner face of cover. Shims are available in thicknesses of .0015 and .0025 inch (.04 and .06 mm). Tighten cover bolts and then tighten differential casing nuts.

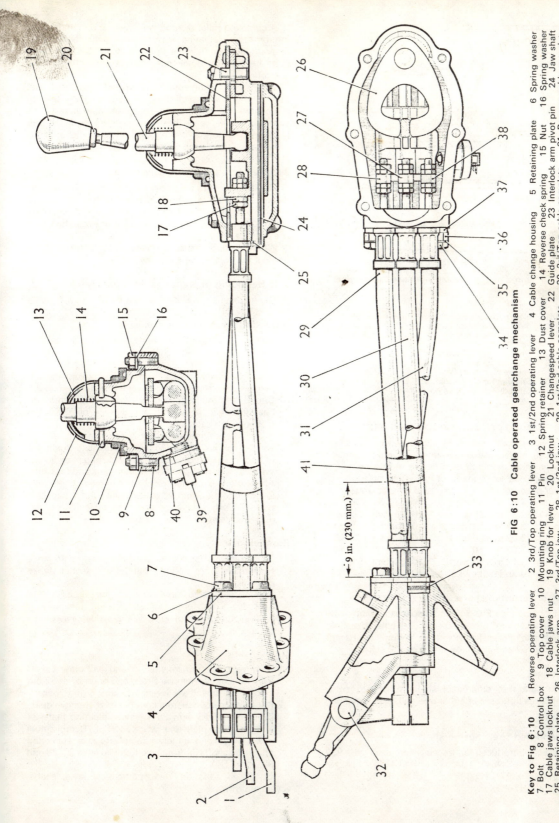

FIG 6:10   Cable operated gearchange mechanism

Key to Fig 6:10   1 Reverse operating lever   2 3rd/Top operating lever   3 1st/2nd operating lever   4 Cable change housing   5 Retaining plate   6 Spring washer
7 Bolt   8 Control box   9 Top cover   10 Mounting ring   11 Pin   12 Spring retainer   13 Dust cover   14 Reverse check spring   15 Nut   16 Spring washer
17 Cable jaws locknut   18 Cable jaws nut   19 Knob for lever   20 Locknut   21 Changespeed lever   22 Guide plate   23 Interlock arm pivot pin   24 Jaw shaft
25 Retaining plate   26 Interlock arm   27 3rd/Top jaw   28 1st/2nd jaw   29 1st/2nd cable complete   30 3rd/Top cable complete   31 Reverse cable complete
32 Operating levers pivot   33 Cables O-ring   34 Screw   35 Spring washer   36 Spacer   37 Retaining plate   38 Reverse jaw   39 Reverse light switch*
40 Joint washer*   41 Retaining band   *Plug and fibre washer when switch is not fitted

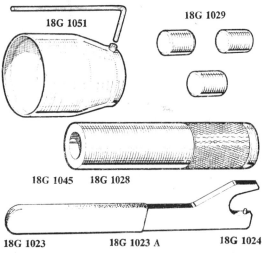

18G 1051

18G 1029

18G 1045   **18G 1028**

18G 1023   **18G 1023 A**   **18G 1024**

FIG 6:11   Some of the special tools used to service the gearbox

Key to Fig 6:11

18G.1051	Sleeve to protect clutch shaft oil seal
18G.1029	Selector shaft assembly guides
18G.1028	Drift for third motion shaft (up to engine No. 18AMW/U/H301)
18G.1045	Drift for third motion shaft
18G.1023	Spanner for clutch shaft nut (larger nut up to engine Nos. 18AMW/U/H42439, L20592)
18G.1023A	Spanner for clutch shaft nut
18G.1024	Spanner for third motion shaft nut

Setting bearing preload (second method):

Fully tighten casing nuts. Eliminate end clearance by driving differential case and bearings towards righthand end cover. Measure depth from casing to bearing with a depth gauge. Select shims from following table:

Depth of bearing	Shim thickness
.113 to .114 (2.87 to 2.90 mm)	None
.115 to .116 (2.92 to 2.95 mm)	.0025 inch (.06 mm)
.117 to .118 (2.97 to 3.00 mm)	.004 inch (.10 mm)
.119 to .120 (3.02 to 3.05 mm)	.006 inch (.15 mm)
.121 to .122 (3.07 to 3.10 mm)	.008 inch (.20 mm)
.123 to .124 (3.12 to 3.15 mm)	.010 inch (.25 mm)

Insert shims and refit end cover and joint washer.

Fitting differential shafts:

On first type (see **FIG 6:7**) coat splines of shafts with Duckham's Lammol grease. On second type, clean out old grease and refill each cavity in shafts with $\frac{3}{8}$ oz (10 gm) of Duckham's Lammol grease and coat the splines.

Final check:

Make sure that differential shafts turn with equal resistance, as tightness of either one will lead to steering pull.

6:7 Modified first motion shaft

This was introduced at transmission case No. 937 or at engine Nos. 18AMW/U/H114425/L114219, 18H197/H110897/L108006, 18C/U/H213 and 18WB/SbU/H7667.

A complete roller bearing was fitted to a modified first motion shaft, retaining washer, drive gear, lockwasher, retaining nut and flywheel housing (see **FIG 6:8**). These parts are not individually interchangeable with the original assembly.

When dismantling, pull housing and bearing off first motion shaft. When refitting, fit housing with bearing in position and drift bearing up to retaining ring. In the case of the alternative bearing shown in the inset, drift the bearing onto the first motion shaft with the lip of the outer race towards the clutch housing.

6:8 Servicing speedometer drive

The components are shown in **FIG 6:9**. To remove, disconnect cable from bush 8. Remove end plate 3 and withdraw drive wheel 1. Release plate 9 and withdraw screwed bush 8, pinion 4 and bush 5. Renew parts if wear is excessive.

When refitting, use spring plate 9 in preference to the original flat washer on early gearboxes.

6:9 Servicing gearchange mechanism (cable)

The mechanism is shown in **FIG 6:10**.

Adjusting from inside vehicle:

1 Pull gaiter up gearlever. Depress spring retainer 12 to release its bayonet fixing and withdraw lever 21 complete.
2 Pull floor covering clear and remove coverplate and joint washer. Remove top cover 9 and guide plate 22. Check that interlock arm 26 swings freely through change speed jaws with a clearance of .030 inch (.76 mm) on each side.
3 If jaws do not line up, adjust cables. Slacken nuts 17 and 18. Set jaw correctly, then move cable to and fro to find mid-point of backlash in cable and relay levers. With cable in mid-position, tighten nuts and locknuts. An easy check on mid-position is to move cable fully in one direction and screw adjusting nut up to jaw, repeat in other direction and then set cable so that gaps between nuts and jaw are equal.

Removing:

1 Drain transmission oil. Remove floor covering. Remove heat shield from floor (3 nuts). Release handbrake cable from lever.
2 Release cable housing 4 from differential casing. Let heat shield drop onto exhaust pipe and remove four bolts securing control box 8. Withdraw cable assembly complete.

Dismantling:

1 Remove bolts and retainers 5 and withdraw cables from housing 4. Remove circlip and press pivot 32 out of housing to release levers 1, 2 and 3 and spacers.
2 Remove top cover 9 from control box 8. Remove guide 22 and interlock arm 26. Release retaining plate 37 and withdraw plate and two spacers 36. Remove nuts and locknuts and withdraw cables. Release retainer 25 and press shafts 24 from box. Remove jaws 27, 28 and 38.

Check all parts for wear, particularly jaws, shafts, levers and pivots.

Reassembling:

1 Refit operating levers, spacers and pivot. Refit circlip. Insert cables and fit retainers.

2 Position jaws in cable control box, press in shafts and fit retainer. Plunger of reverse light switch 39 should just touch contact face of reverse jaw 38.

3 Insert cables and fit nuts and locknuts. Apply liberal coating of grease. Refit cable retainer, spacers and interlock arm. Fit band 41 to cables (see dimension in **FIG 6:10**). Note that reverse cable has a yellow band and is longer than the other two.

4 Set operating levers in neutral position, ease cable housing into differential cover and fit nuts and spring washers. Refit control box to heat shield and secure heat shield assembly to floor. Connect handbrake cable.

5 Adjust cables as already instructed. Refit change speed guide, control box cover, floor cover and gearlever assembly. Check for selection of all gears.

Mk 3 models:

Since March 1972 the Mk 3 models have been modified and have a single rod and steady bar instead of cables. The selector rod, from the lever to the gearbox selector shaft, is roll-pinned into position at each end and no adjustment is allowed for, and neither should it be necessary with a positive selector mechanism of this type.

6:10 Fault diagnosis

(a) Jumping out of gear

1 Broken spring behind selector rod ball
2 Worn groove in selector rod
3 Worn synchromesh coupling dogs
4 Worn selector fork
5 Excessive backlash in gearchange mechanism

(b) Noisy transmission

1 Insufficient oil
2 Excessive end float of laygear
3 Incorrect end float of idler and mainshaft gears
4 Incorrect preload on differential bearings
5 Worn or damaged bearings
6 Worn bushes on third motion shaft
7 Worn or damaged gear teeth
8 Worn splines on drive shafts and gears

(c) Difficulty in engaging gear

1 Faulty clutch or clutch withdrawal mechanism
2 Worn synchromesh cones
3 Backlash or incorrect adjustment of gearchange mechanism
4 Worn selector forks and couplings

(d) Oil leaks

1 Faulty joint washers or joint faces
2 Worn or damaged oil seals or running surfaces

(e) Steering pulls to one side

1 Check for stiffness of one differential shaft

NOTES

CHAPTER 6a

AUTOMATIC TRANSMISSION

6a : 1 General description

This Borg Warner transmission incorporates a fluid torque converter coupled by chain and sprockets to a hydraulically operated gearbox which gives three forward ratios and reverse. The forward ratios are automatically engaged according to accelerator position and the speed of the vehicle. By selecting 'L' it is possible to override the automatic control in first and second ratios and this will give engine braking.

The layout of the system is shown diagrammatically in **FIG 6a : 1**. The hydraulic torque converter is a casing filled with fluid and carrying impeller vanes 5. The casing is bolted to the crankshaft 1. As the casing revolves, fluid is impelled against the vanes of stator 3 and turbine 4. As the stator is virtually stationary at starting, the effect is of torque multiplication. At first this multiplication is about 2 to 1 but as the stator picks up speed this gradually falls to 1 to 1 when it is turning at the same speed as the impeller and turbine. The converter is then turning as a unit and transmitting engine torque to input shaft 8 by way of chain 7.

Front clutch 9 connects the converter to the gears for forward ratios. Rear clutch 11 is for reverse. Bands 12 and 14 are operated by hydraulic pressure and hold elements of the gear set stationary for the ratios required. In 'L', band 14 holds the pinion carrier stationary for first ratio. Band 12 holds reverse sun gear 15 stationary for second ratio.

One-way clutch 13 operates in the first ratio to stop pinion carrier from turning in opposite direction to engine. This allows the gear set to freewheel and ensures smooth changes from first to second and back.

Power flow:

Refer to diagrams in **FIG 6a : 2**.

'L' selected (first ratio):

Front clutch applied, converter connected to forward sun gear (diagram 'A'). Rear band is applied. Pinion carrier gives reaction on drive and overrun to provide engine braking. Reverse sun gear turns in opposite direction. Ratio 2.39 to 1.

'D' selected (first ratio):

Front clutch applied (diagram 'B'). One-way clutch operates to hold carrier stationary. Freewheel on the overrun. Ratio 2.39 to 1.

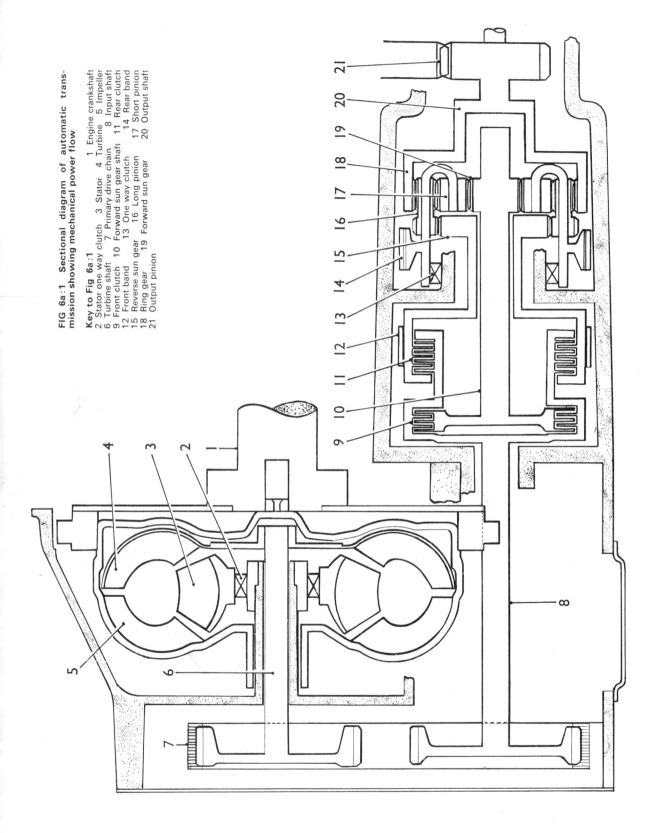

FIG 6a:1 Sectional diagram of automatic transmission showing mechanical power flow

Key to Fig 6a:1
1 Engine crankshaft
2 Stator one way clutch
3 Stator
4 Turbine
5 Impeller
6 Turbine shaft
7 Primary drive chain
8 Input shaft
9 Front clutch
10 Forward sun gear shaft
11 Rear clutch
12 Front band
13 One way clutch
14 Rear band
15 Reverse sun gear
16 Long pinion
17 Short pinion
18 Ring gear
19 Forward sun gear
20 Output shaft
21 Output pinion

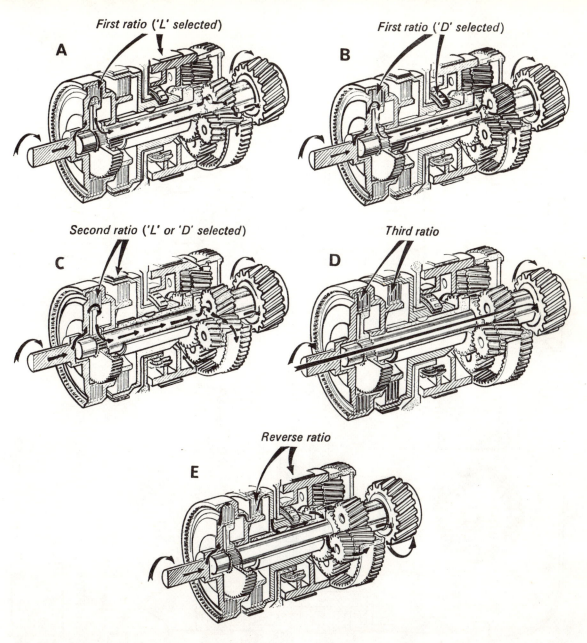

FIG 6a:2 Diagrams showing the power flow through the transmission in the various ratios. The input shaft is on the left

'L' or 'D' selected (second ratio):

Front clutch and front band applied (diagram 'C'). Reverse sun gear provides reaction on drive and overrun, giving engine braking. Ratio 1.45 to 1.

Third ratio:

Front and rear clutches applied (diagram 'D'). Both sun gears are locked together, the gear set turning as a unit. This provides drive and engine braking. Ratio 1 to 1.

Reverse:

Rear clutch and rear band applied (diagram 'E'). Pinion carrier provides reaction on drive and overrun, giving engine braking. Ratio 2.09 to 1.

Hydraulic control:

This is shown diagrammatically in **FIG 6a:3**. Hydraulic control is achieved by directing hydraulic fluid pressure through valves that are under the combined influences of

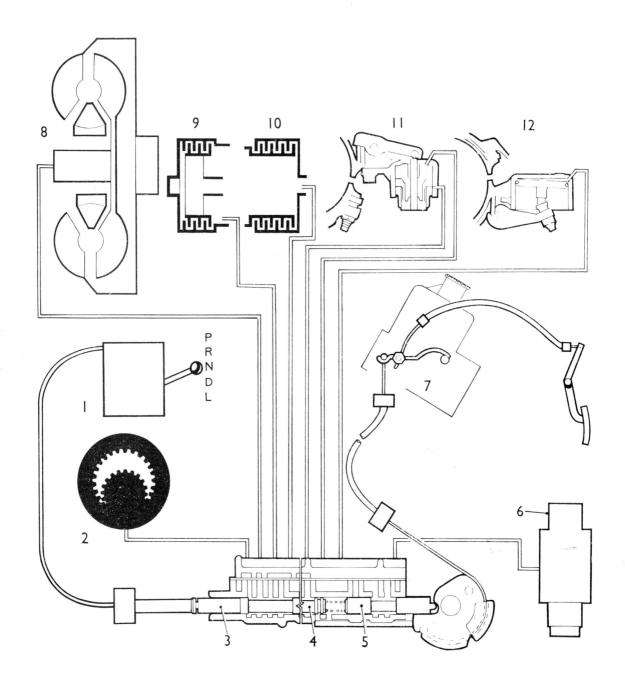

FIG 6a:3   How the automatic transmission system is hydraulically controlled

Key to Fig 6a:3   1 Selector lever   2 Pump   3 Manual valve   4 Downshift valve   5 Throttle valve   6 Governor
7 Throttle lever   8 Torque converter   9 Front clutch   10 Rear clutch   11 Front servo   12 Rear servo

selector lever and throttle pedal, and also a governor which is sensitive to road speed. Pump 2 supplies the hydraulic and lubrication needs of the converter and transmission.

Moving selector lever 1 to 'D', 'L' or 'R' moves valve 3 which then directs fluid to, or exhausts it from, the appropriate valves, clutches or bands.

The downshift cam is connected by cable to carburetter throttle lever 7. Movement of downshift valve 4 modifies pressure from throttle valve 5 to produce a pressure that is related to engine torque and road speed. Full movement of the downshift valve by pressing the throttle pedal through the 'kickdown' position produces up-changes at preset maximum road speeds, or gives a down-change at speeds just below the maximum according to governor pressure.

The governor 6 regulates pressure according to road speed. This pressure decides the points at which ratio changes occur.

6a:2 Routine maintenance

Refer to **FIG 6a:4**. Keep stoneguards 'A' free from dirt. Clean converter and transmission casings to encourage natural cooling.

Every 3000 miles (5000 km) or 3 months, check fluid level. Have vehicle parked on level ground, with engine and transmission at normal running temperature. Select 'P' (3) and let engine idle for 2 minutes. Wipe dipstick (4), and with engine still idling, insert it and withdraw again immediately. If necessary add correct automatic transmission fluid to bring level to 'high' mark (5). Difference between marks is one pint (1.2 US pints, .6 litre).

If draining is necessary, take great care if transmission is at running temperature. **The fluid will be extremely hot and may scald.** Do not refill with used fluid if contaminated. Amount needed will depend on fluid that is trapped in the converter and this may be up to 5 pints (6 US pints or 2.8 litres). Total capacity of system is 13 pints (15 US pints or 7.4 litres).

The selector linkage must be checked every 6000 miles (10,000 km) or 6 months.

6a:3 Selector lever positions

To prevent direct selection from 'N' the lever must be moved to the left against spring pressure, before engaging 'L' or 'R'. Move lever fully to left before engaging 'P'.

'P' (Park): No engine power to wheels. Transmission locked. Use for parking or for running engine for tuning or adjustment. **Do not select when vehicle is moving.**

'R' (Reverse): Gives reverse with full engine braking. Do not select while vehicle is moving forward.

'N' (Neutral): No power to wheels. Apply handbrake when vehicle is at rest.

'D' (Drive): For all normal driving. Fully automatic gearchanges according to speed and to position of accelerator pedal.

'L' (Low): Overriding control for first and second ratios. Gives engine braking.

6a:4 Towing

When vehicle is used for towing, always select 'L' before going up or down steep hills.

To tow the vehicle, add an extra 3 pints ($3\frac{1}{2}$ US pints or 1.7 litres) of fluid to the transmission. Do not tow at

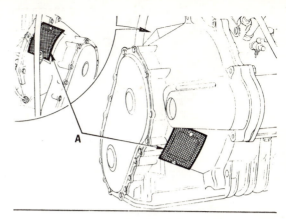

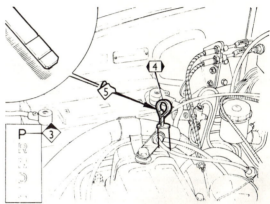

FIG 6a:4 Converter housing stoneguards 'A' must be kept clean. Lower view shows sequence for checking level of transmission fluid. Numbers are referred to in text

speeds higher than 30 miles/hr (50 km/hr) or for more than 40 miles (65 km).

Do not tow with front wheels on road if transmission is excessively noisy. The vehicle cannot be tow-started.

6a:5 Stationary tests

These tests are essential to determine the nature of defects. **In most cases, rectification is work for a properly equipped service station.** However, the tests may help an owner to check what is wrong. The engine and transmission must be at normal running temperature.

Starter:

Check that starter operates only in 'P' and 'N'.

Reverse light (if fitted):

Should operate in 'R' only.

With brakes applied:

Select 'N' to 'D', 'N' to 'L' and 'N' to 'R' with engine idling. Transmission engagement should be felt with each selection.

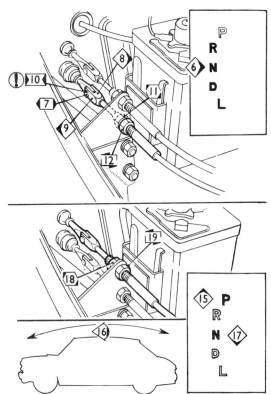

FIG 6a:5 Top view shows sequence for adjusting the manual control cable. Lower view is sequence for adjusting the parking cable. Numbers are referred to in text

'Creep':

Select 'N' and release brakes. Check that 'creep' does not occur with engine idling and with it revving.

Stall test:

The duration of this test must not exceed 10 seconds. The test is made only when transmission slip or poor acceleration is suspected.

Stall speed is the maximum engine speed obtained at forced throttle opening ('kickdown') with the converter turbine held stationary.

1 Drive for 5 miles (8 km) so that engine and transmission are at running temperature. Set handbrake and chock the wheels.

2 Connect up a tachometer (revolution indicator) so that it can be seen from the driver's seat. Select 'P'. Check that fluid level is correct (see **Section 6a:2**). Apply footbrake.

3 Select either 'L' or 'R' (whichever is required for the process of elimination). Force throttle through 'kickdown' position for not more than ten seconds. Note highest rev/min reading. If under 1150, a slipping stator is indicated. If over 2100, there is transmission slip. If between 1950 and 2050, the condition is normal.

Converter condition is analysed by road testing, engine condition and transmission performance together with a stall test.

A slipping stator is due to its freewheel not holding (see 2 in **FIG 6a:1**). Condition is confirmed by inability to pull away on a steep hill or poor acceleration from rest.

If stall test shows a normal condition, the converter is probably satisfactory but there is a rare condition of a seized stator freewheel that may still be present. This will show by reduced maximum speed in all gears (more pronounced in top ratio) with severe overheating of converter and transmission.

Transmission slip indicates slip in components employed in the selected gear ('L' or 'R'). Slip in both positions may be due to low pressure. In one position only, it suggests a faulty component.

As pointed out at the beginning of this section, rectification of defects is a matter for a service station equipped to deal with automatic transmission.

6a:6 Cable adjustments and servicing

Adjustment of the downshift/throttle cable cannot be made without hydraulic pressure testing. This is work for service station.

Adjusting manual control cable:

Refer to top view in **FIG 6a:5**. First check operation by selecting 'R', 'N', 'D' and 'L'. A positive hold must be felt in each position with no overriding of the detent in the control valve (see 3 in **FIG 6a:3**). If unsatisfactory, adjust as follows:

1 Select 'N' (6). Remove pin 7 and push cable in as far as possible (8). Pull cable out by two stops (9). This should give correct 'N' position.

2 Holes for pin should now line up (10). If they do not, adjust at nuts 11 and 12. Recheck by selecting positions as before.

Adjusting parking cable:

Refer to lower half of **FIG 6a:5**. Select 'P' (15). Check for full engagement by rocking car backwards and forwards (16). If parking pawl ratchets out of engagement, adjust as follows:

1 Select 'N' (17). Release nuts 18 and 19.

2 Increase effective length of outer cable for better engagement.

3 Decrease effective length of outer cable to disengage, when there is fouling in 'N'.

4 Tighten nuts and recheck.

Renewing parking control cable:

This is the only cable that is renewable without removing the valve bodies cover from the transmission. Refer to **FIG 6a:6** and do the following:

1 Put lever in 'N' (23). Remove washer bottle and bracket (24 and 25).

2 Remove pin 26 and nut 27 to release cable 28. Drain transmission (29).

3 Unscrew outer cable from transmission casing (30) and unhook cable eye from parking pawl lever (31).

4 Refit cable by pushing inner cable right down from above. Hook cable eye over lever (32). Reverse rest of dismantling instructions and check parking action. If necessary adjust as previously described. Refill transmission (see **Section 6a:2**).

Servicing selector control:

Refer to **FIG 6a:7**. To remove starter inhibitor and reverse light micro switches only, do operations (3), (4) and (5) and (11), (12) and (13). Note in operation (4) that bottom of panel is pulled clear and lowered to release the top pegs. To remove selector control, proceed as follows:

1 Remove washer bottle 1. Remove pin 2, screw 3, pull panel out and down to release pegs 4. Remove speedometer drive 5.

2 Remove knob 6 and pull off cables 7. Remove pin 8. Remove bolts 9, noting spacer on top bolt. Remove control rearwards and down (10).

Dismantle the control by referring to lower view in **FIG 6a:7**. Remove clips and pins 11 and 12. Remove micro switches 13. These are not adjustable and must be renewed if defective. Remove clips and pins 14 and 15. Remove selector and park controls 16, remove pin 17 from selector rod, and spring and pin 18 from lever.

To reassemble, reverse the dismantling sequence. Make sure that selector lever spring presses against lefthand side of lever (19). Check selector operation and micro switch operation. High spots on the selector cams operate the starter inhibitor switch in 'P' and 'N' positions. A second high spot on the manual control cam operates the reverse light switch (when fitted) in position 'R'. Check for faulty switch by shortcircuiting the switch terminals. If the circuit operates, renew the switch.

6a:7 Removing and separating transmission

The operations of removing the power unit and lifting the engine from the transmission are fully described in **Chapter 1, Sections 1:8** and **1:9** in the Engine chapter. For servicing of the transmission and final drive assembly it is necessary to secure the services of a properly-equipped organization.

6a:8 Servicing the primary drive

Refer to **FIG 6a:8**. Remove the power unit (see **Chapter 1, Section 1:8**). Drain the transmission and refit the drain plug 1 (see **Section 6a:2**). Remove 17 bolts (2). Remove cover and gasket (3). Knock back

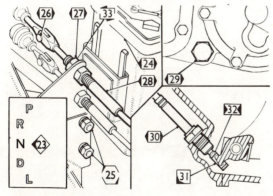

FIG 6a:6 Operations to remove and refit the parking cable. The numbers are referred to in text

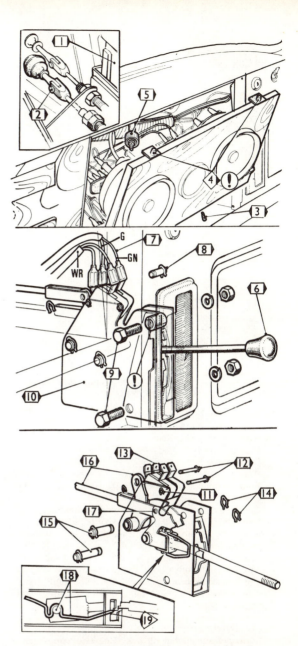

FIG 6a:7 Removing and dismantling the selector lever control and micro switches. Numbers are referred to in text. Cable colours are 'G' for green, 'GN' for green and brown and 'WR' for white and red

tabs of washers 4. Stop top shaft from turning by inserting a wedge between the sprocket and the pump suction boss. Remove nut 5. Remove nut 6 from input shaft. Lever off chain 7 and sprockets 8.

Inspect chain and sprockets for wear, and renew parts. Do this if chain is noisy. When refitting, use new tabwashers and gasket. Torque wrench figures are given in **Technical Data**.

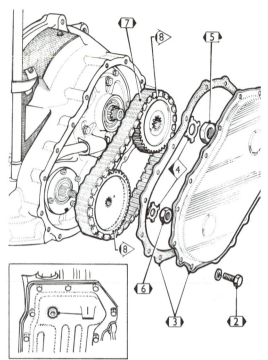

FIG 6a:8 Removing primary housing and chain drive. Numbers are referred to in text

6a:9 Servicing speedometer drive

Refer to **FIG 6a:9**. Do the following:

1 Release cable (1). Remove bolt 2 and lift off plate 3, bush and gasket 4 and oil seal 5. Renew seal if faulty. Extract bush 6 and pinion 7.
2 Drain fluid and refit plug (8). Remove 7 bolts 9. Remove housing and gasket (10). Remove collar and O-ring.
3 Check sealing rings 12. They must be undamaged and free in their grooves. If gear 13 is worn or damaged, use a nut-splitter to remove it. Take care not to damage shaft or put side pressure on it.

Start reassembling by tapping new gear up to shoulder using a copper hammer (14). Refit housing, making sure governor pressure tube enters the seal (15). Continue in reverse order of dismantling. Refill with fluid (see **Section 6a:2**).

6a:10 Driving tests

These are carried out on the road. **The speeds are true and may not be those recorded by the speedometer.**

Do not select 'L' from 'D' at speeds above 55 mile/hr (88 km/hr) or the engine may be over-revved.

'Kick-down is obtained by depressing accelerator pedal fully until it touches the carpet. A slight resistance will be felt as the pedal passes through the point of normal full travel. **Use delicate pressure on the pedal to determine minimum upward shifts or the shift speeds may seem too high.**

1 Select 'D', use 'kick-down' acceleration and check that 1 to 2 shift occurs between 37 and 43 mile/hr

(60 to 70 km/hr). 2 to 3 shift should occur between 62 and 68 mile/hr (100 to 110 km/hr). If no drive in 'D' (1st ratio not operating), select 'L', accelerate to 20 mile/hr (30 km/hr) and select 'D' to verify drive in 2nd and 3rd ratios.
2 Between 53 and 56 mile/hr (85 to 90 km/hr) in 3rd ratio (D3), 'kick-down' and check downshift to 2nd ratio (D2).
3 Between 25 and 30 mile/hr (40 to 48 km/hr) in 3rd ratio (D3), 'kick-down' and check downshift to 1st ratio (D1).
4 Using minimum throttle, check for 1 to 2 shift between 10 and 15 mile/hr (16 to 24 km/hr). Check for 2 to 3 shift between 18 and 25 mile/hr (30 to 40 km/hr).
5 At 30 mile/hr (50 km/hr) in 3rd ratio (D3), release accelerator and select 'L'. Check for 3 to 2 engagement and a subsequent 2 to 1 downshift occurring at approximately 5 mile/hr (8 km/hr) and come to rest.
6 Leave 'L' selected. Accelerate to about 20 mile/hr (30 km/hr), release accelerator and check that upshift does not occur (L1 is retained) and engine braking can be felt.
7 Select 'D'. Accelerate to 30 mile/hr (50 km/hr), release accelerator to ensure 3rd ratio (D3) and select 'L' to get L2. 'Kick-down' between 25 and 30 mile/hr (40 to 48 km/hr) and check for L2 to L1 downshift.
8 At rest, select 'R'. Reverse with full throttle (if possible). Release throttle and confirm engine braking.
9 Stop on steep hill, select 'P'. Check that vehicle is held and selector is trapped by gate. Repeat when facing the other way.

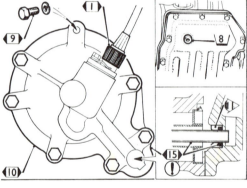

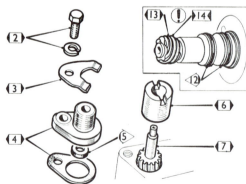

FIG 6a:9 Servicing the speedometer drive gear. The numbered sequence is referred to in the text

6a:11 Fault diagnosis

It is impossible to give a detailed fault analysis because most of the innumerable tests for faults and their cure are a matter for a service station. Those that are given may be rectified with the help of instructions in this chapter.

(a) Starter will not operate in 'P' or 'N' or operates in all positions

1 Test inhibitor switch(es), circuit(s) and check cam action

(b) Faulty operation of reversing light (when fitted)

1 See 1 in (a)

(c) Excessive bump on engagement of 'D', 'L' or 'R'

1 Reduce idling speed of engine (see **Chapter 2**)
2 If no cure, consult experts

(d) Stall test speed less than 1150 rev/min (slipping stator)

1 Renew torque converter (see experts)

(e) Parking pawl does not hold vehicle

1 Adjust/examine parking cable
2 If no cure, consult experts

(f) 'P' operates, but no drive in 'D', 'L' or 'R'

1 Check fluid level
2 Check manual cable selector cable/adjustment
3 If no cure, consult experts

(g) Reduced maximum speed in all ratios, converter overheats

1 Fit new torque converter (see experts)

NOTES

CHAPTER 7

DRIVE SHAFTS AND SUSPENSION

7:1 General description of drive shafts

The drive shafts connect the differential shafts of the transmission to the front hubs. The universal joint at the wheel end is of the constant velocity type as shown in **FIG 7:2**. At the inner end, the first type of resilient coupling had a flange or yoke that was solid with the shaft. The second type had a flange and sliding joint that was splined to the shaft so that the differential shafts no longer moved in and out, as in the earlier type (see **FIG 7:4** and **Chapter 6**). When automatic transmission is fitted, this inner joint is of the Hardy Spicer needle roller type (see **FIG 7:5**).

7:2 Routine maintenance of joints

There is no need for regular lubrication, but it is advisable to check the condition of the rubber boot that encloses the constant velocity joint. Renew at once if it is damaged or cracked, as dirt may enter and cause rapid wear. Every 6000 miles (10,000 km) check all nuts and bolts connected with the universal joints.

7:3 Removing drive shafts

Early type with fixed flange:

This is the type with no sliding splines at the inner end. These shafts are a push fit in the hub bearings. Remove as follows:

1 Fit a $\frac{1}{2}$ inch (13 mm) block between upper arm of suspension and lower rebound rubber. Jack up, fit a stand under front sidemember and remove wheel.
2 Disconnect steering ball joint from steering arm (see **Chapter 8**). Release brake caliper from swivel hub (see **Chapter 9**).
3 Remove splitpin and nut from drive shaft (see 3 and 4 in **FIG 7:10**). Tap end of shaft with copper hammer and remove outer cone 5.
4 Mark flexible couplings for correct reassembly and remove U-bolt nuts. In the case of flanged differential shafts, mark flanges before undoing the nuts.
5 Release upper ball joint from hub (see suspension details and **FIG 7:11**). Let swivel hub pivot outwards, disengage the drive shaft coupling and pull the shaft out of the hub assembly.

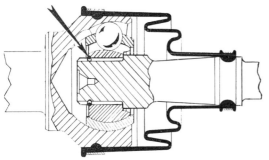

FIG 7:1 Section through constant velocity joint showing retaining circlip on shaft

Later type with sliding joint:

This is the type of shaft with the joint shown in **FIG 7:4**. This is a press-fit in the hub and removal is covered in **Section 7:8**.

7:4 Servicing drive shafts

Dismantling constant velocity joint:

Remove boot clips and turn back out of the way (**FIG 7:3** shows how clip is fitted). Hold shaft with joint downwards. Give top outer edge of joint a sharp blow with a copper hammer. This should drive joint over circlip arrowed in **FIG 7:1**. Check end float of joint. It must not exceed .025 inch (.6 mm).

Put paint mark on cage and races for correct reassembly. Tilt inner race until a ball is released (see lefthand view in **FIG 7:2**). Repeat to remove remaining balls. Swivel cage until the two elongated windows coincide with lands of outer race (bellhousing). Manoeuvre land into window and lift out cage and inner race (central view). Turn inner race as in righthand view to remove inner race.

Note that a damaged joint is unserviceable if it cannot be dismantled by hand.

Inspection of joint:

When parts are clean and dry, check them for wear. Normally this should be even, and end float must be within figures given previously. Balls and races must be free from rust, pitting and flats. The race tracks will be marked but should not be indented. Reject a cage with outer surfaces that show signs of 'picking up'. If cage windows are worn, this will probably cause knocking on extreme lock. Fit a new cage.

Reassembling joint:

Most cages are standard, but a .010 inch (.25 mm) oversize cage and bellhousing may be fitted in production. Make sure replacement cage is correct. Gauge 18G.1064 is available for checking cage size. A standard cage will pass through the gauge, an oversize one will not. Do not try to fit a new cage without checking. Service kits are available, the standard cage being colour-coded white (Part No. 18G.8069) and the oversize one red (Part No. 18G.8070).

Parts should go together without undue force. Smear lightly with Duckham's M-B grease (pack No. AKF.1540).

Having reassembled the cage and inner race into the outer race (bellhousing) in the reverse manner to dismantling, turn races until original marks are aligned. Tilt cage and insert a ball, repeating until every ball is in place. Taking care not to release balls, check that joint articulates freely. Fill joint with rest of grease (total quantity 1.9 oz or 54 gm). **Do not use any other type of lubricant.**

Refitting joint to drive shaft:

Smear inside new rubber boot with Duckham's M-B grease. Fit new circlip to end of shaft (see arrow in **FIG 7:1**). Hold shaft in vice. Locate inner race of joint on splines, centralize circlip in chamfer in race. Using a soft-faced hammer, tap end of stub axle smartly. This will close up the circlip. Tap assembly right home so that circlip expands against inner race as in illustration.

Pull rubber boot over joint (see **FIG 7:1**). Fit clips as shown in **FIG 7:3**. Tab of large clip must be pulled away from direction of rotation.

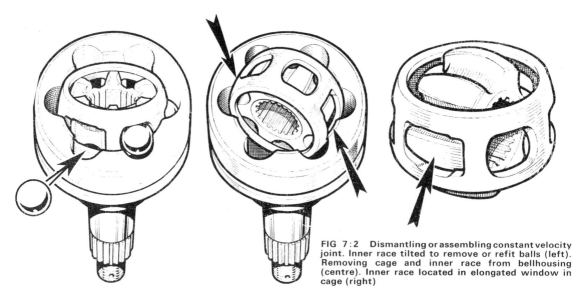

FIG 7:2 Dismantling or assembling constant velocity joint. Inner race tilted to remove or refit balls (left). Removing cage and inner race from bellhousing (centre). Inner race located in elongated window in cage (right)

Refitting shafts to hub and differential:

When fitting early-type shafts to hub, pack hub with grease. For latter-type shafts, refer to **Section 7:8**. Connect the drive couplings at the inner end. On flange-type couplings, fit new nuts and tighten to 28 lb ft (3.9 kg m). If the couplings are flexible, fit new self-locking (Nyloc) nuts. Tighten nuts on each U-bolt evenly until metal faces of coupling touch and at least $\frac{1}{16}$ inch (1.6 mm) of bolt protrudes.

It is important to note that drive shafts with sliding joint (see FIG 7:4) must not be fitted in place of fixed-type shafts unless the differential shafts are modified (see Chapter 6, Section 6:6 in transmission chapter).

Servicing the sliding joint:

This is the later type shown in **FIG 7:4**. To remove from shaft, release clips and pull rubber boot or housing out of the way. Mark shaft and sleeve of flange for correct reassembly. Use two screwdrivers to close ends of circlip together and prise it from groove. Pull out shaft.

Clean parts and check fit of splines. Also check fit if only one part of the pair is being renewed. Renew rubber housing if damaged.

Each joint should hold 1.5 oz (42.5 gm) of Duckham's Laminoid Grease (Q6383). This is available in a $\frac{3}{4}$ oz (21 gm) tube (Part No. 97H.2611) or a 1 lb (.45 kg) tin (Part No. 97H.2465). Grease splines and inside of rubber housing, slide housing and circlip onto shaft. Fill sleeve with rest of grease, fit shaft spring and slide flange into place. Fit circlip. Press shaft right in, holding lip of housing open to let air and surplus grease escape. With shaft still fully closed, check diameter of rubber housing (see 'A' in **FIG 7:4**). If more than 2 inch (51 mm), squeeze by hand until reduced. Partially withdraw shaft and fit clips as in **FIG 7:3**.

Servicing needle roller universal joints:

These are the type fitted to vehicles with automatic transmission. Check for wear by lifting joint and also check for slackness when turning forward and back. After drive shaft is removed, service the joint by removing circlips 4 at exposed ends of bearing cups 3 (see **FIG 7:5**). If removal is difficult, tap face of cup inwards to relieve pressure.

Hold joint and tap yoke near bearing housing until bearing cup starts to emerge. If difficult, peel back seal 2 and tap on inner edge of cup with a small-diameter rod. Remove cup and rollers complete, then remove opposite cup. Tapping exposed ends of spider 1 will enable remaining cups to be removed. Use a soft drift.

Spider and bearings are available as a replacement kit. Check holes in flange and yoke for wear and renew if necessary.

Fill holes in spider with grease, taking care to exclude air. Put $\frac{1}{8}$ inch (3 mm) of grease in bottom of each cup. Fit rollers. Fit seals 2 to spider journals. Insert spider in flanges. Fit a bearing cup and tap it home until it is just possible to fit a circlip. Fit the opposite bearing and circlip. Fit the remaining two. Remove surplus grease and check movement. If tight, tap lightly with a mallet to relieve pressure on journals.

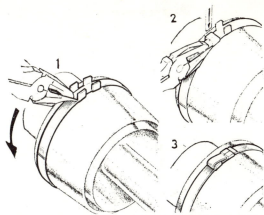

FIG 7:3 Fitting clip on rubber boot. Pull clip tight (1), fold front tabs over (2), bend free end back and secure with rear tabs (3)

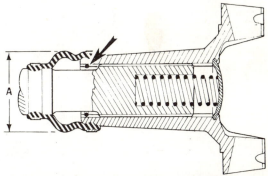

FIG 7:4 Section through sliding joint at inner end of drive shaft (later type). Arrow indicates retaining circlip. Dimension 'A' must not exceed 2 inch (51 mm) diameter

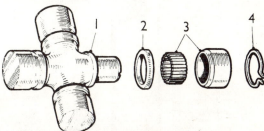

FIG 7:5 Spider and bearing parts of needle roller universal joint (automatic transmission)

Key to Fig 7:5   1 Spider   2 Rubber seal
3 Needle rollers and bearing cup   4 Circlip

7:5 The suspension system

The system is designed to give a smooth flat ride with excellent handling. Each suspension unit consists of a displacer containing a rubber spring (see **FIG 7:7**). The location of these displacers and the operation by push-rods from the suspension radius arms is shown in **FIG 7:8**. The interconnecting pipe and flow of fluid indicated by the arrows will illustrate how the Hydrolastic system works.

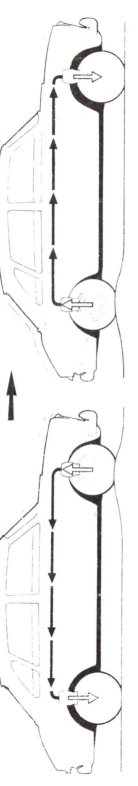

FIG 7:6 Action of suspension system over a bump. Tail rising with upward movement of front wheels (left). Nose rising with upward movement of rear wheels (right)

When the radius arm deflects due to road inequalities the diaphragm is pushed inwards and fluid is forced into the top chamber. The rubber spring is also deflected and pressure causes the fluid to be discharged along an interconnecting pipe to give downward pressure on the other displacer on the same side of the vehicle. The action is shown by the diagrams in **FIG 7:6**. The fluid is a mixture of water and alcohol with an added anti-corrosive agent.

7:6 Routine maintenance of suspension

There is no need for regular lubrication. Every 6000 miles (10,000 km) or 6 months all suspension system nuts and bolts should be checked for tightness.

After the first 12,000 miles (20,000 km) or 12 months the trim height should be checked by a Distributor or Dealer (see **Section 7:14**). See following Section concerning the pressurized system.

7:7 The pressurized system

After the suspension system is assembled it is pressurized through the valves shown in **FIG 7:9**. **Do not tamper with these valves or very high pressure will be released with possible danger to the operator, and the radius arms will drop onto the bump rubbers.** However, if pressure and fluid has been lost as the result of an accident, it is possible to drive the vehicle in this condition at not more than 30 mile/hr (50 km/hr) on metalled roads. The condition must be rectified by a Distributor or Dealer.

It must be understood that many operations on the suspension system cannot be carried out without depressurizing, evacuating and then repressurizing the system. Therefore, the normal owner must entrust such operations to a properly-equipped service station. The following operations are the only ones that can be carried out without depressurizing.

7:8 Servicing the front hubs

Removing:

Refer to **FIG 7:10**. After inserting some packing $\frac{1}{2}$ inch (13 mm) thick and $1\frac{1}{2}$ inch (38 mm) wide between the upper arm of the suspension and the bump rubber, jack up and support the front of the car and remove the wheel, then proceed as follows:

1 Disconnect steering ball joint from steering arm (see **Chapter 8**). Remove brake caliper (see **Chapter 9**).
2 Remove splitpin 4 and nut 3. Lightly tap end of shaft and remove cone 5. Use a puller to withdraw the flange and brake disc assembly 1 and 8 from shaft 11.
3 Disconnect the drive shaft at the inner end, marking the parts for correct refitting (see **Section 7:3**). Release the upper and lower ballpin nuts and plain washers (see 8 and 9 in **FIG 7:11**). Do not try to drive the pins out with a hammer but use the correct tool for the job. Withdraw the hub and shaft assembly.

Dismantling:

Early shafts may be tapped out of the bearings (see **Section 7:3**). The later type are removed with hand press 18G.47C and adaptor 18G.47AT (see **FIG 7:12**).

Note supporting screws indicated by arrows. The halves of the adaptor are placed round the rubber boot so that the hub rests on these screws. With everything centralized, the shaft is pressed out of the hub.

If bearings need renewal, the oil seals must be prised out. This will destroy them. Drive the outer races squarely out of the hub with a soft metal drift. The inner bearing race will remain on the shaft and must be pressed off with the tools shown in **FIG 7:12** without the supporting screws.

Note that some early assemblies may have a washer as well as the spacer 7.

Inspection:

Clean and dry the bearings and check for roughness in action. Check for blueing and chipping and check security of rollers in their cages. Renew oil seals (if they were not removed) if they show signs of deterioration or of leakage.

Check bores and shoulders of hub for burrs and scoring. Remove all high spots that may affect bearing assemblies.

Reassembling:

1 If bearings are not renewed, pack with grease and assemble in hub with spacer (and washer if fitted). Fit new oil seals and fill space between bearings and seals with grease.
2 **If new bearings are to be fitted, make sure that spacer and bearings are a matched set.** Refit as in preceding operation.
3 If drive shaft is a press fit, refer to **FIG 7:13** which shows tool 18G.1104 and guide being used to press hub onto shaft. The driving flange and brake disc assembly are also pressed into place with the same tool and guide.
4 In early assemblies where the shaft is a push fit, there is no need for the special tool, but cone 5 (see **FIG 7:10**) must not be used to press the driving flange home if it is tight on the shaft.
5 Fit cone and tighten nut. Use a dial gauge to check end float of hub assembly. This must lie between zero and .004 inch (.10 mm). If end float is more than this after new bearings are fitted, a new hub must be tried and the float checked again.

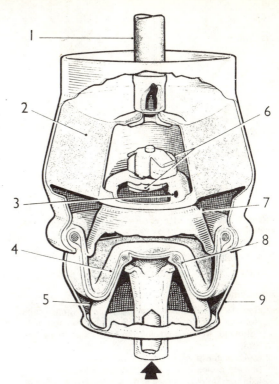

FIG 7:7   Section through Hydrolastic unit (rear)

Key to Fig 7:7 1 Interconnecting pipe 2 Rubber spring
3 Damper bleed   4 Butyl liner   5 Tapered piston
6 Damper valves   7 Fluid-separating member
8 Rubber diaphragm (nylon reinforced)   9 Tapered cylinder

6 Tighten nut to 150 lb ft (20.74 kg m) and check runout of brake disc face at periphery. If more than .008 inch (.20 mm), remove flange and disc assembly and reposition on drive shaft splines. If satisfactory, lock nut with a new splitpin. If necessary, tighten nut still more to align splitpin holes.
7 Refit dust shield, caliper and steering ball joint, using correct torque figures for tightening fixings (see **Technical Data**). Bleed the brakes (see **Chapter 9.**

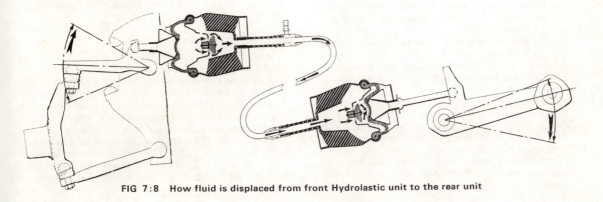

FIG 7:8   How fluid is displaced from front Hydrolastic unit to the rear unit

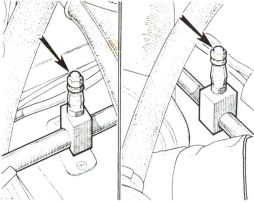

FIG 7:9 Location of pressure valves in Hydrolastic system. These valves must not be unscrewed

7:9 Servicing the rear hubs

FIG 7:14 is a section through the rear hub.

Removing:

1 Remove wheel, brake drum and prise off grease cap 6. Remove splitpin 4 and nut 5. Righthand nut has a righthand thread and lefthand nut has a lefthand thread.
2 Use a puller to withdraw the hub assembly. Leave the bearing cones in the hub and inner bearing race on axle stub unless renewal is necessary. Use a soft metal drift to drive the cones squarely from the hub.
3 Remove the shims 9 (if fitted) and spacer 10.

Inspection:

Refer to the instructions for front hubs in **Section 7:8**.

Reassembling:

If original bearings are to be refitted, pack with grease. If necessary, fit a new oil seal. Fill space between bearing cone and oil seal with grease. Refit hub, spacer and shims (if fitted).

Tighten axle nut to 40 lb ft (5.5 kg m). Use dial gauge to check end float of hub assembly. Correct figure is zero to .002 inch (zero to .05 mm). If it exceeds this, check thickness of shims 9. These are available in thicknesses of .003 inch (.08 mm), .005 inch (.13 mm) and .010 inch (.25 mm).

Finish final assembling and fit a new splitpin. Fit cap, but do not fill with grease. After fitting brake drum and wheel, adjust the brakes.

If new bearings are to be fitted, note that early assemblies used a standard bearing spacer and shims. Later assemblies have a variable spacer. When new bearings are to be fitted, use a standard spacer (BTB.593) and shims. Proceed as follows:

1 Press bearing cones into hub. Press inner bearing onto axle shaft and pack it with grease.
2 Fit spacer and enough shims to give excessive end float. Fit hub, outer bearing packed with grease, flat washer and nut.
3 Tighten nut and check end float with a dial gauge as described earlier. Obtain correct figure by altering shims.

4 Fit a new oil seal and pack space between bearing cone and oil seal with grease. Refit hub. Chamfer in flat washer must face hub. Tighten nut to 40 lb ft (5.5 kg m). Fit a new splitpin.
5 Fit cap without grease. Fit brake drum and wheel and adjust brakes.

7:10 Front support arm (lower)

This is removable without depressurizing system. Insert packing between upper arm and bump rubber. Locate a stand under front sidemember and remove wheel. Release tie rod (see **Section 7:11**). Release outer end of arm from swivel hub. Remove lower support arm (splitpin, nut and washer). Push out pivot pin and rubber bushes.

Check parts for cracks or thread damage. Renew rubber bushes if worn, perished or oil-soaked. Check straightness of arm.

Reassembling:

Fit bushes and pivot pin. Fit support arm to pin and fit nut and washer finger tight. Position tie rod fork, assemble to hub and tighten nut. Pivot pin must be tightened to 45 lb ft (6.4 kg m) with no load on the bushes, but with the lower arm in its normal trim position. Fit a new splitpin.

Bolt tie rod to arm. Fit road wheel and remove stand.

7:11 Servicing tie rod

The parts of the tie rod and bracket are shown in **FIG 7:15**. To remove the rod 6, detach it from the lower support arm. Release bracket from body (4 bolts and nuts). The central outside bolt also secures the towing eye.

Mark tie rod and bracket for alignment. Slacken the forward towing eye bolt. Remove locknut 9 and withdraw rod from bracket.

Check rubber pads 7 for deterioration. Check bracket and rod for cracks or damage. **While rod is detached, do not let suspension system take the weight of the vehicle.**

Reverse dismantling sequence to reassemble the parts. On vehicles with power steering the tie rods must be stamped 'P' at the fork-end. Do not use on other vehicles. Note also that the second-type bracket can only be fitted to a second-type gusset plate. Fit a polythene seal between the bracket and the gusset plate. The forward bolt on the outside also secures the towing eye (if fitted).

Mk 2 and 3 tie rods:

When Mk 2 and 3 vehicles have manual steering, the front suspension upper support arm will have a longitudinal rib on the upper surface near the outer end. There will also be a letter 'M' stamped on the steering lever.

This type of suspension system must have a negative castor angle as given in **Technical Data**. If this is not so, the tie rods must be changed for a pair with the part number of 11H.1942. These are identified by a red paint band near the fork end. The existing locknuts at the front end of the rods must be discarded and new Nyloc nuts LNZ.208 fitted. When reassembled, check front wheel alignment.

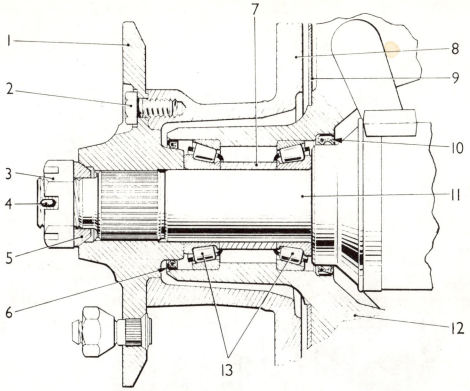

FIG 7:10   Section through front hub

Key to Fig 7:10   1 Driving flange assembly   2 Flange to disc bolt   3 Nut   4 Splitpin   5 Outer cone   6 Outer oil seal
7 Spacer   8 Disc   9 Dust shield   10 Inner oil seal (single lip, second type)   11 Drive shaft   12 Swivel hub
13 Taper roller bearings

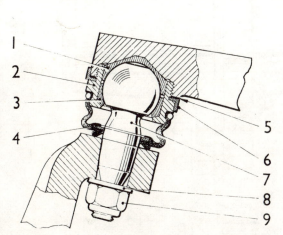

FIG 7:11   Section through ball joint for swivel hub

Key to Fig 7:11   1 Bottom socket   2 Housing
3 Top socket   4 Dust cover   5 Shim   6 Lockwasher
7 Ballpin   8 Flat washer (special)   9 Locknut

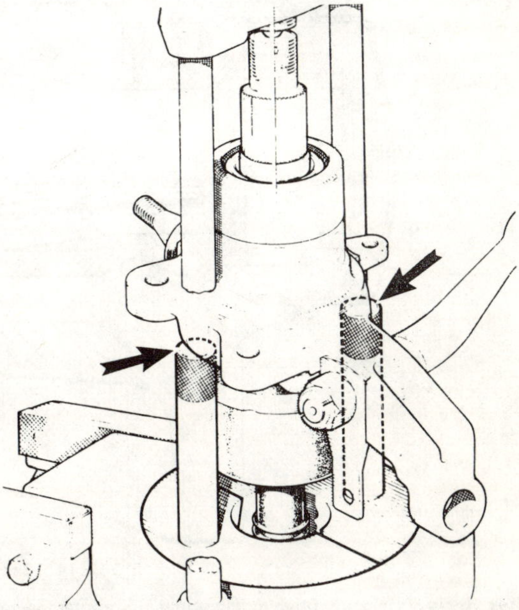

FIG 7:12   Pressing later type of drive shaft from hub,
using press 18G.47C and adaptor 18G.47AT with
screws (arrowed)

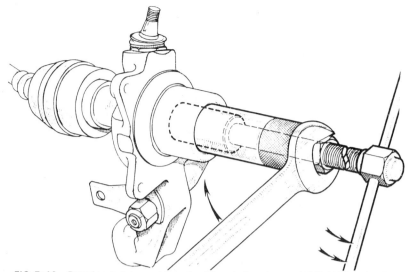

FIG 7:13 Pressing hub assembly onto drive shaft using tool 18G.1104 and guide

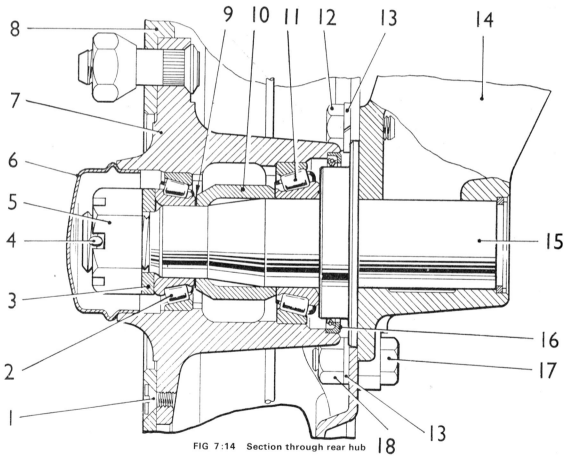

FIG 7:14 Section through rear hub

Key to Fig 7:14   1 Drum to hub screw   2 Outer taper roller bearing   3 Washer   4 Splitpin   5 RH or LH threaded nut
6 Grease retaining cap   7 Hub assembly   8 Brake drum   9 Shims (when fitted)   10 Distance piece or spacer
11 Inner taper roller bearing   12 Backplate setscrew   13 Spring washer   14 Radius arm   15 Stub axle shaft   16 Oil seal
17 Backplate bolt   18 Nut

7:12 Servicing ball joints

A section through a ball joint is shown in **FIG 7:11**. Detach ball joints from swivel hub by following instructions in **Section 7:8**. Knock back tab of lockwasher 6 and unscrew housing 2 to remove ball joint.

Clean the parts and check condition of ball, sockets and dust cover. Check ballpin threads.

Refit the ball joint assembly without lockwasher or shims 5. Screw housing down until there is no end play in the ball. Measure gap between housing and swivel hub or upper arm. Unscrew assembly and select shims to the value measured, less the thickness of the lockwasher which is .036 inch (.91 mm). From this, subtract .009 to .013 inch (.23 to .33 mm) to preload the ball. There are five thicknesses of shim available, .002 inch (.05 mm), .003 inch (.08 mm), .005 inch (.13 mm), .010 inch (.25 mm) and .030 inch (.76 mm).

Assemble joint with selected shims and lubricate freely with Dextagrease Super BP lubricant. Tighten housing to 70 ±5 lb ft (9.6 ±.7 kg m). Lock with three tabs of the lockwasher, turning up one of them on a flat adjacent to the brake disc. Refit dust cover.

Refit ball joint. If ballpin is copper plated, do not use original nut and spring washer but fit a Nyloc locknut and flat washer. The washer is a special one that is .160 inch (4 mm) thick. Use this type on plain steel ballpins too. Tighten nuts to 45 lb ft (6.2 kg m).

7:13 The anti-roll bar

Early vehicles were fitted with an anti-roll bar at the rear. To remove the bar the rear suspension must be in its normal laden position.

Refit the bar under the same conditions, fitting the spacing washers under the bar, tightening the bolts and locking them with tabwashers.

7:14 Suspension geometry and trim height

Castor and camber angles, swivel hub inclination and wheel alignment of front suspension, and camber and wheel alignment of rear suspension are settings that are important if the vehicle is to handle properly. Apart from front wheel alignment, the other settings are not adjustable and if it is thought that something is wrong because of wear or accident damage, the angles must be checked with accurate equipment. Defects must be rectified by fitting new parts. The correct angles are given in **Technical Data**.

Trim height may be checked by measuring from the centre of the wheels to the highest point of the wheel arch. The vehicle must be loaded with coolant, oil and four gallons (4.8 US gallons or 18 litres) of fuel.

Trim height (first type):

This applies to vehicles up to the numbers given in **Technical Data**. Correct trim height is 14.625 + .25 inch (372 + 6 mm) at an approximate fluid pressure of 230 lb/sq in (16.2 kg/sq cm).

Trim height (second type and with automatic transmission):

See **Technical Data** for vehicle numbers where second-type systems are concerned. Correct trim height is 14.875 ±.25 inch (378 ±6 mm) at an approximate fluid pressure of 245 lb/sq in (17.2 kg/sq cm).

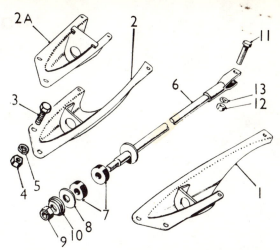

FIG 7:15 Components of tie-rod showing righthand and lefthand brackets

Key to Fig 7:15   1 Lefthand tie rod bracket
2 Righthand tie rod bracket 2A Second type and automatic
3 Bracket to body screw   4 Nut   5 Spring washer
6 Tie rod   7 Tie rod pad   8 Compression cup washer
9 Locknut   10 Plain washer 11 Tie rod to lower arm bolt
12 Nut   13 Spring washer

Trim height (Mk 2 and 3 vehicles):

Trim and pressure figures for these vehicles are the same as those given in the preceding paragraph.

7:15 Fault diagnosis

(a) Wheel wobble

1 Incorrect tracking
2 Worn hub bearings
3 Defective suspension units
4 Worn swivel hub joints
5 Loose wheel fixings

(b) 'Bottoming' of suspension

1 Check 3 in (a)
2 Incorrect pressurizing
3 Rebound rubbers worn or missing

(c) Heavy steering

1 Defective swivel hub joints
2 Wrong suspension geometry
3 Tight differential assembly on one side

(d) Excessive tyre wear

1 Check 1 in (a) and 2 in (c)

(e) Rattles

1 Check 1 in (c)
2 Suspension mountings defective
3 Tie rod or anti-roll bar mountings loose

(f) Excessive rolling

1 Check 3 in (a) and 2 in (b)

NOTES

CHAPTER 8

THE STEERING GEAR

8:1 General description (manual)

The steering column is connected to pinion shaft 18 (see **FIG 8:1**). The pinion engages rack 9 which is thus moved laterally to and fro by steering wheel rotation. The rack ends are connected to steering arms on the swivel hubs by tie rods and ball joints (see lower view). Rack gaiters 36 seal the rack assembly against dirt and maintain the internal supply of lubricant. Correct engagement of rack with pinion is ensured by support yoke 11 and spring 12. Inner ball joint 31 to 35 is adjustable, but the outer ball joints are sealed. The outer ball joints are screwed onto the tie rods to provide a simple means of adjusting the tracking of the front wheels.

8:2 Routine maintenance (manual steering)

Lubrication:

There is no need for regular lubrication of the rack assembly. If lubrication is lost through leakage, rectify the cause and then add $\frac{1}{3}$ of a pint (.5 US pint or .2 litre) of the correct grade of oil by injecting through a nozzle. Remove clip 37 and release gaiter 36 from righthand end of rack housing (see **FIG 8:1**). On lefthand drive cars, do

the lefthand end. Insert nozzle in rack housing and inject the oil. After reconnecting the gaiter, move the rack slowly from side to side to distribute the oil.

If the front wheels are off the ground, do not force the wheels from lock to lock or reverse the motion suddenly or the rack mechanism may be damaged.

Wheel alignment:

Check this every 6000 miles (10,000 km) or 6 months. On Mk 1 vehicles, inflate front tyres to 28 lb/sq in (1.97 kg/sq cm) and rear to 22 lb/sq in (1.55 kg/sq cm). On Mk 2 and 3 vehicles, front tyre pressure should be 30 lb/sq in (2.1 kg/sq cm) and rear 24 lb/sq in (1.7 kg/sq cm).

Correct alignment is with wheels toeing-in by $\frac{1}{8}$ inch (3.2 mm) unladen. The wheels are not parallel by the angular amount of 22 minutes.

With vehicle on level ground and wheels straightahead, measure distance between tyres at wheel centre height, in front and behind. Mark positions on tyres with chalk. Roll vehicle forward by half a turn of the wheels. Take a second set of readings. Dimension across vehicle between

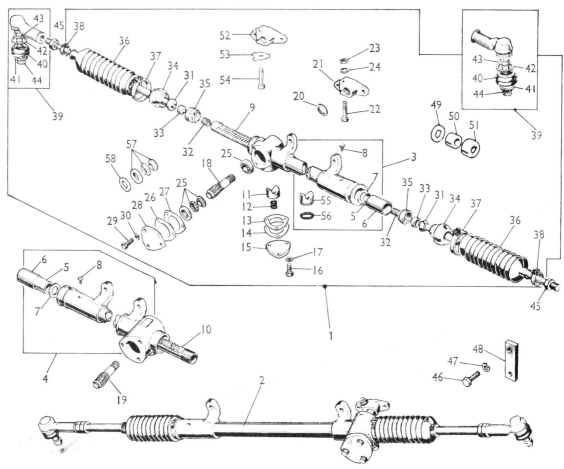

FIG 8:1 Components of the rack and pinion steering gear (manual)

Key to Fig 8:1   1 Righthand drive steering rack assembly   2 Lefthand drive steering rack assembly   3 Righthand housing assembly   4 Lefthand drive housing assembly   5 Felt bush   6 Bush housing   7 Backing disc   8 Retaining screw   9 Righthand drive rack   10 Lefthand drive rack   11 Rack support yoke*   12 Spring*   13 Yoke cover joint washer   14 Yoke cover shim(s)   15 Coverplate*   16 Coverplate bolt   17 Spring washer   18 Righthand drive pinion   19 Lefthand drive pinion   20 Oil seal   21 Pinion coupling   22 Bolt   23 Nut   24 Spring washer   25 Ball cage   26 End cover shim(s)   27 Joint washer   28 End cover   29 Bolt   30 Spring washer   31 Tie rod   32 Thrust spring   33 Ball seat   34 Ball housing   35 Locking ring   36 Rack gaiter   37 Inner clip   38 Outer clip   39 Ball joint assembly   40 Boot   41 Boot ring   42 Boot spring garter   43 Boot retainer   44 Slotted nut   45 Ball joint locknut   46 Rack to body bolt   47 Spring washer   48 Rack to body tapped block   49 Retainer (2nd type bearing assembly)   50 Polyvon bush (2nd type bearing assembly)   51 Housing (2nd type bearing assembly)   52 Pinion coupling (2nd type)   53 Lockwasher (2nd type)   54 Bolt (2nd type)   55 Yoke (2nd type modified)   56 O-ring oil seal (2nd type modified)   57 Ball cage (from 3.8 rack assembly)   58 Shims (from 3.8 rack assembly)

*2nd type damper assembly illustrated

inner walls of tyres must be an average of $\frac{1}{8}$ inch (3.2 mm) less at the front than the back.

This is a rough check only. For real accuracy it is best to entrust the checking to a service station.

To adjust for correct alignment, slacken gaiter clips 38 and tie rod locknuts 45. Turn tie rods an equal amount, noting that they both have righthand threads. The amount of thread visible behind each locknut must be the same on both sides. If it is not, screw one tie rod in, and the other one out by equal amounts until satisfied. **This is essential if the rack is to be central and the steering geometry correct.**

After adjustment, hold outer ball joints square with their ballpins and tighten the locknuts to 35 lb ft (4.8 kg m). Tighten the gaiter clips.

Column clamp bolt:

Every 3000 miles (5000 km) or 3 months, check the tightness of the pinion coupling clamp bolt (see 22 or 54 in **FIG 8:1**). Correct torque is 12 to 15 lb ft (1.7 to 2.1 kg m).

Checking moving parts:

Check these for wear every 12,000 miles (20,000 km) or 12 months.

8:3 Servicing steering wheel and column

Removing and refitting steering wheel:

Unplug the connector for the column switch. The connector is located under the parcel shelf.

Remove horn push by turning anticlockwise. Unscrew wheel nut and mark relative positions of hub and column. Pull off the wheel.

Refit wheel in marked position. With wheels straight-ahead, spokes should be horizontal. Tighten nut to 32 to 37 lb ft (4.4 to 5.1 kg m).

Removing and refitting column:

Later 1800 Mk 2 models are fitted with steering column locks that operate through the ignition switch mechanism. The lock is secured in position by shear-head bolts which also retain the column upper bracket (see **FIG 8:2**). Shearhead bolts are used because, as the name implies, the heads snap off the bolts when the correct tightening torque has been reached. It also makes it a little more difficult to get them out, but this is intentional, to dis-encourage any would-be car thief who would find it a comparatively simple matter to remove normal bolts and disengage the lock.

Before extracting the shear-head bolts, to remove the column or the lock, first ensure that new bolts are available from your local service garage spares department. The methods used to extract the decapitated bolts make them ineffective and they must be scrapped.

1 Centralize the steering and unplug the wiring connectors under the parcel shelf.
2 Refer to **FIG 8:3**, pull back the floor coverings and take out the four setscrews which retain the upper 5 and lower 4 clamp plates to the floor panel. Pull the clamp plates and the bush 6 upwards on the column.
3 Remove the two setscrews and washers 8 and 9 that secure the coupling 1 to the pinion flange (21 or 52 in **FIG 8:1**).
4 Support the steering column and referring to vehicles without a steering lock, release the column upper support clip by extracting the two setscrews. Collect the spring washers, sealing strip and abutment bracket.
5 To remove the shear-head bolts either saw-cut across the heads and use a screwdriver, or drill down the length until an Easiout extractor can be fitted, or, as in some instances, they can be removed with a hammer and a sharp punch.
6 Withdraw the column assembly, complete with coupling, upwards and out of the car.

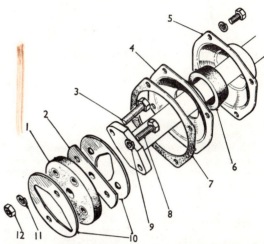

FIG 8:3 Components of the steering column coupling

Key to Fig 8:3 1 Steering column to rack coupling 2 Dimple to column earthing strip 3 Coupling to column screw 4 Lower clamp plate 5 Upper clamp plate 6 Bush 7 Seal 8 Coupling to rack screw 9 Spring washer 10 Coupling plates 11 Spring washer 12 Nut

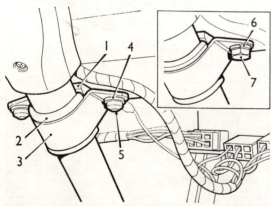

FIG 8:2 The steering column upper support assembly

Key to Fig 8:2 1 Abutment bracket 2 Rubber sealing strip 3 Support clip 4 Plain washer 5 Shear bolt 6 Spring washer 7 Setscrew
Items 4 and 5 are fitted only if the vehicle is equipped with a steering lock.

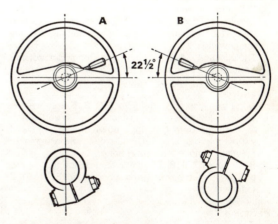

FIG 8:4 The final assembled position of the steering column clamp bolt and the direction indicator clamp stud

A Righthand steer B Lefthand steer

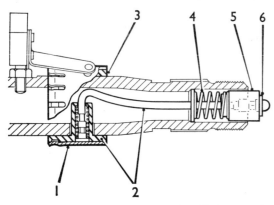

FIG 8:5 The horn slipring assembly (Mk 1 vehicles)

Key to Fig 8:5 1 Slipring   2 Rotor and cable assembly
3 Insulator—half   4 Spring   5 Insulator bush   6 Circlip

7 Refit the assembly in the reverse order of removal noting the following:
Do not tighten the column bracket setscrews or shear-head bolts until the lower coupling plates have been tightened. Ensure that the direction indicator control stud is approximately $22\frac{1}{2}$ deg. above horizontal (see **FIG 8:4**), the road wheels are in the straight-ahead position, and the steering wheel is fitted with the spokes perfectly horizontal.

Column coupling:

The parts are shown in **FIG 8:3**. Keep oil off the coupling. To ensure a good earth for the horn circuit, make sure contact points of strip 2 and end of column are clean and bright. Dimple in strip contacts column.

Column top bush:

Removing:

1 Remove the steering wheel.
2 Take out the two self-tapping screws that retain the cowling to the column and the two screws which secure the two halves of the cowling together. Remove the cowlings.
3 The direction indicator control, trip stud and headlamp flasher switch are secured by two screws and spring washers and a clamp. Remove the screws, clamp and switches.
4 Mk 1 vehicles only: Refer to **FIG 8:5**, remove the circlip 6 and take off the insulator bush 5 and spring 4. Push the horn slipring 1 down the column and extract the rotor assembly and cable 2 from the inner column. Remove the horn slipring.
5 Refer to **FIG 8:6**, lift the retaining tongue 4 and pull out the top bush 1 using service tool 18G 1191/2 (see items 2).

Refitting:

6 Before fitting the new bush smear it with graphite grease. Align it into the outer column so that the cut-out and depression will coincide, then drift it into position with service tool 18G 1191/3. Depress

the tongue 4 to arrest the bush, but not too far, otherwise the tongue will contact the inner column.
7 Measure the length of inner column protruding from the outer column—dimension A. Slacken the clip, if necessary, and adjust to obtain a protrusion of 3.56 inch (90.42 mm) nominal.
8 Refer to the inset and adjust the trip stud to the correct height—dimension B.
9 Refit the remaining parts in the reverse order of dismantling.

Steering lock: ignition switch:

Removing:

1 Complete operations 1 and 2 in the previous sub-section.
2 Remove the shear-bolts as described under 'Removing column'.
3 Remove the lock assembly and the clamp plate.
4 Take out the retaining screws and remove the ignition switch assembly.
Operations 3 and 4 can be carried out either way round if it is necessary to remove the switch without removing the lock.

Refitting:

5 Refit the lock and switch in the reverse order of removal. Ensure the lock spigot is engaged in the steering column. Check the lock and switch operation before shearing the heads off the bolts, a 12 lb ft (1.7 kgm) torque is sufficient to sever the hexagon heads.

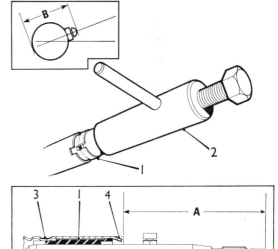

FIG 8:6 Removing the top bush from the steering column

Key to Fig 8:6   1 Top bush   2 Service tool 18G.1191/2
3 Depression in outer column   4 Retaining tongue
'A' dimension=3.56 inch (90.42 mm) nominal
'B' dimension=1.175±.010 inch (29.84±.25 mm)

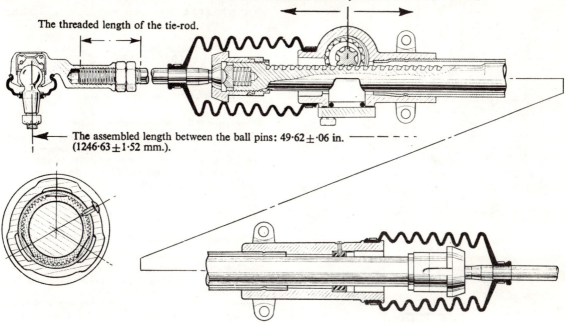

Rack travel from the central position: 3·28 in. (83·3 mm.).

The threaded length of the tie-rod.

The assembled length between the ball pins: 49·62 ± ·06 in. (1246·63 ± 1·52 mm.).

FIG 8:7 Sectioned views of rack and tie rods (manual). Dimensional details (top). Lefthand inset shows flats on Polyvon bush in relation to securing screw and oilways.

8:4 Removing and refitting steering rack

Removing:

Disconnect column from pinion flange (see preceding Section). Remove righthand front wheel on righthand-drive vehicles and the lefthand wheel on lefthand-drive vehicles. Remove splitpins and nuts 44 from outer ball joints (see **FIG 8:1**). Press ball joint pins out of steering levers with tool 18G.1063 (see **FIG 8:19**) or any suitable extractor. Do not try to drive the pins out with a hammer or the threads will be ruined. The tapered fitting is exceedingly tight.

Release handbrake and remove pivot bolt from intermediate lever (see **Chapter 9**). Release rack housing from toeboard (4 bolts). Withdraw assembly through valance, turning to clear the pinion flange.

Refitting:

Reverse the removal procedure. Check that steering wheel and rack are centralized before connecting the coupling flange. Check wheel alignment as in **Section 8:2**.

8:5 Servicing steering rack

Having removed rack assembly as described in preceding Section, do the following:

1 Hold rack housing in a vice. Unlock and unscrew ball joints from outer ends of tie rods after noting amount of tie rod thread exposed.
2 Remove gaiters (clips 37 and 38 in **FIG 8:1**), having a container handy to catch the oil. Set rack in central position. Total rack travel is 6.56 inch (166.6 mm) so

that half this from either end will give the central position. Half the travel is 3.28 inch (83.3 mm) (see **FIG 8:7**). Mark pinion coupling, pinion shaft and rack housing to ensure correct refitting.

3 Remove coverplate 15, shims and washer 13 and 14, spring(s) 12 and yoke 11. Note second-type parts 55 and 56. Remove pinion cover 28, shims 26, washer 27, lower bearing 25 and pinion 18. Top bearing 25 cannot be removed until the rack is withdrawn.

4 Remove oil seal 20 if it has been leaking. Using spanners 18G.1030 (see **FIG 8:19**), unlock and unscrew the rack ball joints after clearing the indentations in the locking ring 35 out of the slots in housing 34.

5 Withdraw rack 9 from pinion end of housing. Withdrawal from the other end may damage bush 5 or 50. Remove screw 8 and withdraw bush and housing. If first-type with felt bush 5, loosen screw two turns, prise up felt at joint and extract.

Inspection:

After cleaning, examine rack and pinion teeth for roughness, chipping or cracks. Renew gaiters on slightest signs of deterioration. Check fit of bush in rack housing and renew to prevent rattling. Check ball seats at inner end of tie rods. Slackness or rough action of the outer ball joints can be cured only by fitting new assemblies. Check condition of ball joint boots 40 as joints will wear rapidly if dirt enters through cracks.

Reassembling:

Insert bush and housing in rack housing so that hole for the screw is between flats in bush (see inset in **FIG**

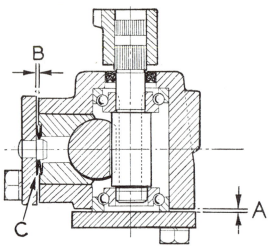

FIG 8:8 Section through first type of rack damper. For bearing preload shims, measure gap at 'A'. Measure gap at 'B' for damper shimming. 'C' indicates spring washers for damper

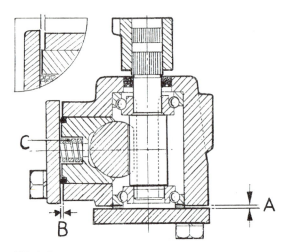

FIG 8:9 Section through second type of rack damper, showing O-ring oil seal. Measure gap at 'A' for bearing preload shims. Measure gap at 'B' for damper shimming. 'C' indicates damper spring. Inset (top left) shows early plain yoke

8:7). Support bush on a mandrel and drill a $\frac{7}{64}$ inch (2.8 mm) hole through from the existing one. If originally fitted with a felt bush, assembly should be modified by fitting Polyvon bush 50 and housing 51 with retainer 49. If the felt bush is retained, the rack housing must be lubricated with SAE.140.EP oil. Secure bush and housing in place with screw 8, putting sealing compound under the head.

Refit pinion bearing 25 into housing, insert rack and refit pinion, aligning the marks made prior to dismantling. Fit lower bearing and prepare to adjust pinion bearing preload.

Pinion bearing preload (first type):

Refer to **FIG 8:8**. Fit cover without shims or washer. Tighten bolts lightly. Measure gap 'A'. Subtract .001 to .003 inch (.03 to .08 mm) from feeler gauge measurement. Result is thickness of shims required. Shims are available in thicknesses of .0024 inch (.06 mm), .005 inch (.13 mm) and .010 inch (.25 mm). Treat joint faces with sealing compound and reassemble using a new joint washer. Pinion bearings will now be preloaded.

Pinion bearing preload (second type):

Refer to **FIG 8:9**. Fit cover with a few shims but without joint washer. Tighten bolts lightly. Measure gap 'A'. Remove end cover and adjust shims until gap is thickness of joint washer plus .001 to .003 inch (.03 to .08 mm). Shims are available in thicknesses of .005 inch (.13 mm), .0075 inch (.19 mm) .010 inch (.25 mm) and .092 inch (2.29 mm). Refit end cover on a new joint washer.

Reassembling (continued):

If necessary, renew pinion oil seal by pressing in a new one until it is flush with top of housing.

Screw a new locking ring onto the rack to the limit of the thread. Refit spring 32, seat 33, tie rod 31 and ball housing 34 (see **FIG 8:1**). Tighten housing until tie rod is nipped. Run locking ring up to ball housing, keeping tie rod still nipped. Slacken ball housing by $\frac{1}{8}$ of a turn so that tie rod can be moved. Relock by tightening locking ring to a torque of 33 to 37 lb ft (4.6 to 5.7 kg m). Make sure ball housing does not turn. If adjustment is correct, preload on rack ball joint will be such that a torque of 32 to 52 lb in (.37 to .6 kg m) will be needed to move tie rod sideways. This is equivalent to a side pull of 3.2 to 5.2 lb (1.45 to 2.35 kg) at a distance of 10 inches from the tie rod ball. Check this by hooking a spring balance on the tie rod at that distance from the ball and pulling at right-angles to the rod. Take the reading the moment the tie rod starts to move.

When satisfied, lock the ball housing to the rack by punching the lips of the locking ring into the slots in the housing and the rack.

Damper adjustment (first type):

The damper is on the left in **FIG 8:8** and the parts are 11 to 17 in **FIG 8:1**. For this operation it is necessary to check the torque required to turn the pinion shaft. This may be done using preload gauge 18G.207 and adaptor 18G.207A (see **FIG 8:19**). As the torque is measured in lb inches it may be possible to attach a lever ten inches long (measured from centre of pinion shaft) to the pinion coupling and use a spring balance pulling at right angles to the lever in the direction of pinion rotation. With a lever of that length, the required torque must be divided by ten to give the reading on the spring balance. Make similar calculations when working in kg m.

1 Check torque needed to turn pinion shaft and add the reading to the preload figure of 15 lb in (.18 kg m).
2 Fit yoke 11 and spring washers 12 (see **FIG 8:1**). Do not fit shims. Tighten bolts in damper cover with rack in central position until it is just possible to turn the pinion shaft with the preload gauge set to the combined figure obtained in the preceding operation.

3 Use feelers to measure the gap at 'B' and select shims and a new joint washer with a total thickness of the width of the gap. Shims are available in thicknesses of .0025 inch (.06 mm), .005 inch (.13 mm) and .010 inch (.25 mm).

4 Apply sealing compound and refit the cover, shims and joint washer. Check torque load needed to turn pinion shaft. **Figure must not exceed 25 lb in (.3 kg m).**

Damper adjustment (second type):

The damper is on the left in **FIG 8:9** and the parts are 11 to 17 or 55 and 56 in **FIG 8:1**. Adjust as follows:

1 Fit yoke 55 and spring 56. Fit cover and lightly tighten the bolts.

2 Centralize the rack, adjust bolts to give a gap of .001 to .006 inch (.03 to .15 mm) between the face of the yoke and the inner face of cover. Turn pinion half a turn in each direction and check clearance again.

3 Measure gap at 'B'. Select shims and joint washer to a total thickness of the gap measurement.

4 If yoke is plain as part 11, put sealer on joint faces and refit cover on selected shims and the new joint washer. If yoke is like part 55 with O-ring, fit the O-ring and refit the cover on shims to the thickness of the gap measurement.

Final assembling:

Refit gaiters and clips. Leave clip off gaiter at pinion end, stand assembly upright and pour in about $\frac{1}{3}$ pint (.4 US pint or .2 litre) of Extreme Pressure (EP) oil. Refit gaiter and clip.

Centralize the rack (see **FIG 8:7**). If pinion shaft is not marked, make a mark so that the central position can be

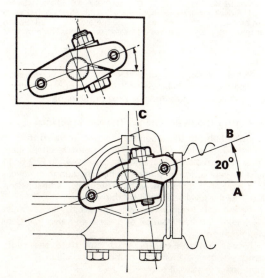

FIG 8:10 With the rack in the central position the pinion flange coupling should be set at 20 deg. to the rack centreline. The inset shows the 1st type flange assembly

'A'=Centreline of rack   'B'=Centreline of flange coupling
'C'=Centreline of pinchbolt

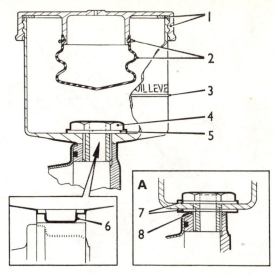

FIG 8:11 Pump reservoir header tank

Key to Fig 8:11   Inset 'A' represents 1st type with 2.5 inch (64 mm) header tank.
1 Cap and sealing ring   2 Bellows and retaining ring
3 Fluid level mark   4 Retaining bolt   5 Plain washer
6 Header tank lugs (at right angles to pump axis)   7 Steel washer   8 Fibre washer (items 7 and 8 fitted to 1st type only)

checked after fitting assembly to vehicle. Note that full travel of the rack gives 4.4 turns of the pinion (early rack) or 3.8 turns (later rack). Keeping rack centralized, fit flange coupling 21 or 52 in original position as marked. If new parts have been fitted, correct position for flange can be found by fitting it to the pinion shaft so that centre line through flange bolt holes is in line with the centre line of the rack and housing. Rack must be central. Now withdraw the flange and refit it by turning it anticlockwise by two splines. The position should then be as shown in **FIG 8:10**. Tighten the clamp bolt to 12 to 15 lb ft (1.7 to 2.1 kg m).

Refit outer ball joints, screwing them up to the original position if possible. This helps in tracking adjustments. Check that distance between ballpins is $49.62 \pm .06$ inch (1246.63 ± 1.52 mm) as shown in **FIG 8:7**. Tighten locknuts just enough to prevent movement. **If two locknuts are fitted, remove one of them.** Later assemblies have one locknut only.

Refit the assembly to the vehicle as explained in **Section 8:4**.

8:6 Ball joints and steering lever

The outer ball joints are sealed and lubricated for life. Renew the complete joint if the rubber boot has allowed dirt to enter. If boot is damaged but joint remains clean, fit a new boot, smearing the adjacent area with Dextagrease Super GP lubricant.

The original steering levers are attached to the swivel hubs by keyed tapers and locknuts. Under each nut is a brake hose bracket.

Renew a lever bent in an accident. **Do not attempt to straighten it**. Before refitting a lever, especially if it became loose on the road, check the tapered surfaces and

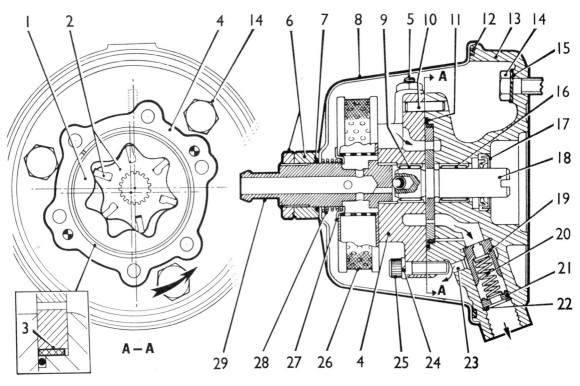

FIG 8:12 Section through the steering pump—generator mounted

Key to Fig 8:12   1 Annulus   2 Hub and vane assembly   3 Bearing bush (when fitted)   4 Cover   5 Pressure relief valve   6 Knurled nut and locknut (locknut not fitted on early pumps)   7 Reservoir O-ring seal   8 Reservoir pump   9 Short needle bearing   10 Dowel   11 Cover O-ring seal   12 Reservoir O-ring seal   13 Body   14 Pump to adaptor setscrew   15 Pump to adaptor seal washer   16 Long needle bearing   17 Oil seal   18 Shaft assembly   19 Flow control valve plunger   20 Flow control valve spring   21 Flow control valve abutment   22 Flow control valve circlip   23 Bypass port   24 Spring washer   25 Allen screw   26 Filter   27 Plate   28 Spring   29 Return union   30 Bearing bush (when fitted)   **AA** View of pumping members looking towards drive end. The hub must be assembled in position shown

the keyway for wear. Renew parts if fit is impaired. If key is plain steel, discard it and fit later copper-plated type.

After reassembling, slightly oil the nut and tighten to a minimum torque of 85 lb ft (11.7 kg m).

The second type of steering lever is attached by two special bolts, the longer bolt being on the lever side of the hub. Lever is stamped 'M' for vehicles with manual steering and 'P' for those with power steering.

8:7 General description (power steering)

Power to assist steering is provided by the fluid pump shown in **FIG 8:12**. This is mounted on the rear end of the generator. It pumps fluid from a reservoir (see **FIG 8:11**) to flow control valve 19 to 23 in **FIG 8:12**. This valve controls the flow rate from the pump, returning surplus fluid to the reservoir. A constant flow rate to the steering gear is thus maintained. Pressure relief valve 5 keeps pressure at around 1000 lb/sq in (70 kg/sq cm). **The setting of this valve must not be disturbed.**

Turning the steering wheel turns pinion 1 in **FIG 8:14**. Reaction moves housing 9 sideways and rod 14 moves spool valve 22. This valve directs fluid to the appropriate side of rack piston (parts 27, 28a, 30 and 37).

When pressure on the steering wheel is released, pressure becomes balanced and the valve spool centralizes. Normal castor action then centres the steering.

8:8 Routine maintenance (power steering)

In addition to the recommendations in **Section 8:2**, every 3000 miles (5000 km) or 3 months, check fluid level in reservoir. Clean round the cap shown in **FIG 8:11** and be careful to exclude dirt when the cap is removed. If necessary, replenish with Automatic Transmission Fluid to the level indicated by the arrow.

Periodically examine the system for leaks. Hoses must be secure and free from oil or grease, and also free from deterioration.

Never run the engine with the fluid reservoir empty. When dismantling components, clean the outside first and seal all ports.

8:9 Servicing power steering

Refer to instructions for manual steering to lubricate the rack, set front wheel alignment, remove the steering wheel, work on the tie rod joints and service the outer ball joints.

The only adjustment that may be made with the rack unit in situ is to the rack damper (see **Section 8:15**). **All other adjustments and servicing must be made with the units removed.**

8:10 Fault diagnosis

Before checking, see that fluid level in reservoir is correct, that fan belt is correctly tensioned, that the tyre pressures are correct and that the wheel alignment and castor angle are correct.

Heavy steering:

1 Steering linkage binding. Adjust and lubricate.
2 Pump output low. Check flow control valve (see **Section 8:14**)
3 Pump hub wrongly assembled (see **Section 8:14**).

Poor self-centring

1 Steering linkage binding. Adjust and lubricate
2 Excessive friction. Check alignment of inner column and upper bush. Check rack with tie rods detached. Load required to pull rack from lock to lock must not exceed 28 lb (12.7 kg). Check pinion housing and rack seals.

Steering pulls to one side:

1 Operating rod damaged or out of adjustment
2 Control valve spool out of centre. Replace assembly.

Excessive free play in steering wheel:

1 Incorrect yoke adjustment
2 Pinion coupling loose
3 Tie rod joint(s) loose
4 Spool reaction spring out of adjustment. Replace assembly

Lack of power assistance:

1 Pump output low. Check flow control valve
2 Hub incorrectly assembled (see **Section 8:14**)
3 Pinion housing seized on rack
4 Assistance in one direction only. Operating rod damaged or out of adjustment. Control valve spool out of centre. Replace assembly

Intermittent assistance when turning:

1 Engine idling too slowly
2 Air in system. Bleed as in **Section 8:11**
3 Pump output low. Check flow control valve
4 Internal fault. Check oil seals

Excessive noise:

1 Leak in system
2 Air in system. Bleed system (see **Section 8:11**)
3 Hose fouling or damaged
4 Yoke wrongly adjusted
5 Worn pump. Check as in **Section 8:14**

8:11 Bleeding the system (power steering)

If a hose has been disconnected, bleed the system before starting the engine.

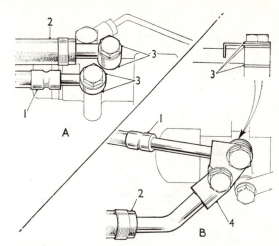

FIG 8:13 Banjo connections to power steering rack

Key to Fig 8:13 **A** Righthand drive
B Lefthand drive   1 High pressure hose   2 Low pressure hose   3 Joint washers   4 Location plate

Priming:

Set steering straight-ahead. Operate starter several times with ignition switched off, while filling reservoir up to level mark (see **Section 8:8**). Do not move steering or air will be drawn into the system.

Bleeding:

Let engine idle while turning steering slowly from lock to lock. Keep topping up the reservoir to correct level. System is bled when fluid level is stable and there is no frothing or bubbling.

8:12 Servicing the hoses

Hoses must lie naturally in the clip in front of the battery. They must not touch the engine or any other part. Where rear of hoses might contact flange of engine mounting there must be protection strips. The top or high pressure hose is fitted with an insulator in two parts.

Deterioration or damage calls for renewal of hoses. Fit new insulators if hydraulic knocks develop in high pressure hose.

8:13 Servicing steering wheel and column (power steering)

Remove and refit the steering wheel as described in **Section 8:3**.

Removing column:

Set steering straight-ahead. Disconnect wiring connectors under parcel shelf. Release clamping plates at toe-board (4 bolts). Push plates and bush up column out of the way. Release column to pinion clamp bolt. Remove two bolts, column clip and abutment and withdraw column. Remove shear-bolts as described in **Section 8:3**.

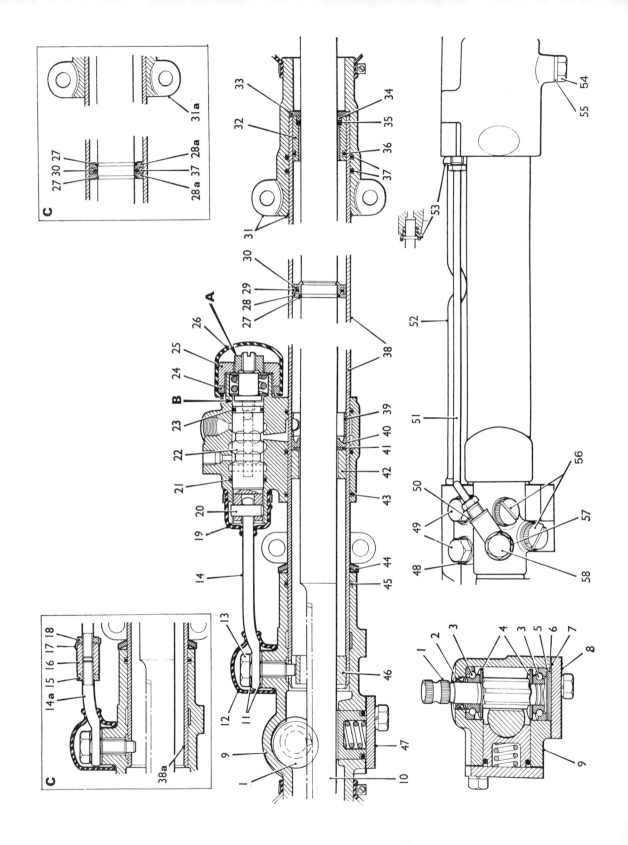

Key to Fig 8:14 1 Pinion 2 Oil seal-pinion 3 Bearings 4 Washers 5 Shims 6 Distance piece 7 Gasket 8 End cover 9 Pinion housing 10 Rack 11 Belleville washers and tab washer 12 Dust cover 13 Retaining bolt 14a Operating rod 15 Locknut-L.H.T. 16 Adjusting nut 17 Tab washer 18 Locknut 19 Dust cover 20 Dowel pin 21 O-ring seal—large 22 Operating spool valve 23 O-ring seal—small 24 Locknut 25 Retaining nut 26 Dust cover 27 Circlip 28 Piston 28a Backing washers 29 Piston ring 30 O-ring 31 End housing with undercut for sealing mastic 32 Bush 33 Backing washer—steel 34 Anti-extrusion ring 35 Seal—Nu-lip 36 O-ring seal—bush to tube 37 O-ring seal—tube to housing 38 Valve body and rack tube assembly 38a Valve body and rack tube assembly 39 Seal retainer 40 Seal 41 Anti-extrusion ring 42 Seal abutment 43 O-ring oil seals—valve body to tube 44 Dust excluder 45 O-ring seal 46 Bush—rack support, tube end peened over 47 Damper assembly 48 Washer 49 Locating pegs—valve body 50 Bonded sealing washer 51 Bundy tube—fluid transfer 52 Bypass tube—rack oil 53 Seals 54 Locating peg—end housing 55 Bonded seal 56 Caps—inlet and outlet ports 57 Bonded sealing washers 58 Banjo bolt **A** The reaction spring nut and screw setting must not be tampered with **B** The small clearance between spool and extension must not be altered **C** Insets show the first-type components and assembly

Refitting:

Centralize rack. Set column with clamp bolt and direction indicator stud horizontal. Engage pinion splines and push column down. Tighten clamp bolt to 12 to 15 lb ft (1.7 to 2.1 kg m). Refit clip, plates and wiring connectors. Check that column aligns with pinion shaft as misalignment may bias the power steering in one direction and give loss of centring in the other. Make sure steering wheel spokes are horizontal in straight-ahead position. Refer to **Section 8:3** to fit the shear-bolts.

8:14 Servicing the pump (power steering)

Refer to **FIG 8:12**. Remove pump as follows:
1 Release outlet hose banjo and drain fluid into a container. Release return hose from union 29. Blank off openings to keep out dirt.
2 Remove generator and pump assembly (see **Chapter 10**). Release nuts and seal and withdraw reservoir 8. Locknut not fitted to early pumps.
3 Mark pump and generator end bracket for correct reassembly. Release pump (3 bolts). Retrieve flexible coupling. Before proceeding to dismantle the pump a warning should be given that individual components may not be available, in which case a new pump will have to be fitted.

Dismantling pump:

1 Withdraw spring 28, plate 27 and filter 26. Release cover 4 (Allen screws 25). Unscrew return union 29 and extract bearing 9. Remove O-ring.
2 Pull out shaft 18. Lift out hub 2 and annulus 1. If necessary, extract seal 17 and press out bearing 16. Do not remove bearings and seal unless they need renewal.
3 Extract circlip 22 and remove flow control valve parts 19, 20 and 21.

Inspection:

Clean the parts and dry them. Check body and rotor for wear. Fit hub and annulus in body and lie a straight-edge across assembly to check end clearance of hub and annulus. If over .002 inch (.05 mm), renew hub and annulus. If end clearance is too much with the new parts, fit a new body or pump assembly. In an emergency it is permissible for a skilled person to lap the body face to reduce the clearance to .011 inch (.025 mm). Check the clearance between the annulus 1 and the bearing bush 3, which should be .001 to .004 inch (.02 to .10 mm), if the clearance is excessive after fitting a new annulus renew the pump body.

Tension of flow control valve spring 20 should be around 3.75 lb (1.7 kg) at a length of .687 inch (17.4 mm).

Worn shaft or bearings must be renewed.

Reassembling:

Reverse dismantling procedure. Be scrupulously clean and coat all parts with Automatic Transmission Fluid.

Fit new bearings with maker's marks facing hub 3. Press them in so that they are .040 to .050 inch (1.0 to 1.3 mm) below faces adjacent to hub. Tool 18G.1115 with details '1' and '2' is available for this purpose. Fit a

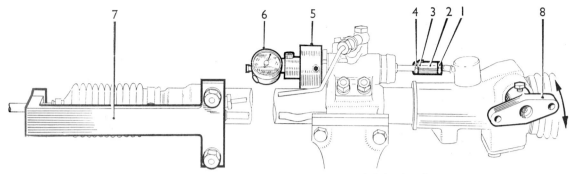

FIG 8:15 Checking and adjusting movement of pinion housing

Key to Fig 8:15 1 Locknut (lefthand) 2 Operating rod adjust nut 3 Tabwasher 4 Locknut 5 18G.1132 fitted to retaining nut 6 Dial gauge 7 18G.1131 holding rack 8 Pinion with flange fitted

new oil seal with the same tool and detail '3'. Lubricate seal and location in body. Leave detail '3' in the seal to keep it expanded while the shaft is pushed home. This ensures that the lip of the seal is not pulled back along the shaft. Assemble hub and annulus in position shown by 'AA' in illustration.

When assembled; pump should turn freely by hand. Fit reservoir, tightening knurled nut by hand. Hold nut and tighten locknut. Refit hoses, fill system with Automatic Transmission Fluid and bleed the system (see **Section 8:11**).

8:15 Servicing steering unit (power steering)

Note that rack lubrication, front wheel alignment, attention to steering wheel, tie rod joints and outer ball joints are all serviced by referring to similar items in the 'Manual' section.

Removing:

1 Release steering column to pinion clamp bolt. Slacken off bolts in outer column abutment clip. Release handbrake.
2 Remove cap from fluid reservoir. Remove righthand wheel on righthand drive car and the lefthand one on a lefthand drive car.
3 Remove splitpins and nuts and release outer ball joints from steering levers (see **Section 8:4**).
4 Clean all round the banjo connections and note positions of hoses. **FIG 8:13** shows the connections to the rack housing. Have a container handy to catch fluid draining from the valve body when the banjo bolts are withdrawn. Note that lefthand drive vehicles have a location plate with extra joint washer (see 3 and 4).
5 Release rack housing from toe-board (4 bolts). A separate two-part bracket is used at the valve end. Withdraw unit sideways through valance aperture, turning it to clear the pinion shaft, the valve body and the balance pipe banjo.

Checking movement of pinion housing:

This is part 9 in **FIG 8:14**. When pinion 1 is turned, housing should move an equal amount in each direction. Check this as follows:

Fit tool 18G.1131 (see 7 in **FIG 8:15**) to end housing bracket. Remove dust cover 26 from retaining nut 25 (see **FIG 8:14**). Fit a dial gauge 6 to tool 18G.1132 (see 5 in **FIG 8:15**), fit tool to retaining nut and zero the gauge. Fit tool 18G.207D or a suitable lever to pinion shaft or coupling 8.

Turn pinion shaft to move housing fully in each direction. The two readings should be equal within ±.005 inch (.13 mm).

Adjustment, 1st type:

To make adjustments, slacken off operating rod locknut 4 (lefthand thread). Release adjusting nut 2. Alter length of operating rod as required, turning adjusting nut half a turn at a time, tightening the locknut and checking as before.

Spool valve movement is restricted by the pinion housing retaining bolt 13 which locates in a slot in the rack tube, however, this movement must be centralized by also adjusting the control rod 14a (inset C); refer to next operation on 'servicing oil seals'.

2nd type:

Referring to the rod 14 in **FIG 8:14** it will be seen that it is non-adjustable. Spool valve movement on this type is restricted by the reaction spring and not by the slot in the rack tube. **It must not be adjusted.**

Servicing oil seals on spool:

Note that the reaction spring nut and extension screw are set and must not be moved (see 'A' in FIG 8:14).

Dismantle by removing dust covers 19 and 26. Unlock and remove retaining bolt 13 and washers 11. Remove dowel pin 20. Scribe a line across the valve body and retaining nut 25 for correct reassembly. Release locknut 24 and remove retaining nut, then pull spool assembly 22 straight out of body. **Do not alter the small clearance between spool and extension indicated at 'B'.**

Renew all seals. Fit new dust covers if deteriorated. Use a fine oilstone to remove burrs and sharp edges from operating fork.

Lubricate parts with Automatic Transmission Fluid. Fit the O-ring seals and push the spool assembly into the bore. Screw up retaining nut until it just contacts reaction washer with original scribed marks aligned. Do this carefully by feel. **There must be no load on the washer, nor any free movement.**

Hold retaining nut and tighten locknut. Refit operating rod. Dowel pin enters chamfered end first. Fit retaining bolt so that flat of tab washer locates with flat on bolt.

Recheck pinion housing movement as in preceding instructions. Smear silicone grease inside lips of dust covers.

Servicing rack and pinion assembly:

Refer to **FIG 8:14**. Note that the valve body is bonded to the rack tube and must not be moved. The 1st type operating rod must be adjusted as in 'Checking movement of pinion housing'.

Dismantling:

The following operations refer to two types, the later type having slight modifications. The differences can be seen in **FIG 8:14** between the main subject and the insets C.

High standards of cleanliness are absolutely necessary when working with hydraulic components, this criterion has been pointed out in the clutch and brake sections of the manual and the principle applies no less on these components.

1 Refer to **Section 8:5** and remove both tie-rods.
2 Remove the damper assembly 47 noting that when working on the first type there is a distance piece between the cover plate and yoke.
3 Remove pinion housing cover 8, gasket 7 and extract distance piece 6 and shims 5. Push out the pinion 1, tail bearing and washer. The top bearing and washer will remain inside the housing.
4 Take off the dust cover 19, release the locking tab and remove the retaining bolt 13 and special Bellville washers 11. Slide the pinion housing 9 off the tube complete with O-ring 45.
5 2nd type rack: Refer to **FIG 8:16** and using a pair of pliers ease back the four peened indentations in the rack tube to allow the support bush 2 (46) to come through.
6 Take out the two dowel bolts 49 from the valve body and collect the bonded steel washers 50. The dowel bolt at the pinion end locates the seal abutment 42 and the second bolt, away from the pinion end, locates the seal retainer 39. To avoid scoring the end housing bush 32 remove all burrs from the locking groove in end of rack.
7 1st type rack: Withdraw the rack from the pinion end. Cover the transfer ports and dowel holes as there will be a quantity of fluid expelled as the rack is withdrawn.
8 2nd type rack: Drain the fluid by tipping the rack over, then pull the rack to the pinion end to abut the rack piston 28 and support bush 46. Using a soft faced drift carefully drive the rack and support bush from the tube. An approximation of the size of the drift would be 12 inch x $\frac{1}{2}$ inch diameter (300 mm x 13 mm).
9 1st type rack: Take out the piston ring 37, break circlips 27 to remove them—do not try to withdraw them over the finished surface of the rack and extract washers 28a and O-ring seal 30. Withdraw retainer 39, oil seal

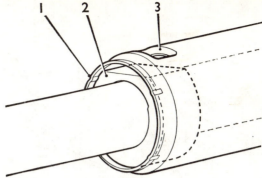

FIG 8:16 The rack support bush (2nd type rack assembly)

Key to Fig 8:16   1 Peened in four places   2 Bush
3 Enlarged slot

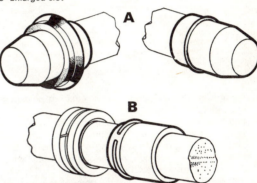

FIG 8:17 Fitting the oil seals and piston circlips

Key to Fig 8:17   A Thimble tool 18G.1129 fitted over the threads of the rack to protect the seals   B 1st type rack only: Protector sleeve 18G.1130 is used to protect rack surface from cutting edges of circlips

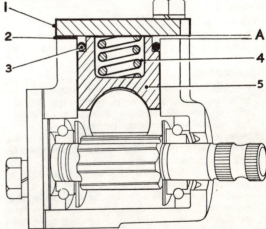

FIG 8:18 Section through the rack damper assembly —to clarify adjustment only

Key to Fig 8:18   1 Cover   2 Shims   3 O-ring
4 Spring   5 Yoke
'A' dimension=Measured gap made up with selective shims, plus .001 to .003 inch (.03 to .08 mm)

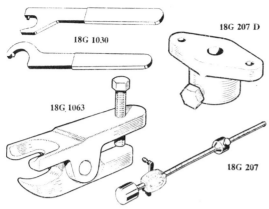

FIG 8:19 Special tools used when working on manual steering gear

Key to Fig 8:19

18G.1030   Spanners for rack ball joint
18G.1063   Remover for ballpin of outer ball joints
18G.207D   Adaptor for pinion when checking preload (drill through $\frac{35}{64}$ inch (13.9 mm) to modify early adaptors)
18G.207   Bearing preload gauge

40, anti-extrusion ring 41, which must not pass over the rack teeth, and seal abutment 42.

10 2nd type rack: Take off the piston ring 29 and O-ring seal 30 from the piston assembly. Extract the seal abutment 42, anti-extrusion ring 41, oil seal 40 and retainer 39, all of which, on this type, can be withdrawn over the rack teeth.

11 Release the Bundy tube 51 at the end housing, remove the dowel bolt and washer 54 and 55, and slide the end housing and backing washer from the tube.

12 Withdraw bush 32, anti-extrusion washer 34, Nu-lip seal 35 and O-ring seal 36 from the rack tube.

Inspection:

13 Renew all seals and dust covers. Examine pinion bearing and rack bush for wear. Check the teeth of the pinion and rack and inspect all dowel holes for burrs.

Reassembling:

14 Reassemble in the reverse order of dismantling but before starting, clean all the parts thoroughly and dry them off. Assemble all the internal parts, particularly seals, coated with automatic transmission fluid.

15 Refer to **FIG 8:17** and fit tool 18G.1129 over the threaded end of rack. This will protect the rack and O-ring seals during assembly.
1st type rack: Fit circlips 27 onto tool 18G.1130 to protect the finished surface of the rack.

16 Insert the rack into the tube from the end housing end, ensure the holes in the seal abutment 42 and retainer 39 align with the valve body dowel bolt holes, (see operation 6). Note also that the elongated slot in the retainer is a fluid passage.

17 Centralize the rack and refit the end housing bush 32, fit the tool 18G.1129 over the threaded ends of the rack and assemble the Nu-lip oil seal 35, refit the anti-extrusion washer 34—align the locating hole—and

press the bush flush with the end of the tube. Fit the backing washer 33 before fitting the O-ring seals 36 and 37.

18 2nd type rack: Use Sealastic to fill the undercut in the end housing.

19 Insert pinion top bearing and washer before assembling pinion housing 9 to tube. With the rack centralized fit the pinion so that the stamped line, on the top end of the shaft is below the centreline and vertical within 5 deg.

20 2nd type rack: Adjust the pinion preload (see **Section 8:5**).

21 Adjust the rack damper as described under the next heading.

22 During the refitting of the operating rod retaining bolt 13 ensure the tabs of the washer engage correctly with the flats of the bolt head.

23 Check the pinion housing movement.

Adjusting rack damper:

Note that adjusting the rack damper is the only operation that may be carried out on steering gear while it is in situ on the vehicle (see **Section 8:9**).

Damper assembly is shown in **FIG 8:18**. Fit yoke 5 without O-ring or spring. Refit cover without shims 2. Tighten cover bolts lightly and turn pinion to check for tight spots. Adjust bolts as necessary. Use feelers to check gap between cover and housing (A).

Remove cover and fit O-ring and spring and shims to thickness of measured gap plus .001 to .003 inch (.03 to .08 mm). Three shims (as fitted to standard rack) are available as follows:
.0025 inch (.06 mm), .005 inch (.13 mm) and .010 inch (.25 mm).

Final assembling of rack and pinion:

After adjusting the rack damper, fit retaining bolt to operating rod, engaging the flats on tab washer and bolt correctly.

When assembly is complete, check pinion housing movement as described under that heading earlier in this Section.

8:16 Tracking and steering geometry

Adjustment of front wheel alignment is covered in **Section 8:2**. As steering performance is profoundly affected by the various angles built into the suspension system, the owner is advised to read the relevant details given in **Section 7:14** in the preceding Chapter.

8:17 Fault diagnosis

(a) Faults in power steering

1 These are covered in **Section 8:10**.

(b) Wheel wobble

1 Unbalanced wheels and tyres
2 Slack steering ball joints
3 Incorrect steering geometry
4 Excessive play in steering gear
5 Faulty suspension
6 Worn hub bearings

(c) Wander

1 Check 2, 3 and 4 in (b) and check (e)
2 Uneven tyre pressures
3 Uneven tyre wear

(d) Heavy steering

1 Check 3 in (b)
2 Very low tyre pressures
3 Neglected lubrication (damaged dust covers)
4 Wheels out of track
5 Rack damper too tight

6 Excessive pinion bearing preload
7 Steering column bent or misaligned
8 Column bushes tight

(e) Lost motion

1 Loose steering wheel, worn splines
2 Defective column coupling
3 Worn rack and pinion teeth
4 Worn ball joints
5 Worn swivel hub joints
6 Slack pinion bearings

NOTES

CHAPTER 9

THE BRAKING SYSTEM

9:1 General description

There are hydraulic disc brakes at the front and drum brakes at the rear. The handbrake operates mechanically on the rear brakes only. A vacuum-servo unit boosts brake pedal effort to give powerful braking. The original Mk 2 servo unit is separately mounted and may be dismantled for repairs (see **FIG 9:9**). This was superseded by the Mk 2B unit which is sealed and must be renewed as an assembly. Later lefthand-drive cars were fitted with the 'Super Vac' unit acting directly on a single or tandem master cylinder bolted to it (see 'B' and 'C' in **FIG 9:1**). The tandem master cylinder shown in **FIG 9:8** has the advantage that failure in the circuit to the front brakes still leaves the rear brakes in operating condition and vice versa.

The various systems employ either a reducing valve or a limiting valve to control pressure to the rear brakes while allowing full power on the front brakes during heavy braking. This reduces the risk of skidding due to locked rear wheels (see **FIGS 9:13** and **9:14**).

The calipers fitted to Mk 2S vehicles have three pistons, as shown in **FIG 9:5**.

9:2 Routine maintenance

Topping up brake fluid:

Every 3000 miles (5000 km) or 3 months, check the fluid level in the reservoir for the master cylinder. **FIG 9:1** shows locations 'A', 'B' and 'C'. 'A' is the reservoir for the system with a separate servo unit. 'B' shows the reservoir and single master cylinder that are bolted direct to the servo unit, and 'C' shows a similar arrangement for the tandem cylinder.

In every case, clean the area round the cap before unscrewing it. If fluid is below the level indicated on the outside of the reservoir, top it up with Castrol Girling Fluid Amber. An alternative is fluid to specification SAE. J1703a (grade 1). **Do not use any other fluid, and never introduce mineral oil or the results will be disastrous.** If there is a need for frequent topping-up, check at once for leaks and rectify them.

Note that brake fluid will dissolve body paint-work, so be careful of drips. Before refitting the cap, make sure that vent hole 3 is clear.

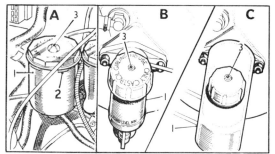

FIG 9:1 The three types of brake master cylinder reservoir, the cylinder at 'A' being separate from the servo unit. 'B' shows a single cylinder mounted on the servo unit and 'C' is a tandem cylinder, also mounted on the servo unit

Key to Fig 9:1   1 Reservoir   2 Fluid level mark
3 Vent in cap

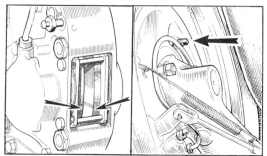

FIG 9:2 Disc brake pad thickness is indicated by arrows (left). On right, arrow points to squared adjuster for rear brake shoes

Brake adjustment:

Every 3000 miles (5000 km) or 3 months, check travel of brake pedal. If excessive, adjust at point indicated by arrow on right in **FIG 9:2**. The square is an adjuster behind each rear brake backplate. Release the handbrake and chock the front wheels. Jack-up the rear wheels and turn the adjuster clockwise until wheel is locked, then turn it back until the wheel turns freely without rubbing. Do both brakes. This will also set the handbrake.

If handbrake movement is still excessive, refer to **Section 9:11**. On early models, apply the grease gun to the nipple about halfway along the handbrake cable under the vehicle. On all models, lubricate the handbrake linkage at the intermediate lever and rear axle (see **FIG 9:15**).

Inspection:

Every 3000 miles (5000 km) or 3 months, make a visual inspection of all brake pipes and hoses.

Disc brake pads:

Every 6000 miles (10,000 km) or 6 months, inspect the front brake pads for thickness at locations indicated by arrows on left in **FIG 9:2**. It is advisable to renew pads if thickness is down to $\frac{1}{8}$ inch (3.2 mm). **Never continue to run with pads that are down to a thickness below $\frac{1}{16}$ inch (1.6 mm). To fit new pads refer to Section 9:4.**

Rear brakes:

Every 12,000 miles (20,000 km) or 12 months, chock the front wheels, release the handbrake, jack-up and remove the rear wheels and the brake drums (2 crosshead screws). Blow dust from drum and backplate. Check brake linings. If they are worn down to the rivets, renew the shoes and linings complete (see **Section 9:5**).

It may be helpful to slacken off the brake adjusters before removing the drums. After refitting, adjust the brakes.

Servo unit filter:

Renew this every 36,000 miles (60,000 km) or 3 years. If a separate servo unit is fitted, refer to lefthand view in **FIG 9:3**, clean filter area, release screw indicated by arrow and remove filter cover and element. Fit a new element.

If master cylinder and servo unit are combined, refer to righthand view in **FIG 9:3**. From below parcel shelf, pull back dust cover 1, remove cap 2 and prise out filter 3. Cut a new filter as shown at 4, fit it over the pushrod, press it into place, refit the cap and finally refit the cover.

Preventive maintenance:

It is recommended that brake pads and linings, and hydraulic pipes and hoses should be examined at intervals no longer than those laid down in the Passport to Service.

Change all the brake fluid every 18 months or 24,000 (40,000 km) whichever is the sooner.

Check all fluid seals and hoses in the hydraulic system every 3 years or 40,000 miles (65,000 km) whichever is the sooner. At the same time check the working surfaces of pistons and bores in the master and wheel cylinders. The brake servo filter element must be renewed at the same mileage.

Always use the recommended fluid and do not leave it in unsealed containers because it absorbs moisture, which can be dangerous. It is best to discard fluid drained from the system or fluid used for bleeding. **At all times observe absolute cleanliness when dealing with brake fluid and the internal parts of hydraulic systems.**

9:3 Bleeding the brake system

If brake pipes have been disconnected or air has entered the system because of extremely low fluid level in the reservoir. the entrained air must be eliminated or the brake pedal will feel 'spongy'.

To prepare for the operation, make sure that the reservoir is filled with fluid. Keep it topped-up so that it is never less than half-full, because air will enter the system if the reservoir becomes empty and the operation will then need to be restarted. Check that the rear wheel cylinders are free to slide in the backplates (see **Section 9:5**) and apply the handbrake. All connections and bleed screws must be tight. Make sure the brake pedal has full movement and is not impeded by the carpet.

Do not use reclaimed fluid and do not pressure-bleed the system.

On single master cylinder systems, start with the front brakes. If a tandem master cylinder is fitted, start with the rear brakes. Proceed as follows:

1 Attach a length of rubber or clear plastic tubing to the bleed screw on the front caliper farthest from the

master cylinder. Immerse the free end in a little clean brake fluid in a clear glass container.

2 Open the bleed screw half a turn (**FIGS 9:4** and **9:6** show the location). Get a second operator inside the car to depress the brake pedal fully for a fast stroke, followed by three short rapid strokes. The pedal should then be released to fly back freely.

3 Air bubbles will emerge from the immersed tube, but these will eventually cease. At this point close the bleed screw during a last slow depression of the pedal. Tighten bleed screws to 4 to 6 lb ft (.5 to .8 kg m). Do not overtighten.

4 Repeat on second front caliper. When operating on the rear brakes, use slow pedal applications so that the ball in the reducing or limiting valve does not close. Let the pedal rise slowly and then wait three or four seconds before the next application. If the ball does move it can usually be heard to do so and the pedal becomes solid before reaching the floor. In this case, tighten the bleed screw, keep pressure on the pedal and release the handbrake. This will displace the ball. Apply handbrake and continue bleeding.

5 When all air has been eliminated from the system, top up reservoir to correct level and adjust rear brakes. Apply strong pressure to the pedal and check all pipe connections for leaks.

6 If air bubbles persist when bleeding a particular brake, try closing the bleed screw at the end of pedal down stroke, let pedal rise fully and then reopen the screw. Close screw finally during last pedal down stroke. If the pedal feels 'spongy', there is still air in the system.

9:4 Servicing front brakes

Renewing pads:

The pads must be renewed before the friction material reaches the minimum thickness of $\frac{1}{16}$ inch (1.6 mm). Refer to **FIG 9:4** and proceed as follows:

1 Apply handbrake and remove front wheel. Remove pins 1 and withdraw retaining pins 2. Lift pads 3 and anti-squeal shims (when fitted) from caliper recess.

2 Clean inside of recess and ends of pistons 6. Release bleed screw 9 and press pistons back into bores with a lever or clamp. Fluid will rise in master cylinder reservoir (see **FIG 9:1**) so watch for overflowing. It may be necessary to syphon off some of the fluid.

3 Insert new pads (they are interchangeable). Refit pins and splitpins. File off high-spots if pads are not free in the recess. If anti-squeal shims are also fitted, make sure the arrow points in the direction of forward rotation. Pump brake pedal several times to set pistons and check level of fluid in reservoir.

Note that pads may not need renewal and yet may be worn unequally. In this case it is permissible to change them over to even up the wear.

Servicing caliper (Mk 1 and 2):

Refer to **FIG 9:4**. Do the following:

1 Open bleed screw to drain fluid from brake pipe. Release metal brake pipe from inner end of flexible hose. Never try to unscrew hose from caliper without releasing inner end first. Release caliper from hub (2 bolts).

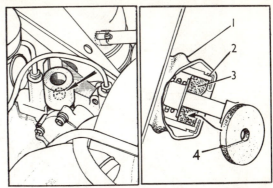

FIG 9:3 Arrow points to securing screw for filter on a separate servo unit (left). Later direct-acting units have filter shown on right

Key to Fig 9:3   1 Dust cover   2 End cap   3 Filter
4 Diagonal cut in replacement filter

2 Remove pads. Clean caliper, removing all dirt and drying off all cleaning fluid. **Use only Girling Cleaning Fluid or methylated spirit.**

3 Apply a clamp to the piston in the caliper half with the mounting lugs. Reconnect brake pipe and gently apply brake pedal. Opposite piston will start to emerge. Disengage dust cover 4 and remove piston by hand. Catch draining fluid.

4 Remove seal 5 with blunt tool, taking care not to scratch bore or groove. Remove clamp. To remove other piston, temporarily refit piston just removed and clamp it, using pedal pressure as before.

The caliper halves must not be separated. Remove bleed screw and clear all fluid passages with compressed air. Reassemble the caliper as follows:

1 Dry a new piston seal and then coat it with clean brake fluid. Seat it carefully in its groove. Refit dust cover.

2 Slacken bleed screw one turn. Apply brake fluid then fit piston squarely into cylinder. Press it in until about $\frac{5}{16}$ inch (8 mm) protrudes, then fit lip of dust cover in piston groove.

3 Press piston home and tighten bleed screw. Repeat process to refit second piston.

4 Fit caliper, tightening bolts to 45 to 50 lb ft (6.2 to 6.9 kg m). **Do not apply brake pedal while pads are out.** Refit pads and then bleed system (see **Section 9:3**).

Servicing caliper (Mk 2S):

Follow the preceding instructions but refer to **FIG 9:5**. The most noticeable difference is the use of two pistons 11 in the outer half of the caliper. Note also the anti-rattle springs 5 which clip over the backing plates.

Brake discs (all models):

Front hub and disc assemblies are removed and refitted as described in **Chapter 7, Section 7:8** of the Suspension chapter. If runout of disc face at outer edge exceeds .008 inch (.2 mm) remove disc and try another position on the drive shaft splines.

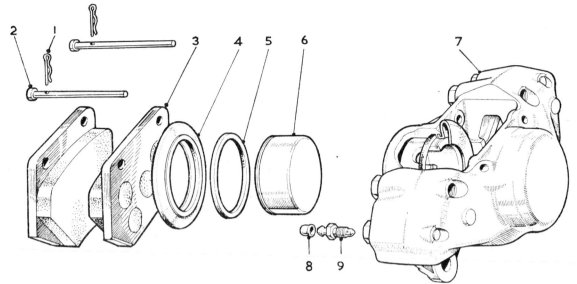

FIG 9:4 Components of front brake caliper fitted to Mk I and Mk II vehicles

Key to Fig 9:4   1 Splitpin   2 Retaining pin   3 Pad assembly   4 Dust cover   5 Sealing ring   6 Piston   7 Caliper body
8 Bleed screw dust cover   9 Bleed screw

Concentric scoring that is even and not excessive is not detrimental. Worn discs may be reground to a surface finish of 63 micro-inch. Equal amount to be removed from each side. Reduction from thickness of .500 to .505 inch (12.70 to 12.83 mm) not to exceed .040 inch (1.02 mm). Faces must be true within total runout of .002 inch (.05 mm) and parallel within .001 inch (.0254 mm).

9:5 Servicing rear brakes

Refer to **FIG 9:6**. Inset (top right) shows correct fitting of linings and shoes.

Removing and refitting brake shoes:

Chock front wheels, release handbrake, remove rear wheel. Pull off drum 28 (screws 29). Remove springs 10 and slacken off adjuster 13. Pull one shoe outward until ends clear abutments on adjuster and cylinder and then relieve tension on springs. Both shoes can then be removed. Put wire or rubber band round cylinder to stop piston 17 falling out of cylinder. **Do not depress brake pedal.**

If linings are worn, fit replacement shoes. It is not advisable to rivet new linings to old shoes as they may not be concentric. Do not fit new linings to one brake

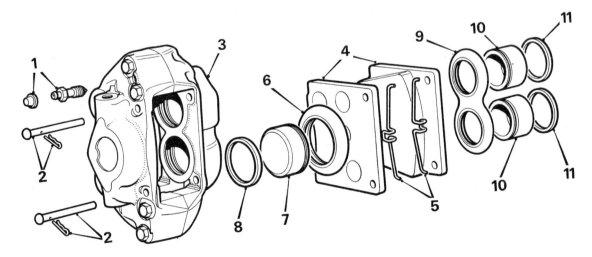

FIG 9:5 Components of front brake caliper fitted to Mk 2S models

Key to Fig 9:5   1 Dust cover and bleed nipple   2 Pad retaining pin and splitpin   3 Caliper body   4 Brake pads
5 Anti-rattle springs   6 Dust cover   7 Piston   8 Seal   9 Dust cover   10 Pistons   11 Seals

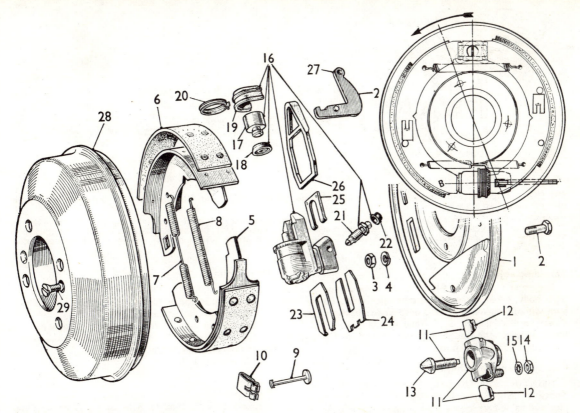

FIG 9:6 Components of rear brake. Inset (top right) shows how linings are offset on shoes. Note direction of wheel rotation

Key to Fig 9:6   1 Backplate   2 Bolt—backplate   3 Nut   4 Spring washer   5 Brake shoe assembly   6 Liner
7 Spring—shoe return—cylinder end   8 Spring—shoe return—adjuster end   9 Pin—brake shoe steady
10 Spring—brake shoe steady   11 Adjuster assembly   12 Tappet   13 Wedge   14 Nut   15 Washer (shakeproof)
16 Cylinder assembly—wheel   17 Piston   18 Seal   19 Dust cover   20 Retainer   21 Bleed screw   22 Dust cover
23 Spring—retaining—wheel cylinder   24 Plate—locking   25 Washer—distance   26 Dust cover   27 Handbrake lever
28 Drum   29 Screw

only, and ensure that linings are of the same make, grade and condition. Grades are given in **Technical Data**.

At all times keep oil, grease, paint or brake fluid off the linings. Do not handle with greasy fingers and do not try to clean oil-soaked linings.

Refit shoes in reverse order of dismantling, referring to inset in the illustration for correct position of shoes and linings. Note direction of wheel rotation. Put smear of Girling White Brake Grease on ends of shoes and on steady pins 9. **Keep grease off rubber parts and linings.** Inset shows correct position of interrupted spring. Fit one shoe of assembly of shoes and springs, pull springs until second shoe can be dropped into place and check that shoes register correctly.

With new linings, slacken adjuster right off and fully-release handbrake. Fit drum and adjust brakes. This will also set the handbrake.

Servicing wheel cylinder:

Refer to assembly 16 in **FIG 9:6**. After removing the brake shoes, disconnect pipe and cable behind backplate 1 and remove rubber dust cover 26. Prise plates 23, 24

and 25 apart and tap the retaining plate from under the neck of cylinder. Withdraw lever 27, plates and cylinder. Remove dust cover 19 and extract piston and seal 17 and 18.

Clean cylinder parts in methylated spirit. Check that bore is smooth and bright. Renew the seal. Fit seal with the fingers, flat face to shoulder of piston. Wet with brake fluid and insert piston, taking care not to trap or turn back lip of seal.

Refit cylinder to backplate after smearing contact surfaces with Girling White Brake Grease. Fit plate 25 as shown. Fit handbrake lever. Fit spring plate 23 and insert locking plate 24 between spring 23 and plate 25 with its open end towards the brake lever. Tap locking plate in until lips of spring plate 23 locate in locking plate. Check that cylinder will slide in slot in backplate.

Fit rubber cover. Connect pipe and cable. Refit remaining parts, adjust brakes and bleed system (see **Section 9:3**).

Cylinder bores must be the same on both brakes. Bodies are marked .7 (for .7 inch diameter), or $\frac{3}{4}$ (.75 inch diameter) up to A17S.12614A.

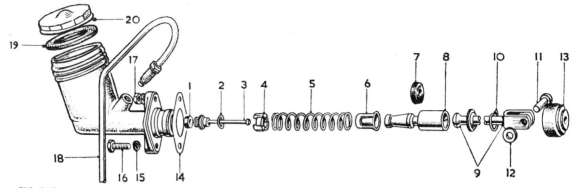

FIG 9:7 Components of single master cylinder of type **bolted to bulkhead.** When cylinder is bolted to servo unit, internal parts **1 to 8** are similar

Key to Fig 9:7   1 Valve seal   2 Spring washer—curved   3 Valve stem   4 Valve spacer   5 Spring   6 Spring retainer   7 Plunger seal   8 Plunger   9 Pushrod and retaining washer   10 Circlip   11 Clevis pin   12 Plain washer   13 Dust cover   14 Packing   15 Spring washer   16 Screw   17 Nut—stud   18 Master cylinder to servo unit pipe   19 Filler cap gasket   20 Filler cap

Servicing adjuster:

See parts 11 to 15 in **FIG 9:6**. Remove wedge 13 from body, clean all parts and check for wear. Smear parts with Girling White Brake Grease when reassembling. Check position of tappets 12. They should move simultaneously when the wedge is turned. Tighten nuts 14 to 4 to 5 lb ft (.55 to .69 kg m).

Removing and refitting backplate:

This is part 1 in **FIG 9:6**. After removing hub (see **Section 7:9** in Suspension chapter), disconnect brake pipe and cable and release plate from radius arm. When refitting, put sealing compound on mating faces of plate and radius arm. Adjust brakes and bleed system.

9:6 Servicing master cylinder (single)

When a separate servo unit is fitted the master cylinder is as shown in **FIG 9:7**. The master cylinder fitted direct to the Super-Vac servo unit shown in **FIG 9:11** has similar internal parts from 1 to 8. The reservoir, however, is not integral with the cylinder, being secured in place by a hollow adaptor bolt. Servicing instructions will apply to both types with due allowance for the absence of pushrod 9 in the type bolted direct to the servo unit.

When plunger 8 is pushed down the cylinder bore, the initial movement presses valve seal 1 against a transfer port between the reservoir and the cylinder. Fluid is then forced out of the cylinder through pipe 18, going to the servo unit in the first type and to the brake pipes in the second. When the brake pedal is released the plunger returns up the bore and the last part of its movement opens the valve so that fluid from the reservoir can replenish any lost in the system by leakage.

Removing:

1 Attach a tube to one of the bleed screws (see **FIG 9:4**). Open screw one turn, depress pedal, close screw and let pedal return. Repeat this till fluid has been drained from reservoir. Disconnect pushrod (clevis pin 11).

2 Clean round pipe connection and disconnect, plugging port in cylinder to exclude dirt. Detach cylinder from bulkhead or servo unit.

Dismantling:

1 After detaching cover 13, prise out circlip 10 and remove pushrod 9. Use gentle air pressure to blow out plunger and valve 1 to 8.

2 Lift leaf in side of thimble 6 and detach plunger. Remove seal 7. Compress spring 5, release stem 3 through keyhole slot in thimble.

3 Separate parts 1 to 6.

Inspection:

Clean in methylated spirit or Girling Cleaning Fluid. Cylinder bore must be polished and free from pitting or scores. Check ports. Renew both seals.

Reassembling:

1 Dip all internal parts in clean brake fluid. Seal 1 has flat face to valve head. Fit curved washer 2 with domed side against valve head as shown. Fit spacer 4, legs first (see 'A' in **FIG 9:8**).

2 Fit spring to spacer, insert thimble and compress spring so that stem can engage keyhole slot.

3 Fit seal 7 with flat face against plunger shoulder. Insert plunger into thimble and press thimble leaf home behind plunger collar (see 'B' in **FIG 9:8**).

4 Insert plunger, taking care not to trap or turn back lip on seal 7. Refit pushrod and cover. Pack cover with Girling Rubber Grease.

5 Refit cylinder to bulkhead or servo unit and bleed the system (see **Section 9:3**).

9:7 Servicing master cylinder (tandem)

Refer to **FIG 9:8**. The section (top right) shows the two plungers, the primary on the right operating the front brakes and the secondary the rear brakes. If one circuit fails, pressure will still be applied to the other. Primary valve at 'C' is tipped open when pedal is fully released, thus allowing fluid to replenish primary circuit if fluid has been lost. Secondary valve parts 11 to 16 are similar in action to those in the single master cylinder shown in **FIG 9:7**.

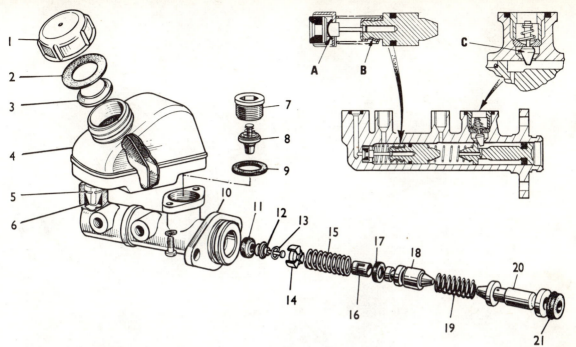

FIG 9:8 Components of tandem master cylinder. **Sections** (top right) show correct position of curved washer **13** at 'A', leaf of thimble **16** behind plunger shoulder 'B' and **tipping** valve in sealed position at 'C'

Key to Fig 9:8   1 Filler cap   2 Gasket   3 Baffle   4 Reservoir—dual   5 Circlip—internal   6 Seal   7 Securing nut
8 Tipping valve   9 Face seal   10 Cylinder body   11 Valve seal   12 Valve stem   13 Spring washer—curved
14 Valve spacer   15 Secondary spring   16 Spring retainer   17 Seal   18 Secondary plunger
19 Intermediate spring (black)   20 Primary plunger   21 Gland seal

Removing:

Drain fluid as instructed for single cylinder in preceding Section, but open a front bleed screw and a rear one to empty both circuits.

Dismantling:

1 Do not remove reservoir (see later). Remove two screws, turn reservoir to one side and remove nut 7 to release seal 9 and valve 8.
2 Blow out plungers with gentle air pressure and dismantle secondary plunger as described for single cylinder in preceding Section.

Inspection:

Follow the instructions under the same heading in **Section 9:6**.

Reassembling:

Valve assembly 11 to 14 is assembled as described under the same heading in **Section 9:6**. **FIG 9:8** shows curved washer 'A' and thimble leaf 'B' correctly fitted. Continue assembling in reverse order of dismantling. Bleed the system as in **Section 9:3**.

The reservoir:

If damaged, renew as follows:
Remove master cylinder and dismantle internal parts. Lever reservoir from cylinder. Remove seal 6 and circlip 5.

Fit new seal and circlip. Lubricate neck of new reservoir with brake fluid and press it home. Reassemble the cylinder. Blank off outlet ports and fill reservoir with correct fluid. Apply 30 to 35 lb/sq in (2.1 to 2.4 kg/sq cm) air pressure to vent hole in filler cap to check for leaks.

9:8 Servicing separate servo unit

The unit is shown exploded in **FIG 9:9**. This is the original type 'Powerstop' Mk 2. **Later units of the Mk 2B type cannot be dismantled for servicing.** They have no end cover 45, the cylinder halves being joined by a crimped ring. The air valve and filter of the Mk 2B are serviced in the same way as those on the Mk 2.

Very briefly, the action is that application of the brake pedal produces hydraulic pressure on control valve 3. This moves to the left and rocks valve assembly 20 so that the lefthand side of piston 42 is subjected to inlet manifold depression through valve 31 and the righthand side of the piston is open to atmospheric pressure. This pressure forces the piston into the cylinder 37 and the piston rod pushes output piston 13 or 46 (first- and second-types) down the bore of a hydraulic cylinder in the braking circuit and powerfully augments the effect of pedal pressure.

Removing:

Unit is mounted on bulkhead. Disconnect vacuum hose from valve 31. Disconnect both hydraulic brake pipes. Release unit from brackets (3 bolts).

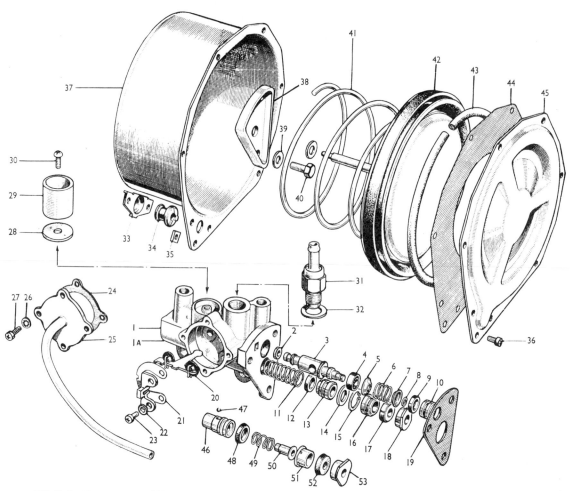

FIG 9:9 Components of 'Powerstop' Mk 2 servo unit, as fitted to vehicles with separate master cylinder

Key to Fig 9:9   1 Body—with circlip groove*   1a Body†   2 Control piston seal—small   3 Control piston
4 Control piston seal—large   5 Spring abutment   6 Piston return spring   7 Spring retainer   8 Circlip—retainer
9 Taper seal—plug   10 Plug   11 Piston return spring   12 Taper seal*   13 Output piston*   14 Flat washer   15 Circlip*
16 Spacer*   17 Gland seal*   18 Guide bush*   19 Gasket—cylinder to body   20 Valve assembly   21 Valve return spring
22 Flat washer   23 Setscrew   24 Gasket—vacuum pipe to body   25 Vacuum pipe   26 Shakeproof washer   27 Setscrew
28 Seal—air filter to body   29 Air filter element   30 Screw   31 Non-return valve   32 Gasket   33 Retaining plate
34 Rubber grommet   35 Nut   36 Setscrew   37 Vacuum cylinder   38 Clamping plate   39 Washer—copper
40 Setscrew   41 Vacuum piston spring   42 Vacuum piston   43 Seal—backing ring   44 Joint washer—2 off
45 End cover   46 Output piston†   47 Ball—fluid return†   48 Taper seal†   49 Spring—sleeve return†   50 Sleeve†
51 Spacer†   52 Gland seal†   53 Guide bush†
*First-type output piston   †Second-type output piston

Dismantling:

1 Remove cover 45, supporting it against spring pressure. Release pressure and remove cover, joints 44, piston 42, seal 43 and spring 41. If piston rod is scored, complete servo unit must be renewed.

2 Release clamp plate 38 and body 1. Remove filter 29. Remove pipe and cover 25. Release valve assembly 20 to 23.

3 Remove gasket 19 and tap body face on a wooden block until plug 10 emerges and releases control piston assembly 2 to 9. Dismantle piston by compressing spring and removing circlip 8.

4 Dismantle first-type output piston 13. Extract bush 18. Ease up gland seal 17 and extract nylon spacer 16. Remove circlip 15 to release parts 11 to 15. Use great care because of spring pressure.

5 Second-type output piston assembly 46 to 53 is removed by extracting bush 53. Keeping thumb over side of bore, prise up seal 52 and let spring 49 eject the parts. Retrieve ball 47. Apart from seal 48, there is another seal in the piston for the piston rod. This seal is not renewable, so that a complete output piston assembly must be fitted.

Inspection:

Do not clean the bore of vacuum cylinder 37. It is pre-lubricated. Remove old seals from body. Clean all parts in methylated spirit or Girling Cleaning Fluid. Fit new seals if piston bores are smooth. Fit new unit if bores are pitted or scored. Do not take chances if condition is doubtful. Check tension of piston return springs.

Reassembling:

Be as clean as possible during this operation. Dip internal parts in clean brake fluid.

1 Fit new taper seal to output piston with taper facing away from seal in end of piston (see **FIG 9:10**). On first-type assemblies, assemble return spring, piston and washer. Press down in bore and fit circlip. Fit seal spacer, large end first, fit gland seal with taper towards guide bush and push guide fully home.

2 With second-type assemblies, fit ball and assemble sleeve return spring and sleeve. Using the piston rod as a guide, hold the spacer, gland seal and guide bush against the sleeve and push assembly down bore.

3 Fit new seals to valve control piston. Large seal must have taper facing spring and small seal with taper away from spring (see **FIG 9:10**). Fit abutment washer, spring and retaining washer. Press spring down and insert circlip. Fit piston assembly in bore, aligning hole in piston with hole in body.

4 Fit valves to rocking lever, refit lever with ball-end engaged with valve control piston. Fit valve retainer. Depress and release piston to check that valves move freely. In normal position the valve nearest the body flange should be open and the other one closed.

5 Fit new seal in groove in plug for valve control bore. Insert plug, leaving about $\frac{1}{16}$ inch (1.6 mm) standing proud of body face. Fit cover and vacuum pipe. Fit new air filter element.

6 Fit retaining plate to vacuum pipe, insert gasket between body and cylinder and fit cylinder, easing vacuum pipe into grommet. Refit clamp plate. Tighten bolts on copper washers to 10 to 12 lb ft (1.4 to 1.6 kg m).

7 Lubricate piston seal lightly with servo lubricant (Rocol 'Moly Cue'). Renew sponge rubber backing ring. Insert return spring, piston and seal assembly into cylinder. Be careful not to damage rod or guide bush. Press piston home. Fit end cover with new joint washers. Refit unit and bleed brakes as in **Section 9:3**.

9:9 Servicing 'Super Vac' servo unit

This is the type that is directly connected to a single or tandem master cylinder and is fitted to lefthand drive vehicles.

The operation can be followed in **FIG 9:11**. Operating rod 17 is connected to brake pedal and rod 4 contacts piston in master cylinder. Inset 'A' shows control valve closing vacuum port as pedal is depressed and opening the atmospheric port. Atmospheric pressure behind diaphragm 9 assists rod in pushing plate 10 and pushrod 4 forward to give augmented pressure on the master cylinder plunger. At inset 'B', the brakes are held on and reaction disc 22 extrudes by pressure to force back the valve rod and thus close the atmospheric port. Increased

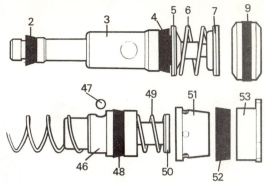

FIG 9:10 Location of seals on the central piston and the second type output piston

Key to Fig 9:10   Refer to the key in **Fig 9:9**

pressure on the brake pedal will open the port again to give a further boost. Release of pedal opens vacuum port 11 and there is vacuum on both sides of diaphragm, which then moves to right under pressure of spring 5.

Removing:

1 Remove pin connecting rod 17 to brake pedal. Drain fluid from master cylinder (see **Section 9:6**). Release brake pipes. Disconnect vacuum hose.

2 Release unit from bulkhead bracket (4 nuts). Remove master cylinder.

Dismantling:

Generally, it is better to fit a replacement servo rather than carry out repairs. To separate the shells it is necessary to make up the tools shown in **FIG. 9:12**. Do not try dismantling without these tools.

1 Non-return valve 7 may be serviced without removing unit from bulkhead. To fit a new valve, note angle of nozzle. On first-type valve, press down and turn anticlockwise one-third of a turn, using a spanner on the flats. Fit dry O-ring and press and turn valve to engage lugs.

2 Second-type valve has no spanner flats and is not interchangeable. Lever valve out with screwdriver. Do not damage shell. Smear new grommet with Girling Grease 64949009. Use no other. Fit grommet to shell and push in valve.

3 Scribe alignment mark across shells. Secure unit to tools by studs. Connect non-return valve to inlet manifold with vacuum hose. Start engine.

4 Turn tool anticlockwise until indentations are in line with recesses in rim of rear shell. Press down on top of unit, detach vacuum hose, and depress operating rod. Halves should part, but tap front shell with hide mallet if necessary. Switch off engine.

5 Lift off rear shell, return spring, dust cover, end cap and filter (see parts 8, 5, 15, 16 and 14 in **FIG 9:11**). Withdraw diaphragm plate 10. Remove diaphragm. Depress valve rod and shake out retaining plate 21. Pull out valve rod.

6 Prise sprag washer 3 from diaphragm plate. Withdraw rod 4 and reaction disc 22. Press out seal 2.

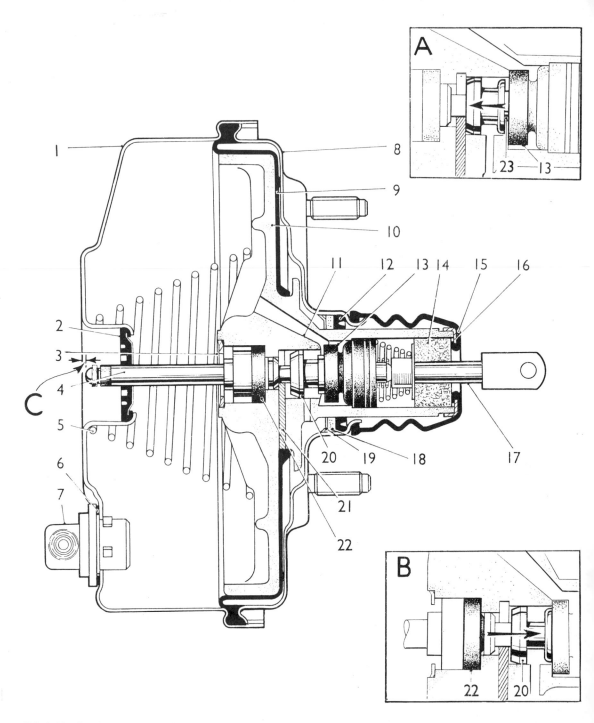

FIG 9:11 Sectioned views of 'Super Vac' servo unit. Master cylinder is bolted to lefthand face. Inset 'A' shows control valve closed, control piston moved forward and atmospheric port open. Inset 'B' shows how reaction disc extrudes to press control piston back to close the atmospheric port. A replacement pushrod is set to dimension at 'C' (see text)

Key to Fig 9:11   1 Front shell   2 Seal and plate assembly   3 Retainer (sprag washer)   4 Pushrod—hydraulic
5 Diaphragm return spring   6 O-ring   7 Non-return valve   8 Rear shell   9 Diaphragm   10 Diaphragm plate
11 Vacuum port   12 Seal   13 Control valve   14 Filter   15 Dust cover   16 End cap   17 Valve operating rod assembly
18 Bearing   19 Retainer   20 Control piston   21 Valve retaining plate   22 Reaction disc   23 Atmospheric port

Inspection:

Clean all parts in Girling Cleaning Fluid. Check sealing surfaces on neck of diaphragm plate and in rear shell.

Reassembling:

Use a major repair kit containing the two essential greases. **Note that the greases are not interchangeable. Use as directed or damage will result.**

1 Smear seal 12 and bearing 18 with grease 64949008 and fit to rear shell. Fit retainer 19. Smear disc 22 and pushrod 4 with grease 64949008. Fit into diaphragm plate and press in the large sprag washer. Discard alternative small sprag washer in kit.

2 **Do not try to alter the length of the original pushrod.** If a new rod is fitted, adjust the length after the unit is assembled (see operation 6).

3 Smear inner and outer surfaces of diaphragm plate neck with grease 64949008. Insert valve rod assembly and fit plate 21. Fit the diaphragm. Fit the non-return valve (see 'Dismantling' operations 1 and 2).

4 Smear seal 2 with grease 64949008 and fit with plate inwards. Fit tools as in **FIG 9:12**. Connect vacuum hose. Fit diaphragm return spring. Smear outer bead of diaphragm with grease 64949009 and fit assembly into rear shell. Locate rear shell assembly on spring and set scribe marks for correct alignment.

5 Start engine, press shells firmly together and turn clockwise to lock. Remove vacuum hose. Fit filter 14, end cap 16 and dust cover 15.

6 If a new pushrod 4 is fitted, adjust height. Connect vacuum hose and start engine. Coat threads of bolt with Loctite (grade B) and fit to rod. Adjust so that face of bolt is .011 to .016 inch (.28 to .40 mm) below face of front shell (see 'C' in **FIG 9:11**). Stop engine. Leave for 24 hours until Loctite has set.

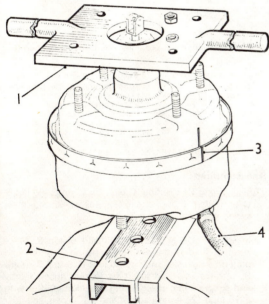

FIG 9:12 Handmade tools used to dismantle 'Super Vac' servo unit

Key to Fig 9:12   1 Lever   2 Base plate
3 Scribe line   4 Vacuum applied

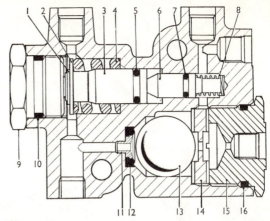

FIG 9:13 Section of reducing valve fitted to early vehicles

Key to Fig 9:13   1 Circlip—retainer   2 Abutment washer
3 Primary piston   4 Main spring   5 O-ring—large
6 Secondary piston   7 O-ring—small   8 Spring—secondary
9 End plug   10 Seal   11 Valve insert   12 Valve seal
13 Ball   14 Spacer   15 Inlet plug   16 Seal

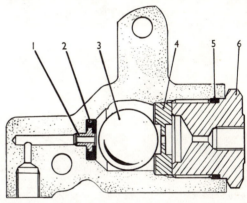

FIG 9:14 The limiting valve fitted to vehicles with 'Powerstop' Mk 2B and 'Super Vac' servo units

Key to Fig 9:14   1 Valve insert   2 Valve seal   3 Ball
4 Spacer   5 Seal   6 End plug

Refitting:

Reverse removal procedure. Bleed the brakes (see **Section 9:3**). Check operation by running engine for two minutes. Switch off. After ten minutes, apply brake pedal. Entry of air into unit should be heard if unit is working.

9:10 The reducing and limiting valves

Reducing valve:

A section is shown in **FIG 9:13**. It is mounted on the righthand wing valance at an angle so that the ball has to run uphill during deceleration. If the brakes are applied and the ball moves to close valve 11 and 12, increasing pedal pressure acts fully on the front brakes and on a differential piston to produce a progressive drop in rear brake pressure to avoid rear wheel locking.

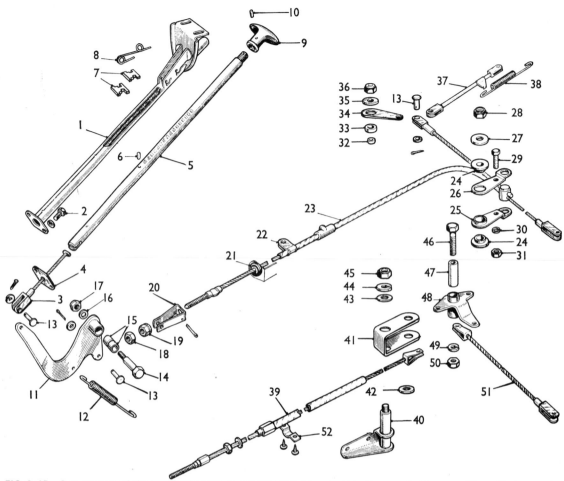

FIG 9:15 Components of the handbrake system. Mk 3 models have a centrally mounted lever positioned between the front seats

Key to Fig 9:15   1 Control body   2 Screw   3 Control cable   4 Joint washer   5 Pullrod   6 Pin   7 Pawls
8 Spring—pawl   9 Tee handle   10 Pin   11 Intermediate lever assembly   12 Tension spring   13 Clevis pin
14 Pivot pin   15 Bushes   16 Plain washer   17 Locknut   18 Locknut   19 Adjusting nut (use with splitpin)   20 Fork
21 Grommet   22 Clip   23 Cable—intermediate to relay lever   24 Bush   25 Compensator lever—bottom
26 Compensator lever—top   27 Plain washer   28 Locknut   29 Bolt   30 Spring washer   31 Nut   32 Distance piece
33 Bush   34 Relay lever   35 Plain washer   36 Locknut   37 Brake rod   38 Return spring   39 Cable—intermediate to
relay lever   40 Pivot assembly   41 Bracket   42 Anti-rattle washer   43 Plain washer   44 Spring washer   45 Nut   46 Bolt
47 Distance tube   48 Compensating lever   49 Spring washer   50 Nut   51 Cable right- or lefthand   52 Clip
Items 39-52 Handbrake cable and compensator assembly from A17S—042816A, M17S—000671A

Removing:

Clean exterior, drain system at a bleed screw (see **Section 9:4**). Disconnect wires and pipes. Release unit (2 bolts).

Dismantling:

1 Observe extreme cleanliness. Remove plug 15, spacer 14 and ball 13. Remove insert and valve 11 and 12, using an extractor.
2 Remove plug 9. Shake out piston assemblies.

Inspection:

Discard old seals. Clean all parts in methylated spirit or Girling Cleaning Fluid. Piston bores must be smooth. If scored or pitted renew unit.

Reassembling:

1 Use Girling Red Rubber Grease on O-rings. Fit larger O-ring after fitting circlip 1, washer 2 and main spring 4. Fit smaller ring 7.

2 Insert piston 6 and spring 8. Insert piston 3. Make sure no fluid is trapped under piston. Tighten end plug on a new seal to 25 to 30 lb ft (3.5 to 4.8 kg m). Refit valve seal and insert by tapping insert lightly and squarely into place, using a mild steel drift with a .10 inch (2.54 mm) spigot and a 120 deg. shoulder (included angle).

3 Fit ball and spacer. Tighten inlet plug on a new seal to same torque as end plug.

Refitting:

Early units are mounted at 17 deg. on an unstamped bracket (up to No. A17S.15245A). Later units are mounted at 13 deg. on a bracket stamped '13'. Angle is measured across top outlet faces. **Do not alter angle.**

Connect pipes and wires, fill master cylinder reservoir and prime and bleed brakes as in **Section 9:3.**

Limiting valve:

See **FIG 9:14**. This is fitted to systems using 'Power-stop' Mk 2B and 'Super Vac' servos. Valve is set at 25 deg. so that ball must run uphill during deceleration to close hydraulic circuit to rear brakes. Increasing fluid pressure will then go to the front brakes only.

Removing:

Clean unit and drain fluid from rear brake bleed screw (see **Section 9:5**). Disconnect unions and release unit (2 bolts). Dismantle by unscrewing plug 6 and extracting parts 1, 2, 3 and 4. Use an extractor on insert 1.

Clean parts and examine ball and ramp for wear or pitting. Reassemble by lubricating and fitting new seals to the insert and plug, using brake fluid. Fit insert as in preceding operation 2. Fit ball and spacer. Tighten inlet plug to 25 to 35 lb ft (3.4 to 4.8 kg m).

9:11 Servicing handbrake

Refer to **FIG 9:15**. If handbrake is ineffective or travels too far on ratchet, giving excessive pedal travel, adjust as follows:

1 Chock front wheels, raise rear wheels clear, release handbrake. Wheels should turn freely. Adjust rear brakes as in **Section 9:2.**
2 If handbrake is still ineffective, with excessive travel, likely cause is worn linings or stretched cables. If necessary, renew linings (see **Section 9:5**). If travel is still excessive, adjust cables.
3 Check rear brake adjustment. Pull up handbrake three or four notches. Turn adjusting nut 19 until heavy hand pressure on the wheels will just turn them with equal resistance.
4 Release handbrake. Wheels should be free. If one brake binds, remove drum and check fitting and condition of pull-off springs. Make sure wheel cylinder can slide in backplate slot (see **Section 9:5**).

Servicing handbrake:

The illustration will enable dismantling to proceed without much explanation. Note that a splitpin is necessary if adjusting nut 19 is to work. After disconnecting cables pull them through heat shield guides. Detach spring 38 before disconnecting the rod.

When refitting the parts coat the inner cable with graphite grease where it contacts the outer casing. Grease at the nipple (if fitted). Lubricate all linkage points. Check adjustment.

9:12 Stop lamp switch

This is operated by brake pedal if a direct-acting ('Super Vac') servo unit is fitted. **It must not act as a pedal stop.** To adjust, set so that body of switch protrudes $\frac{3}{16}$ inch (4.7 mm) from face of bracket. Slacken bracket fixings. With plunger contacting pedal, take up free play in switch and tighten bracket fixings. Screw switch into bracket until contacts open. Screw in one more turn and tighten locknut.

9:13 Fault diagnosis

(a) 'Spongy' brake pedal

1 Leak in hydraulic system
2 Worn master cylinder
3 Leaking wheel cylinder
4 Air in brake fluid
5 Gaps between rear brake linings and shoes

(b) Excessive pedal movement

1 Check 1 and 4 in (a)
2 Rear brakes need adjusting
3 Very low fluid level in reservoir

(c) Brakes grab or pull to one side

1 Distorted or badly worn discs or drums
2 Wet or oily pads or linings
3 Disc loose on hub
4 Worn suspension or steering connections
5 Mixed linings, wrong grade or different thicknesses
6 Unequal tyre pressures
7 Broken shoe return springs
8 Wheel cylinder not sliding on backplate
9 Seized piston in one brake cylinder
10 Loose caliper or backplate

(d) Excessive pedal pressure needed

1 Check 5 in (c)
2 Leak in vacuum hose to servo unit
3 Defective servo unit
4 Servo filter blocked
5 Brake linings water soaked
6 Linings glazed due to heat
7 Defect in one circuit of dual line system

(e) Loss of pedal pressure

1 Defective master cylinder, worn bore, piston or seals
2 Leaking wheel cylinder or servo unit
3 Leaking brake pipes or connections
4 No fluid in master cylinder reservoir

NOTES

CHAPTER 10

THE ELECTRICAL SYSTEM

10:1 General description

The 12-volt system has the positive battery terminal earthed on all models except the later Mk 3, the latest models have a negative earth system. The generator is type C40/1 on earlier models and type C40/PS on later models (including the Mk 2S). Alternator, type 11AC, is fitted as an alternative but it cannot be fitted if power steering is incorporated.

Charging output from the generator is controlled by three units in an RB.340 regulator. The units are a cut-out, a current regulator and a voltage regulator. The alternator is controlled by a separate unit and a relay (see **FIG 10:5**). The generator control unit may be adjusted, but accurate moving-coil meters will be needed.

Wiring faults may be traced by referring to the diagrams in **Technical Data**. Gauges that are voltage-controlled are supplied by a bi-metal resistance unit (see **Section 10:9**). Battery and fuses are mounted on the righthand side of the engine compartment.

In spite of servicing instructions, it must be stressed that equipment that is seriously defective is best replaced by new units on an Exchange basis.

10:2 Routine maintenance

The battery:

Clean corrosion from all parts with dilute ammonia. Top of battery must be clean and dry. Use anti-sulphuric paint on affected metal parts.

Every 3000 miles (5000 km) or 3 months check electrolyte level, on some types by lifting manifold and checking that liquid is just above the separators. On A11, A13 'Pacemaker' types, level should be $\frac{1}{4}$ inch (7 mm) below red top as seen through transparent side of battery, or by lifting cover. Top-up if level is below tops of plates. Do not use tap water. Keep naked lights away. **Do not add acid, but use only distilled water.**

On batteries with a trough under the cover, add distilled water until the filling slots are full and bottom of trough just covered.

Every 6000 miles (10,000 km) or 6 months, check specific gravity of battery electrolyte with a hydrometer. Readings indicate battery condition as follows (for climates below 27 deg. C (80 deg. F):

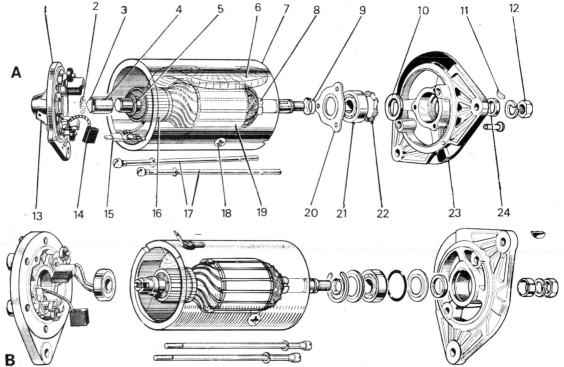

FIG 10:1 Components of C40/1 generator at 'A'. Lower view shows C40/PS generator with ball bearing at commutator end and bracket with mounting for power steering pump

Key to Fig 10:1   1 Commutator end bracket   2 Felt ring   3 Felt ring retainer   4 Bronze bush   5 Thrust washer   6 Field coils   7 Yoke   8 Shaft collar   9 Shaft collar retaining cup   10 Felt ring   11 Shaft key   12 Shaft nut   13 Output terminal 'D'   14 Brushes   15 Field terminal 'F'   16 Commutator   17 Through-bolts   18 Pole-shoe securing screws   19 Armature   20 Bearing retaining plate   21 Ball bearing   22 Corrugated washer   23 Driving end bracket   24 Pulley spacer

Cell fully charged	1.270 to 1.290
Cell about half-discharged	1.190 to 1.210
Cell completely discharged	1.110 to 1.130

Figures given are for electrolyte temperature of 16°C (60°F). For every 2.7°C (5°F) above this, add .002. Subtract .002 if below.

Do not leave battery in discharged condition. If vehicle is not used, give battery a short freshening charge every fortnight.

The lights:

Check headlamp alignment every 3000 miles (5000 km) or 3 months (see **Section 10:8**). Check that all lights work every 6000 (10,000 km) or 6 months.

The generator:

If generator has a small hole in centre boss at rear end, add a few drops of engine oil every 6000 miles (10,000 km) or 6 months. Do not over-oil.

10:3 Servicing the generator
Testing:

If no charge, check belt tension for slipping. Adjust as advised in **Chapter 4**. Check that generator 'D' terminal is connected to 'D' terminal on control box (see **FIG 10:3**). Check small 'F' terminals too.

Switch off all lights and accessories. Disconnect 'D' and 'F' cables from generator, then connect terminals with short length of wire. Start engine and run at normal idling speed. Clip negative lead of 0 to 20 voltmeter to one generator terminal and positive lead to good earth on generator. Gradually speed-up engine. Voltage should rise steadily without fluctuation. Reading must not be allowed to reach 20 volts. A generator speed of about 1000 rev/min is enough.

No reading—check brushgear.

Low reading (about $\frac{1}{2}$ to 1 volt)—suspect faulty field coils.

Reading about 4 to 5 volts—suspect faulty armature.

If readings are good, leave temporary link connected and restore 'D' and 'F' leads. Remove 'D' lead from control box. Connect voltmeter between detached cable and a good earth. Run engine as before. Reading should be same as one recorded directly on generator. If no reading, 'D' cable is broken. Test 'F' in same way. Remove temporary link. If reading is correct, test control box (see **Section 10:4**).

Removing:

Disconnect leads, slacken mounting and link bolts, move generator inwards and remove belt. Remove three attachment bolts and lift generator away.

Dismantling (refer to FIG 10:1):

1 Remove pulley and key 11. Remove bolts 17. Lift or prise off bracket 1.

2 Remove bracket 23 complete with armature 19. If bearing 21 is faulty, press armature shaft out after removing keyway burrs.

Brushes:

Minimum length $\frac{1}{4}$ inch (7 mm). Check that brushes are free in holders. Ease sides on fine file if necessary. Wrap fine sandpaper round commutator and rotate under a new brush to give correct curvature to contact face.

Tension of new brush springs is 34 oz (963 gm). On minimum brush length, tension may fall to 13 oz (370 gm). Check with a spring balance.

Commutator:

Clean with a fuel-moistened cloth. If necessary, polish with very fine glasspaper (not emery cloth). Have a badly worn commutator skimmed in a lathe. Undercut insulation as in 'C' in FIG 10:2. Use a hacksaw blade ground on sides to correct width between copper segments. Undercut fabricated commutators $\frac{1}{32}$ inch (.8 mm) and moulded types .020 to .035 inch (.51 to .89 mm), (see 'A' and 'B' in FIG 10:2). Do not skim a moulded commutator below a diameter of 1.45 inch (36.83 mm), but if bearing collar is stamped K64 or later, it may be reduced to a diameter of 1.43 inch (36.4 mm).

Burnt commutator segments are a sign of a breakdown in armature windings.

Armature:

A suspected armature must be tested on a 'growler' at a service station. Do not try to machine an armature core or straighten a bent shaft.

Renew a worn plain bearing 4 by screwing in a $\frac{5}{8}$ inch tap and pulling on it. Stand a new bush in SAE.20 engine oil for 24 hours or for 2 hours in oil heated to 100 deg. C (212 deg. F), allowing oil to cool before removing.

Press bush in until flush with inner face of bracket, using a shouldered mandrel. Part of mandrel in bore must be highly polished and same diameter as armature shaft. Do not ream bush after insertion.

Renew ball bearing 21 by drilling out retaining plate rivets on early models (see 20 in FIG 10:1). For later generator shown at 'B', remove circlip and retainer to reach bearing at drive end. Bearing at commutator end is a press fit and is sealed and packed with lubricant for life.

Pack drive end bearing with high-melting point grease. Fit felt washer, corrugated washer or retainer and O-ring in order shown. Fit bearing into bracket, securing later type with circlip. Fit rivets of same size as originals, on early type.

Ball bearing at commutator end must be fitted so that the collar precedes it on the armature shaft. There are no fibre thrust washers on generator 'B'.

Note when fitting drive-end bracket 23 on generator 'A' that inner race of bearing must be used to press assembly onto armature shaft. Do not apply pressure through the end bracket.

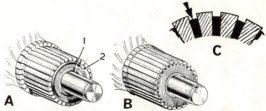

FIG 10:2 Generator commutators. Fabricated type ('A') and moulded type ('B'). Note metal roll-over (1) and insulating cone(2). View 'C' shows insulation undercut between copper segments

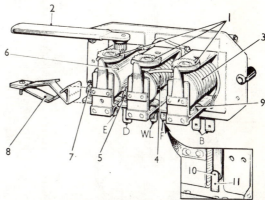

FIG 10:3 Control box RB.340 showing setting tool for cams. Clip 8 is used to keep contacts 7 closed

Key to Fig 10:3   1 Adjustment cams   2 Setting tool
3 Cut-out relay   4 Current regulator   5 Current relay
contacts   6 Voltage regulator   7 Voltage regulator contacts
8 Clip—contacts   9 Armature back stop   10 Cut-out
contacts   11 Fixed contact bracket

Field coils:

Test coils for resistance without removing them. Correct figure is 6 ohm. Alternatively, connect a 12-volt battery and ammeter in series with terminal 15 and yoke 7. Reading should be about 2 amp. Coils are defective if no reading, or if more than 2 amp (or below 6 ohm). Have field coils renewed by a service station.

Reassembling and refitting:

Reverse the dismantling sequence. Before fitting end bracket 1, lift brushes in their holders until springs bear on brush sides, thus holding them in raised position. Push bracket into place until about $\frac{1}{2}$ inch (13 mm) from yoke. Insert a thin screwdriver and lift brush springs so that brushes drop onto commutator. Let springs down onto tops of brushes. Push bracket home.

Refit in reverse order of removal, noting that some upper mounting bolts have flat washers under their heads. Tension the driving belt.

10:4 Servicing generator control box

FIG 10:3 shows control box RB.340 with cover removed. Note special Lucas tool 2 for turning adjusting cams 1. Before disturbing the box, check for no charge as in Section 10:3. Check all wiring in charging circuit and all earth connections. If control box is still suspect,

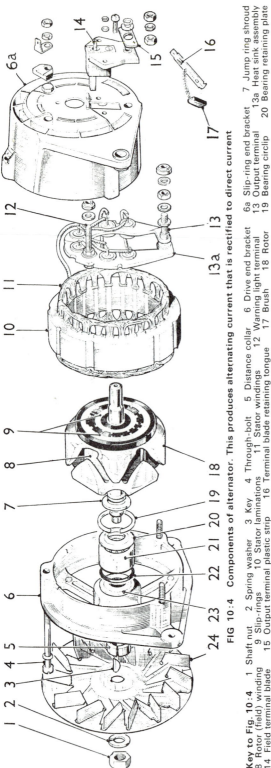

FIG 10:4 Components of alternator. This produces alternating current that is rectified to direct current

Key to Fig. 10:4 1 Shaft nut 2 Spring washer 3 Key 4 Through-bolt 5 Distance collar 6 Drive end bracket 6a Slip-ring end bracket 7 Jump ring shroud 8 Rotor (field) winding 9 Slip-rings 10 Stator laminations 11 Stator windings 12 Warning light terminal 13 Output terminal 13a Heat sink assembly 14 Field terminal blade 15 Output terminal plastic strip 16 Terminal blade retaining tongue 17 Brush 18 Rotor 19 Bearing circlip 20 Bearing retaining plate 21 Ball bearing 22 O-ring oil seal 23 O-ring retaining washer 24 Fan

check and adjust as follows, using a good moving coil 0–20 voltmeter and a moving coil 0-40 ammeter:

1 **Check and adjust quickly to avoid overheating errors.** Check voltage regulator 6 by withdrawing both cables 'B' and cable 'WL'. Connect voltmeter between 'WL' and earth. Join detached cables 'B' together.

2 Run generator at 3000 rev/min (Mk 1) or 2250 rev/min (Mk 11 and 11S). Reading should be 14.5 to 15.5 volts at 20 deg. C (68 deg. F). If reading fluctuates more than ±.3 volt, contacts may be dirty, or there may be dirt in the air gaps.

3 If outside limits, adjust with engine running at original speed, turning cam clockwise to raise and anticlockwise to lower voltage. Stop engine and restart to check.

4 Check current regulator 4 by clipping voltage regulator contacts together (see 7 and 8 in **FIG 10:3**). Detach cables 'B' and join them together. Make sure all electrical loads are switched off. Connect ammeter between cables 'B' and terminal blades 'B'.

5 Run generator at 4500 rev/min with headlamps on. Ammeter should read 22±1 amp. If, unsteady, check for dirty contacts or dirt in air gaps. If outside limits, adjust as follows:

6 Turn cam clockwise to raise and anticlockwise to lower setting. When satisfied, stop engine and refit cover and connections.

7 Check cutout 3. Check cut-in voltage by detaching 'WL' cable. Connect voltmeter between terminal and earth. Switch on headlamps. Gradually increase engine speed. Voltage should rise steadily then drop slightly as cutout contacts close. At this point, voltmeter should read between 12.7 and 13.3 volts.

8 If incorrect, adjust by reducing engine speed and turning cam clockwise to raise and anticlockwise to lower setting. Check as before, then restore connections.

9 Check cutout drop-off voltage by detaching 'B' cables and joining them. Connect voltmeter to terminal 'B' and earth. Run generator at 3000 rev/min. Slowly decelerate. Needle should drop to zero when voltage between 9.5 and 11 is reached. If outside limits, bend fixed contact breaker 11. Reduced gap will raise and increased gap will lower drop-off voltage. Restore connections.

10 Check cutout drop-off current by connecting ammeter instead of voltmeter. Start engine and run it up until meter shows a charge. Slowly decelerate and watch needle. It should momentarily show a reverse current of 3 to 5 amp and then flick back to zero as contacts open. Adjust by stopping engine, disconnecting ammeter and then bending fixed contact bracket. Reduced gap will raise and increased gap will lower setting. Check setting. Restore connections.

11 Check air gap settings. If adjusted, check electrical settings (operations 1 to 10). Detach cables 'B'. Turn cam on voltage regulator to give minimum lift on spring. Slacken locknut and unscrew contact 7. Spring is riveted to armature. Insert .058 inch (1.47 mm) feeler under armature as far back as rivets on underside. Screw contact in until feeler is just trapped. Tighten locknut. Check electrical setting. Leave current regulator until cutout has been checked.

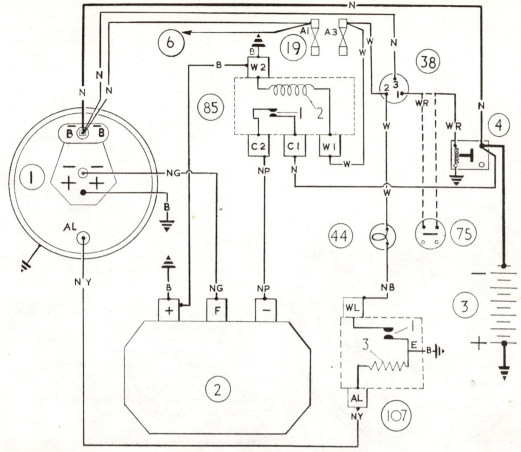

FIG 10:5 Alternator circuit diagram

Key to Fig 10:5 1 Alternator 2 Control unit 3 Battery 4 Starter solenoid 6 Lighting switch 19 Fuses
38 Ignition/starter switch 44 No charge warning lamp (2.2 watt) 75 Automatic gearbox—safety switch 85 Isolating relay
107 Warning light simulator 1 Points 2 Operating coil 3 Ballast resistor
Cable Colour Code **B** Black **U** Blue **N** Brown **R** Red **P** Purple **G** Green **W** White **Y** Yellow
When a cable has two colour code letters the first denotes the main colour and the second denotes the tracer colour

12 Check cutout air gap with 'B' cable detached. Insert
.015 inch (.38 mm) feeler under cutout armature as
far back as rivet heads. Press armature in and bend
fixed contact breaker 11 until contacts just touch.
Resultant blade deflection should be .010 to .020
inch (.25 to .50 mm). Remove feeler and insert one
.040 inch (1.02 mm) thick. Press armature in and
bend armature back stop until it just touches back of
armature. Resultant gap between armature and core
should be .035 to .045 inch (.90 to 1.15 mm). Restore
connections and check cutout electrically.

13 Check current regulator air gap as instructed in
operation 11.

Cleaning contacts:

Use a fine carborundum stone or silicon carbide paper
on regulator contacts. Use fine sandpaper on cutout
points (never carborundum stone or emery paper). Wipe
contacts with a cloth moistened with methylated spirit.

10:5 Servicing the alternator

Components are shown in **FIG 10:4** and the circuit
in **FIG 10:5**.

Precautions:

1 Polarity of replacement alternator must be same as
original.

2 Connect battery earth terminal first. Reversed battery
connections will damage alternator rectifiers.

3 If high-rate battery charging is necessary, first disconnect the control unit. If starting an engine with
the high-rate charger connected and control unit
disconnected, run engine at idling speed, disconnect
charger and then reconnect control unit.

4 **Never disconnect battery with engine running.**
Never run alternator with main output cable disconnected at alternator or battery.

5 Cable between battery and alternator is always 'live'.
Take care not to earth alternator terminal or detached

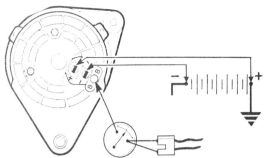

FIG 10:6 Ammeter connected between output terminal 'B' and connectors to check alternator output

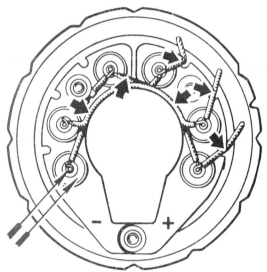

FIG 10:7 Internal connections to heat sink diodes in alternator. Arrows (bottom left) show testing points for checking diodes

cable. **Do not make or break any connections in alternator circuit with engine running.**

6 Disconnect alternator and control unit when arc-welding on vehicle.

Testing:

Since March 1972, Mk 3 models have a negative earth system. The following instructions for testing apply to the earlier models that have a positive earth system. Check the polarity before starting the test and note that **FIGS 10:5, 10:6, 10:7** and operation 3 apply to positive earth systems and for Mk 3 models the polarity will be reversed.

Before testing for faults, first see that belt tension is correct (see **Chapter 4**). Provide an accurate moving coil ammeter reading up to 60 amp and a moving coil 0–30 voltmeter. Use a battery powered ohmmeter. Never test diodes with a generator-type ohmmeter.

1 Disconnect both cables from alternator field terminals (see illustrations). Connect voltmeter to cables and run engine, when battery voltage should be registered. If no reading, check field circuit wiring.

2 Check alternator output by referring to **FIG 10:6**.

Disconnect battery earth. If an ammeter is not fitted, disconnect both connectors from terminal 'B' and connect ammeter as shown. Withdraw cables from field terminals and connect two temporary cables to battery as shown. Reconnect battery earth. Start engine and slowly increase speed to 4000 rev/min (alternator), and check that meter reads about 40 amp. If no reading stop engine and check brushes (see later). If new brush gear gives no cure, service the alternator.

3 If reading is low, wiring or alternator may be at fault. Stop engine. Connect voltmeter between alternator terminal 'B' and battery negative. Start engine and note reading. Transfer voltmeter to alternator frame and battery earth (+ve). Note reading. If either reading exceeds .5 volt there is high resistance in charging circuit. Check and rectify. If there is no undue resistance but output remains low, check alternator.

Removing:

Disconnect battery and alternator cables. Slacken alternator mountings, push alternator towards engine by end bracket and lift off belt. Remove bolts and alternator.

Dismantling:

Refer to **FIG 10:4**. Remove nut 1 and parts 2, 3 and 24. Mark brackets 6 and 6a and stator 10 for correct reassembling. Remove bolts 4. Rotor 18 may be pressed out of bracket if bearing 21 needs renewal. First remove key and collar 5. Remove terminal nuts, brush box (extreme right) and heat sink bolt. Withdraw assembly 10 to 13 from end bracket. Press down tongues 16 to release terminals from brush box.

Inspection of rotor and brushes:

Renew brushes if less than $\frac{5}{16}$ inch (8 mm) long. Push into holder until tongue registers then lever up tongue. Check that brushes slide freely. Tight brushes may be eased by rubbing sides on a smooth file.

Clean slip-rings with fuel moistened cloth. Polish rings with very fine glasspaper. **Do not try to machine rings.**

Check rotor windings with ohmmeter. Resistance should be 3.8±.2 ohm at 20 deg. C (68 deg. F). Connections go to slip-rings. Alternatively connect 12-volt battery and ammeter across rings. Reading should be 3.2 amp.

Check insulation by connecting a 110-volt A.C. 15 watt lamp between one slip ring and a rotor pole. If lamp lights, coil is earthed. Renew rotor. **Do not try to machine rotor or straighten a bent shaft.**

Inspection of stator:

Unsolder the three stator cables from heat sink 13a. Connect any two in series with 12-volt battery and 1.5 watt lamp. Replace one cable by the third and test again. If lamp does not light, coils are faulty. Renew stator.

Check stator coils with mains test lamp. Connect across one stator lead in turn and stator laminations. If lamp lights, coil is earthed. Renew stator. With cables disconnected, check diodes.

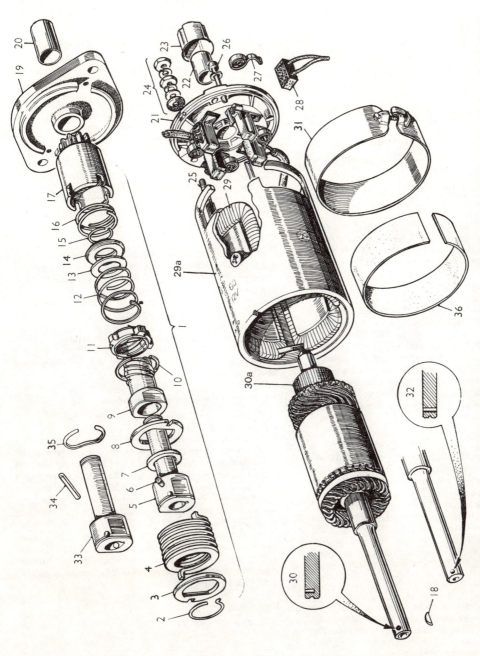

FIG 10:8 Components of starter motor. Insets (bottom left) are of alternative shaft drillings for long and short sleeve pins

Key to Fig 10:8 1 Drive assembly   2 Retaining ring   3 Anchor plate—front   4 Main spring   5 Centre sleeve*   6 Retaining pin   7 Thrust washer (fibre)
8 Anchor plate—rear   9 Screwed sleeve   10 Retaining ring*   11 Control nut   12 Restraining spring   13 Thrust washer   14 Locating collar   15 Retaining ring   16 Spring
17 Pinion and barrel   18 Woodruff key*   19 Drive end bracket   20 Bush   21 Commutator end bracket   22 Bush   23 Cap—shaft   24 Terminal nuts and washers
25 Terminal post   26 Through-bolt   27 Spring—brush   28 Brush   29 Field coils   29a Yoke   30 Armature*   30a Commutator   31 Cover band   32 Armature†
33 Centre sleeve†   34 Spiral pin†   35 Waved circlip†   36 Seal—cover band†

*For starter motors Serial No. 25555
†For starter motors Serial No. 25599

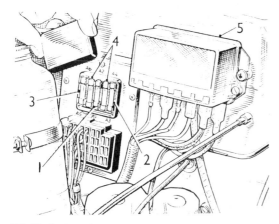

FIG 10:9 Location of fuses and control box. The connector panel is below the fuses

Key to Fig 10:9   1 Fuse A1—A2   2 Fuse A3—A4
3 Fuse A5—A6   4 Spare fuses   5 Control box

The diodes:

Test with a 12-volt battery and 1.5 watt lamp, placing probes across each diode in turn. Long arrows (bottom left) in **FIG 10:7** show test points. Reverse the probes. Current should flow in one direction only. If bulb lights up, or does not, in both directions, diode is faulty. Renew whichever heat sink half is defective.

The heat sink assembly is in two insulated parts, the positive side carrying diodes marked red and the negative side, diodes marked black. Refer to **FIG 10:7** when making connections. Use 'M' grade 45—55 solder and work quickly to avoid overheating the diodes. It helps to grip the diode pins lightly with long-nosed pliers which will carry off heat. Arrange wires clear of rotor and secure them with a suitable heat-resistant adhesive. The three stator connections must pass through the appropriate notches in edge of heat sink.

Bearings:

The needle roller bearing in bracket 6a (see **FIG 10:4**) may be pressed out after checking its depth in the housing. Fit a new one to the same depth and pack with high-melting point grease.

Bearing 21 may be secured by circlip or rivets. File off rivet heads and punch through; or remove circlip. Press out bearing. Pack new one with high-melting point grease and press right home. Refit retaining plate. If a circlip is fitted, press in retainer just enough to allow circlip to enter groove.

Reassembling:

Reverse dismantling procedure, aligning marks on stator and brackets. Support inner race of drive-end bearing on a steel tube and press the rotor into place. Do not use the bracket as a support. Tighten fixings to torque figures in **Technical Data.**

Refitting:

After mounting, tension belt as described in **Chapter 4. Lift alternator by drive-end bracket only.**

Warning light control:

This is a small canister with three tag terminals, electrically connected to the centre point of one pair of diodes and to the warning light. The tags are marked if unit must be renewed.

Alternator control unit:

This is part 2 in **FIG 10:5.** Before testing, make sure that all charging circuit, and battery to relay and control unit wiring is in good order. Battery must be fully charged. Resistance of complete circuit, including relay, must not exceed .10 ohm.

Test by leaving connection to alternator and control unit undisturbed. Connect voltmeter across battery and note reading with all equipment switched off. Connect ammeter in series with the main output cable as shown in **FIG 10:6.** Switch on side and tail lamps to give load of 2 amp. Start engine and run alternator at 3000 rev/min for eight minutes to stabilize voltage. If charging current is then more than 10 amp, keep engine running until correct figure is reached. Voltmeter should read 13.9 to 14.3 volts. Renew control unit if voltage is incorrect.

The relay:

This is part 85 in **FIG 10:5.** It disconnects the alternator field from the battery when the ignition is switched off. The alternator cannot charge if the relay contacts do not close when ignition is switched on.

Test by connecting ammeter as shown in **FIG 10:6.** Remove 'C2' lead and join to 'C1' terminal. If alternator now generates correct output, relay is faulty and must be renewed. Now check continuity of relay winding, relay circuit and earthing. If satisfactory, with leads still joined, but no output from alternator, check alternator and control unit.

10:6 Servicing the starter motor

If starter seems defective, with battery fully charged, test as follows:

Switch on lights and try starter. If lights dim but starter motor does not turn, pinion is probably jammed in mesh with flywheel. This may be freed by turning squared shaft at outer end with a spanner. Alternatively, engage a gear, keep ignition switched off and rock car backwards and forwards until pinion becomes free. This does not apply to lefthand drive cars with a pre-engaged starter or automatic transmissions.

If lights stay bright, check starter switch. If in order, check wiring and connections. Frequent cause of trouble is dirty connections to battery. If starter runs but pinion does not engage, check for dirty drive pinion assembly (see **FIG 10:8**).

Removing:

Disconnect battery earth lead and lead to starter terminal. Release starter flange (2 bolts).

Servicing:

Remove band 31 (see **FIG 10:8**). Pull on brush flexible leads to check that brushes move freely. If sluggish, polish sides of brush by rubbing on a smooth file. Keep brushes in their original positions. Renew brushes if less than $\frac{5}{16}$ inch (7.9 mm) long. Clean commutator (copper segments 30a) with a fuel-moistened cloth.

Test by holding in a vice and connecting to battery with heavy cables. Starter should run at high speed.

Dismantling:

Hook back brush springs and remove brushes. Compress main spring 4 and remove circlip 2, plate 3, spring and plate 8. Withdraw pin 6 or 34, push sleeve along shaft and remove key 18. Slide off drive assembly. Remove ring 10 or 35 and ring 15 to dismantle drive parts. Remove assembly 24 and bolts 26. Remove end brackets 19 and 21 and armature 30.

Brushes:

Hook spring balance on brush springs. Renew springs if tension is below 42 to 52 oz (1187 to 1477 gm). Renew brushes if worn (see 'Servicing'). Unsolder brush leads in order. Two leads go to eyelets on end bracket and two to the field coil junction. Brushes do not require bedding-in.

Drive:

Renew worn or damaged parts. **Assemble parts dry and do not lubricate.**

Commutator:

If not worn or burned, polish with very fine glasspaper (not emery cloth). A badly worn commutator may be skimmed in a lathe. **The mica insulation between the copper segments must not be undercut.**

Field coils:

Test with 12-volt battery and bulb. Connect to joint of two brush leads and terminal 25. Coils are broken if lamp does not light. If lamp lights, check for earthing with one lead on terminal and the other to clean part of yoke 29a. If bulb lights, field coils are earthed. Make sure brushes do not contact yoke in this test. Have faulty coils renewed by a service station.

Armature:

Look for melted solder and lifted conductors at commutator segments. **Do not try to repair a damaged armature, or to straighten a bent shaft.**

Bearings:

Press worn bearings out of brackets. Stand new bush in thin engine oil for 24 hours or for 2 hours in oil heated to 100 deg. C (212 deg. F). Press into place with shouldered mandrel having highly polished spigot of same diameter as armature shaft to ensure a good fit. **Bush must not be reamed or porous qualities will be lost.**

Reassembling:

Do this in reverse order of dismantling. Do not lubricate drive assembly.

10:7 Fuses

These are located as shown in **FIG 10:9.** Fuse 1 (35 amp) protects equipment that operates independent of ignition switch. Fuse 2 (35 amp) protects equipment

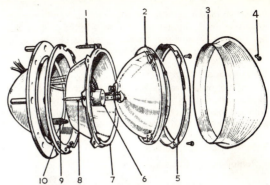

FIG 10:10 The sealed-beam light unit

Key to Fig 10:10   1 Vertical adjustment   2 Sealed-beam unit   3 Rim   4 Rim fixing screw   5 Unit retaining plate   6 Connector plug   7 Seating rim   8 Horizontal adjustment   9 Spring—unit seating   10 Seating washer

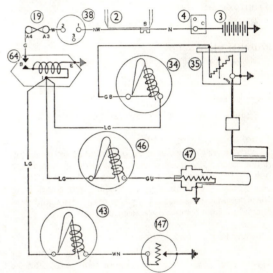

FIG 10:11 Circuit diagram for bi-metal resistance instrumentation

Key to Fig 10:11   2 Control box   3 Battery—(12 volt)   4 Starter solenoid   19 Fuse—(A3–A4)   34 Fuel gauge   38 Ignition switch   43 Oil pressure gauge*   46 Coolant temperature gauge   47 Coolant temperature transmitter   64 Voltage stabilizer   147 Oil pressure transmitter*   *Not Austin/Morris

that operates only when ignition is switched on. Fuse 3 (35 amp) protects pilot and tail lamp circuits. Fuses 4 are spares. Always use correct rating and check for shorts if fuse blows immediately it is renewed.

10:8 Servicing the lights and switches

Headlamps:

A sealed-beam light unit is shown in **FIG 10:10.** To change unit 2, remove rims 3 and 5. Pull out unit and disconnect plug 6. When fitting unit make sure three lugs engage slots in back shell.

If light unit has renewable bulb (European type), remove rim and light unit and withdraw bulb by pinching ends of wire clip together. Fit new bulb with pip on bulb flange engaging in slot in reflector seat. Coils of clip must rest on bulb flange. If vehicle is lefthand drive but not for Europe or North America, twist back shell anti-clockwise and pull off. Withdraw bulb.

Setting headlamps:

Set slightly below horizontal or to accord with local regulations. Setting is best done accurately by a service station properly equipped. Adjust vertically with screw 1 and horizontally with screw(s) 8 (see **FIG 10:10**).

Side lamps and flashers:

Remove lens (2 screws).

Tail, stop and indicator lamps:

Work inside luggage compartment. Remove cover and pull out bulb holders. Bulbs have offset pins and fit one way only.

Front repeater lamps:

Remove lens (1 screw). Pull out capless bulb.

Number plate lamp:

Press and turn lens to detach. Pull capless bulb straight out.

Interior lamp:

Squeeze cover gently inwards and pull off.

Panel and warning lights:

For Austin/Morris vehicles, gain access by removing parcel shelf top cover screws. Lower cover and reach behind facia. For Wolseley, remove screw from lower edge, pull lower edge of panel forward and down. Bulb for automatic transmission selector may be reached from the side (panel removed) or from below.

Flasher unit:

If defective in operation, first check bulbs. Check all wiring and fuse. Switch on ignition and use voltmeter between flasher terminal 'B' (or '+') and earth to check for battery voltage. Connect flasher terminals 'B' and 'L' together and operate indicator switch. If lamps now light, flasher unit is defective.

Unit is mounted horizontally with terminal 'P' at 3 or 9 o'clock.

Flasher and direction indicator switch:

Remove steering column cowl (4 screws). Disconnect wiring connections under parcel shelf. Release switch from column (2 screws).

If an early switch is replaced by one with spring-loaded metal pawls working against spring leaves, fit a square-headed indicator trip stud. Stud must project 1.166 to 1.187 inch (29.9 to 30.5 mm) from underside of column.

Ignition switch:

To remove lock barrel, turn switch to 'ignition on' position. Barrel retaining plunger will now be aligned with hole on body. Depress plunger and withdraw barrel and key.

10:9 Bi-metal instrumentation

The instruments are controlled by a stabilized voltage supply (see **FIG 10:11**). Check faults as follows:

Connect voltmeter to control box terminal 'B' and earth. Should read about 12 volts. With engine at 1000 rev/min and ignition warning light out, reading should be about 12 to 13 volts.

Check wiring for continuity, short circuits and possible earthing. Check that stabilizer 64 and transmitters are earthed. Gauges have common feed wire from stabilizer on Wolseley.

Voltage stabilizer:

After two minutes with ignition on, voltage between terminal 'I' and earth should be 10. Renew stabilizer if faulty. When fitting, ensure that terminals 'B' and 'E' are uppermost and do not exceed 20 deg. from vertical.

Gauges:

Do not shortcircuit a gauge to earth. Check for continuity between terminals with wiring disconnected.

Transmitter:

Check for continuity between terminal and case with lead disconnected.

10:10 Servicing windscreen wipers

There are two types, the single-speed shown in **FIG 10:12** and the two-speed fitted to Mk 2 and 3 vehicles (**FIG 10:13**).

Blades:

Remove arm from spindle by prising off. Note spring clip. Before fitting arm, switch on ignition and turn wiper control on and then off. Press arm into place at correct parking angle. Spring clip should snap into place. Wet screen to check position. If parking mechanism needs adjusting, slacken screws and turn parking switch 3 in **FIG 10:12**. There is no adjustment on two-speed type.

Servicing single-speed type:

In case of faulty operation, test as follows:

Disconnect cable rack 24. Connect moving coil ammeter in lead to wiper motor, switch on and check current. Correct reading is 2.6 to 3.4 amp. After one minute, count speed of final gear 8. Connecting link 6 should make 44 to 48 cycles per minute.

If wiper takes no current check fuse 'A3' to 'A4'. If blown, check wiring. If wiring correct, fit new fuse. If fuse is intact, check wiper switch and wiring.

If wiper takes very low current check battery. Check brush gear 18 after removing cover 17. Brushes must bear firmly on commutator (copper segments) so check spring tension and freedom of levers. Clean commutator with fuel-moistened cloth.

If wiper takes heavy current check freedom of wheelbox assemblies 29. Check freedom of rack cable in outer casing 25, 26 or 27 by taking off wiper arms and hooking a spring balance into hole in crosshead 24. Pull on rack. Force to move must not exceed 6 lb (2.7 kg). If rack is too resistant to movement, check alignment of wheel boxes and check outer casing for damage or sharp

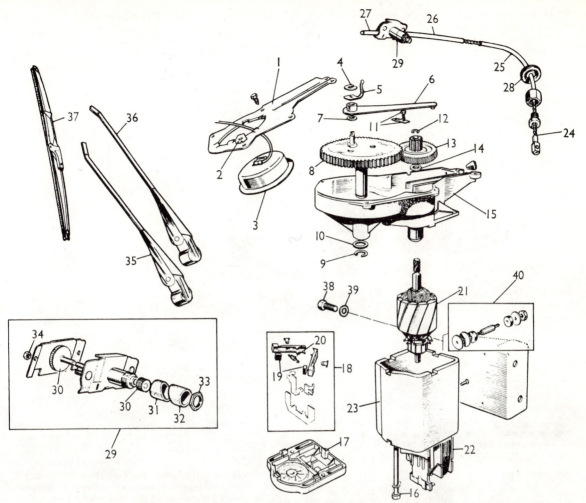

FIG 10:12 Components of single-speed wiper motor and drive

Key to Fig 10:12   1 Gearbox cover   2 Locking plate   3 Parking switch   4 Circlip   5 Earth connector
6 Cross-head connecting link   7 Plain washer   8 Final gear   9 Circlip   10 Plain washer   11 Armature end-play stop
12 Circlip   13 Intermediate gear   14 Plain washer   15 Gearbox   16 Bolts   17 Commutator end bracket
18 Brush assembly   19 Brushes   20 Brush spring   21 Armature   22 Field coil   23 Yoke   24 Cross-head and rack
25 Motor to wheelbox—outer casing   26 Wheelbox to wheelbox—outer casing   27 Wheelbox end—outer casing
28 Grommet   29 Wheelbox assembly   30 Spindle and gear   31 Rear bush   32 Front bush   33 Nut   34 Nut
35 Wiper arm—R.H.D.   36 Wiper arm—L.H.D.   37 Wiper arm blade   38 Screw to valance   39 Shakeproof washer
40 Fixing stud assembly

bends. Another cause of high current consumption may be shorts in wiring, dirty brush and commutator gear or shorted field coil. If resistance of coil is less than 8 to 9.5 ohm at 16 deg. C (60 deg. F), renew coil. Also check end float of armature (see later).

Removing:

Remove battery earth cable, wires to wiper motor and wiper arms. Unscrew union nut joining rack casing to motor. Release mounting bracket and pull motor and rack from casing. To remove casing, slacken cover screws of wheelboxes (see 29). From outside car, remove nut 33 and bush 32. Push on spindle. On Wolseley, remove facia panel to reach nearside wheelbox.

Dismantling wiper unit:

Mark position of parking switch 3 and remove cover 1. Remove circlip 4, connector 5 and link 6. Remove circlip 9, remove shaft burrs and lift out final gear 8. Remove stop 11 and circlip 12 to remove gear 13. Check parts for wear.

Remove connectors and bolts 16 and lift off cover 17. Brush gear 18 may be withdrawn as a unit after carefully noting correct positions of brushes. Withdraw yoke 23 for access to armature 21 and field coil 22. Check resistance of coil. If to be renewed, unsolder cables and release pole-piece from yoke.

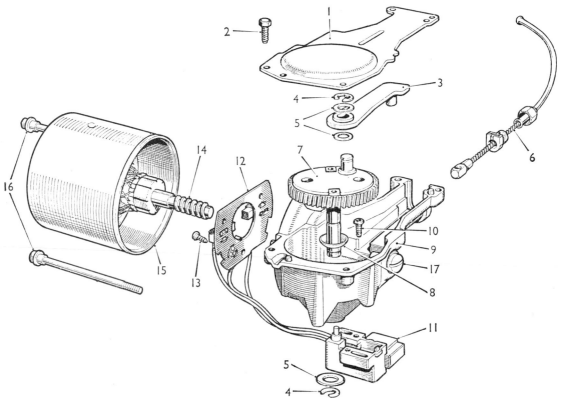

FIG 10:13 Components of two-speed wiper motor and gearbox

Key to Fig 10:13   1 Gearbox cover   2 Screw   3 Connecting rod   4 Circlip   5 Plain washers   6 Cross-head and rack
7 Shaft and gear   8 Dished washer   9 Gearbox   10 Screw   11 Limit switch assembly   12 Brush gear
13 Screw for brush gear   14 Armature   15 Yoke assembly   16 Yoke bolts   17 Armature thrust screw

Reassembling:

Do this in reverse order of dismantling, lubricating armature bearing bushes with SAE.20 oil. Bushes should be immersed in the oil for 24 hours.

Apply SAE.20 oil sparingly to gear shafts. Grease the crosshead and its guide channel, the link, crankpin, cable rack and wheelboxes liberally (preferably with Ragosine Listate 225). Do not forget washers 7 and 10.

Note that new brushes with ridged contact faces must be fitted so that ridges will trace a series of rings round commutator.

Armature end float must be .008 to .012 inch (.20 to .30 mm). Adjust at stop 11.

Servicing two-speed type:

Refer to **FIG 10:13**. Service wiper arms, test motor and remove assembly as described for single-speed type. To remove wheelboxes, remove parcel tray tops (push down on one-piece top), instruments and demister ducts. Then follow single-speed instructions.

Dismantling:

Remove cover 1. Remove circlip 4 and lift off rod 3. Remove circlip 4, remove burrs from shaft and pull out gear 7. Note dished washer 8.

Mark yoke and gearbox then release yoke, storing it away from steel particles, which will adhere to it. Release brush gear 12 and switch 11.

Inspection:

Main brushes (opposite each other) must be not less than $\frac{3}{16}$ inch (4.8 mm) thick. If narrow part of third brush is worn down to full width it needs renewal. In both cases renew complete brush assembly.

Brushes must move freely. Renew assembly if brush base is not level with bottom of slot in brush box under a load of 5 to 7 oz (140 to 200 gm).

Renew armature if open- or short-circuited. Renew gears and link if worn.

Reassembling:

Adopt the reverse order of dismantling. Use Ragosine Listate grease on gear teeth and cam, armature worm gear, connecting rod, crosshead and rack 6 and gears in wheelboxes.

Use Shell Turbo 41 oil on bearings, shafts and crankpin. Soak felt washer in yoke bearing. Be sparing on armature shaft.

Tighten yoke bolts to 14 lb in (.16 kg m). If armature is renewed, slacken screw 17. Fit washer 8 with concave face to gear. Larger of washers 5 goes under rod 3.

Adjust armature end float by tightening thrust screw 17 and turning it back one quarter of a turn. Measure gap under head of screw and fit suitable shim to give end float of .002 to .008 inch (.05 to .2 mm) when screw is tightened.

Refitting:

Fit in the reverse order, leaving wheelbox covers slack until cable rack has been inserted and motor secured.

10:11 Servicing clocks and horns

Transistorized clocks:

These clocks use a 1.35 volt cell. **Do not connect to 12-volt system.** Fit new battery every 12 months or to check failure to operate. Feed cable blade (under insulator sleeve) must not touch casing or battery will discharge rapidly.

12-volt clocks:

Normal clock has green terminal moulding. Rectified type has black. Clocks with rectifiers have polarity of live terminal stamped on case. This will be '—ve' for positive earth system. Do not reverse polarity and do not leave clock not working while connected. Press knob and release smartly.

Mk 11 and 11S clocks:

These 12-volt clocks start automatically upon connection.

Horns:

These may be of Lucas or Clear hooters type. Neither can be dismantled. Do not disturb adjustment points unless note is ineffective.

If two horns are fitted, disconnect one to adjust the other. Insulate detached cables.

If horn does not sound after adjustment, release horn push at once. As fuse may blow due to heavy load, remove fuse and short 'A1' and 'A2' connections.

In the case of failure, first check all wires and connections. Check security of bolts. Horn must not touch anything. Current consumption 3.5 amp. This will be 4 amp on later horn with widely spaced Lucar connectors.

Adjusting Lucas horn:

Unlock and turn screw on top of horn anticlockwise until horn just fails when push is operated. Turn screw back one quarter of a turn.

Adjusting Clear hooter:

For loss of volume turn knurled screw on top of horn clockwise until normal, then turn screw back as far as possible without loss of volume. Current consumption must not exceed $3\frac{1}{2}$ amp.

Removing:

When removing horn, do not remove the horn-to-bracket setscrew.

10:12 Accessory wiring

Supply for accessories may be taken from connector panel seen below fuses in **FIG 10:9.** If purple cables ('A2') are used, supply will always be live irrespective of ignition switch. If green cables ('A4') are used, supply will be live only with ignition switched on.

For an accessory forward of the panel, withdraw selected cable and fit a 'pick-a-back' and cable. Slide existing cable socket onto 'pick-a-back'. Connect up suitable switch. Select an 'LM' position and insert terminal blade from rear. Join switch and terminal blade cables with snap connector. Remove 6-way plug and fit a snap-in socket with cable attached, ensuring that socket and terminal match. Terminate lead at accessory and complete circuit with earth return.

Accessory at rear of panel:

Follow preceding instructions as far as 'Connect up a suitable switch'. Take cable from other side of switch direct to accessory and complete circuit by earth return.

10:13 Fault diagnosis

(a) Battery discharged

1 Terminal connections loose or dirty
2 Shorts in lighting circuit
3 Generator not charging
4 Regulator or cutout units not working properly
5 Battery internally defective

(b) Insufficient charging current

1 Check 1 in (a)
2 Driving belt slipping

(c) Battery does not hold charge

1 Low level of electrolyte
2 Battery plates sulphated
3 Electrolyte leakage from cracked case
4 Plate separators defective

(d) Battery overcharged

1 Regulators out of adjustment

(e) Generator output low or nil

1 Belt broken or slipping
2 Regulator unit out of adjustment
3 Worn bearings, loose pole-pieces
4 Commutator worn, burned or shorted
5 Armature shaft bent or worn
6 Insulation proud between commutator segments
7 Brushes sticking, springs weak or broken
8 Field coil windings broken, shorted or burned

(f) Starter motor lacks power or will not operate

1 Battery discharged, loose cable connections
2 Starter pinion jammed in flywheel gear
3 Starter switch faulty
4 Brushes worn or sticking, leads detached or shorting
5 Commutator dirty or worn
6 Starter shaft bent
7 Engine abnormally stiff, perhaps due to rebore

(g) Starter motor runs but does not turn engine

1 Pinion sticking on screwed sleeve
2 Broken teeth on pinion or flywheel gears

(h) Noisy starter pinion when engine is running

1 Weak or broken restraining spring

(i) Starter motor inoperative

1 Check 1 and 4 in (f)
2 Armature or field coils faulty

(j) Starter motor rough or noisy

1 Mounting bolts loose
2 Damaged pinion or flywheel gear teeth
3 Main pinion spring broken

(k) Lamps inoperative or erratic

1 Battery low, bulbs burned out
2 Faulty earthing of lamps or battery
3 Lighting switch faulty, loose or broken connections

(l) Wiper motor sluggish, takes high current

1 Faulty armature, dirty commutator
2 Bearings out of alignment
3 Wheelbox spindle binding, rack cable tight in casing
4 Lack of lubrication
5 No end float to armature spindle

(m) Wiper motor runs but blades immovable

1 Wheelbox defective, rack faulty
2 Motor gearbox worn

(n) Gauges do not work

1 Faulty wiring or earthing
2 Voltage stabilizer faulty
3 Break in continuity of instruments or transmitters

CHAPTER 11

THE BODYWORK

11:1 Bodywork finish

The restoration of serious body damage must be left to the experts, but small dents and scratches may be filled and then painted with self-spraying cans of colour in the maker's shades. First remove wax polish with white spirit, or if a silicone polish has been used a very fine abrasive will be needed. Use a primer surfacer or paste stopper according to the amount of filling required. When dry, rub down with 400 grade 'Wet or Dry' paper until smooth and flush with surrounding area. A perfect surface is needed for best results. Keep sprayed paint wet in centre and light and dry round the edges. After a few hours of drying, remove dry spray with cutting compound and finish off with liquid polish.

11:2 Fitting seat belts

An owner who has the slightest doubt about his skill should entrust this work to an Authorized Dealer. It is dangerous to take chances.

Fitting static type:

Feel for hole at top of centre pillar and cut hole in trim. Take a $\frac{7}{16}$ inch (11.11 mm) bolt and fit a distance piece, waved washer and bracket to it. Screw bolt into pillar. Trim must not be trapped under distance piece.

Locate fixing point in sill and cut hole in carpet. Fit shouldered distance piece, waved washer and bracket to short bolt and secure to sill. Carpet must not be trapped.

Find plug in side of centre tunnel away from seat being fitted. Cut carpet. Fit parts as before. In each fixing, small diameter of shouldered distance piece must enter hole in bracket. Ensure that bolt on righthand side of tunnel does not foul handbrake cable.

Fitting automatic type:

Locate sill fixing point, cut carpet and fit bracket as in preceding instructions. Reel must be mounted on sill with base horizontal. Drill a $\frac{3}{16}$ inch (4.8 mm) hole through forward position of bracket and tighten a No. 6 self-tapping screw into the sill. With webbing on pillar side, secure reel to bracket with screws, nuts and washer provided. The centre pillar and tunnel points are fitted as in the 'static' instructions.

Test action of reel. It should lock belt only under hard braking or cornering. Brake hard from 15 mile/hr (25 km/hr). Belt should lock. It should free itself when tension on belt is released. Check belt retraction. It may be necessary to help action by moving tongue on long belt towards door pulley bracket. **Never remove the end covers to inspect the reel.**

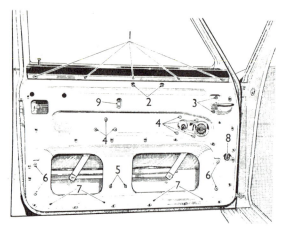

FIG 11:1 Inner panel of front door (first type)

Key to Fig 11:1 1 Screws—trim pad finisher 2 Door-pull securing plugs 3 Screw—door lock remote control 4 Screws—window regulator 5 Screws—window stop 6 Companion box securing plugs 7 Screw holes—low trim pad 8 Screw—window channel 9 Anti-rattle clip—remote control rod

11:3 Servicing doors (first type)

Door trim and interior handles (front):

Pass a blade behind remote control escutcheon to release spring clip from handle assembly. Press window winder escutcheon inwards, push out pin and remove handle. Remove arm-rest (or door pull). Release lower trim pad (4 screws and 6 clips). Prise pad from door. Remove companion box. Inner panel of box is glued to panel round the edge.

Door trim and interior handles (rear):

Remove handle as for front door. Prise lower pad from door (3 screws and clips). Withdraw companion box and panel as for front. A hole under the panel gives access to front channel of window glass.

Refitting trim:

Grease lock parts. Fit plastic cover to door panel. If no cover, tape up all door cutouts. Locate pad clips and drive home with sharp blow.

Servicing door glass:

Refer to **FIG 11:1**. Remove door trim and interior handles. Remove finisher (5 screws 1). Unscrew lock button and withdraw door capping. Clear the door cutouts and remove stop (screws 5). Wind glass right down and clear regulator from channels. Lift glass upwards, keeping front tilted down. Refit in reverse order.

Servicing regulators:

Remove trim and handles. Jam glass in closed position with wooden wedges between glass and door. Release regulator (screws 4). Collapse assembly and remove through cutout (front one on front doors). Refit in reverse order.

Servicing remote control:

Proceed as for servicing regulator. After releasing regulator (screws 4), remove screws 3. Keep regulator clear, push remote control handle through its cutout and remove assembly through regulator cutout.

Refit in reverse order. Ensure that connecting rod is between inner panel of door and the regulator arms, and is engaged in its anti-rattle clip. Control handle should move $\frac{1}{16}$ inch (1.6 mm) before operating the lock mechanism. Move control assembly forward until lock operating lever 7 is against its stop and tighten securing screws (see **FIG 11:2**).

Servicing door lock:

Check that sill rod does not foul. Depress control and look for small clearance between control knob and sill. Gain clearance by bending rod and unscrewing control knob.

If necessary, adjust striker plate on pillar (see 12 in **FIG 11:2**). Door must close easily without rattling, lifting or dropping. **Striker must always be in horizontal plane relative to door hinge axis.** Tighten retaining screws securely.

Before removing lock, check that unsatisfactory action is not due to incorrect striker plate position, wrong adjustment of remote control or incorrect clearance of outside door handle plunger 4. To remove lock, close window and remove trim and interior handles. Release remote control rod 13 (spring clip). Remove locking button (front). Release rear glass

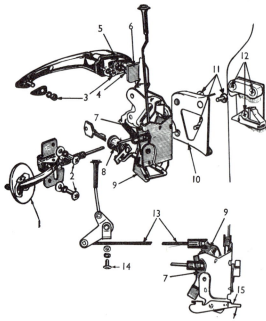

FIG 11:2 Lock mechanisms of front and rear doors (first type)

Key to Fig 11:2 1 Escutcheon 2 Screws—remote control 3 Nuts—outside control 4 Plunger bolt 5 Locknut 6 Lock contact 7 Lock operating lever 8 Twin-legged spring collar 9 Locking lever 10 Dovetail plate 11 Dovetail securing screws 12 Striker plate securing screws 13 Rear lock and remote control 14 Pivot screw 15 Safety catch

channel from its guide and push to one side. Mark position of plate and remove screws 11. Detach lock from private lock shaft (spring clip) and remove lock through access hole.

Refit lock in reverse order. Glue rear glass channel in position.

To remove the interior locking control on rear doors, disconnect connecting rod at lever 7 and detach rod from clip. Remove lock button and the screw securing pivot assembly and withdraw through front cutout in panel. When refitted, connecting rod must pass between inner door panel and regulator arms and must engage in anti-rattle clip.

Front door private lock:

To remove, close window, remove door trim and inside handles. Lock is secured by twin-legged spring collar 8. From inside door, compress legs and withdraw barrel from outside. To remove barrel from cylinder, remove spring clip, push out tapered pin, fit ignition key and pull out barrel.

When refitting, lubricate mechanism sparingly with oil. **Do not use grease.** Fit spring collar, fit lock with its fork inclined towards the door shutting face and engage with lock assembly. A sharp blow on outer face of cylinder will force collar through and engage the spring legs.

Removing doors:

Before releasing door at hinges, remove door check pivot pin and scribe round hinges. After refitting in original position, check striker plate position.

Outside door handles:

To remove, close window and remove trim and inside handles. Remove nuts 3. To adjust position of handle, hold it in place and check that there is a clearance of at least $\frac{1}{32}$ inch (1 mm) between plunger bolt 4 and lock contact. To adjust, release locknut 5 and turn bolt in or out.

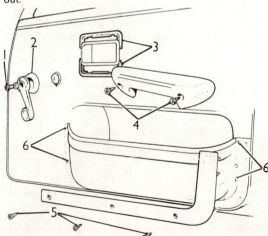

FIG 11 : 3 Interior handles and trim of righthand front door (second type)

Key to Fig 11 : 3 1 Screw—window regulator handle 2 Escutcheon 3 Bezel—remote control 4 Screws—arm-rest 5 Screws—lower trim pad 6 Screws—door pocket

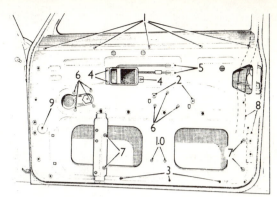

FIG 11 : 4 Inner panel of righthand front door (second type)

Key to Fig 11 : 4 1 Screws—trim pad finisher 2 Arm-rest securing plugs 3 Screw holes—lower trim pad 4 Screws—remote control 5 Guides—remote control rods 6 Screws—window regulator 7 Door pocket securing plugs 8 Window channel out of position for access 9 Screw—window channel 10 Screws—window stop

11 : 4 Servicing doors (second type)

Removing interior handles and trim:

Close window and remove regulator handle (screw 1 in **FIG 11 : 3**). Escutcheon 2 has locating dowel at bottom. Remove bezel halves 3 upwards and downwards. Remove armrest (or door pull). Gently lever trim panel from door along bottom. Lower pad is secured by three screws and three clips. Lever pad from door panel.

When refitting, grease door lock mechanism. Tape plastic cover in place, or tape up all door panel cutouts if plastic sheet not fitted.

Adjusting door striker:

Refer to **FIG 11 : 5**. Latch disc must be open. Ensure this by operating door push button and pushing a screwdriver through the disc (see 'C'). Tighten striker 13 just enough to let door close and latch. Open door and pencil round edge of striker plate. Set plate horizontal to hinge axis and tighten screws. Check door closing. There must be no rattling, lifting or dropping. Do not slam door but press inwards or outwards without pressing button until door lines up with body. It is correctly adjusted if it can be pressed in a small amount, but without rattling on the road.

Servicing door locks:

Refer to **FIG 11 : 5**. Before blaming the lock for unsatisfactory operation, make sure door is correctly adjusted as in preceding notes.

To remove lock mechanism, remove inside handles and trim. Remove remote control unit by pulling latch release and lock control rods from clips and bushes (see 14 and 16, also 'A' and 'B'). Remove screws 4 (see **FIG 11 : 4**).

To remove latch unit 11, pull release rod 14 out of lever bush. Release lock control rod 16 from locking quadrant 10. Leave rods in guides (front doors). Release rods from guides (rear doors). Prise glued window channel from metal channel at bottom of door. Move it to

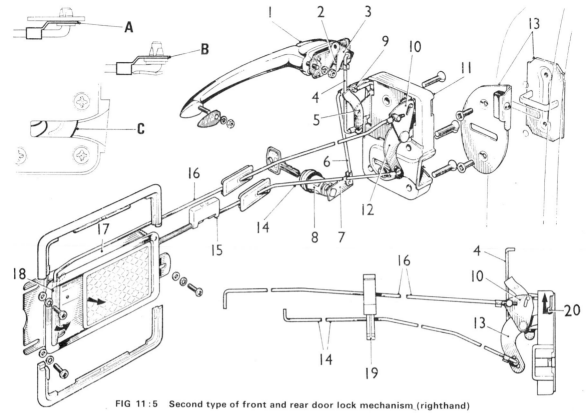

FIG 11:5 Second type of front and rear door lock mechanism (righthand)

Key to Fig 11:5   1 Push button   2 Plunger screw   3 Cranked push button arm   4 Push button link (d)   5 Contactor slide
6 Key-operated link (c)   7 Operating arm   8 Twin-legged spring collar   9 Latch locking lever   10 Locking quadrant
11 Latch unit   12 Latch release lever   13 Striker assembly   14 Latch release rod (b)   15 Plastic clip   16 Lock control rod (a)
17 Remote control unit   18 Safety locking latch   19 Anti-rattle clip   20 Safety catch—children's
A Bush assembly—clip on rod side   **B** Bush assembly—clip other side   **C** Latch disc—latched position

one side. Pull link 4 out of slide 5. On front doors, push key-operated link out of latch lever 9. Remove screws and withdraw latch unit 11.

To remove key-operated lock, prise off spring clip 8. Do not remove self-adhesive washer under lock head.

The adjustment of door striker has been covered earlier. Note that plate which carries loop is inside panel. To reach it on front doors, remove seat belt anchorage and door post liner (6 clips). On rear doors, remove seat squab and peel back the trim.

Refitting:

Rods and links are colour-coded or stamped as follows:

	Right side	Left side
(a) Lock control rod (front)	Black	Black/White
Lock control rod (rear)	Black/Yellow	Black/Yellow/White
(b) Latch release rod (front)	Black/Red	Black/Red/White
Latch release rod (rear)	Black/Green	Black/Green/White
(c) Key operated link	Black/Blue	Black/Blue/White
(d) Push-button link (front)	RF	LF
Push-button link (rear)	RR	LR

Note that items are identified by (a), (b), (c) and (d) in the key to **FIG 11:5**.

Fit correct hand of key-operated link, inserting bush towards lock and spring clip under head (see 'A'). Operating arm 7 must be inclined towards door shutting

face with key slot inverted. Lock units are handed. With spring collar 8 and adhesive washer fitted, press lock home.

Fit latch unit 11 with bushes and clips correctly assembled. For levers 9 and 12, bushes and clips are fitted as at 'B', using centre hole in lever 12. Slide contactor bush is also fitted as at 'B' with bush away from latch. On front doors, bush is inserted towards latch as at 'A'. Secure latch unit to door. Set latch disc as at 'C', and connect links. Check push-button.

Refit remote control unit by pressing correctly-handed latch rod 14 upwards into clip, and end of correct lock control rod 16 downwards into locking latch 18. Locate

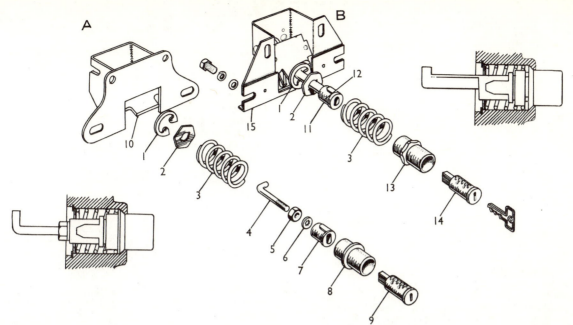

FIG 11:6   First type of trunk lid lock ('A'). Second type ('B'). The insets are plan views of lock assemblies in locked position

Key to Fig 11:6   1 Circlip   2 Bearing washer—push button   3 Return spring   4 Push lever   5 Nut   6 Lock washer
7 Latch push   8 Push button   9 Locking device   10 Lock assembly   11 Latch push   12 Bezel pin   13 Push button
14 Locking device   15 Lock assembly

rods in door guides. On rear doors fit 'peg' type of anti-rattle clip. Loosely fit remote control to door. Press rod 14 into lever 12. Adjust the remote control unit by moving the control towards latch unit 11 without compressing rod spring until latch release lever 12 is against its stop. Tighten control screws. If necessary, elongate slotted hole for control. Close door and check action of release lever 12. It should release striker before its full movement. On rear doors, with latch open, check that children's safety catch 20 can be moved **upwards** to block operation of release lever.

The locking control rod 16 is screwed into pivot on locking quadrant 10. Adjust by setting latch disc in locked position (see 'C'). Set locked positions of locking quadrant towards latch, and locking latch overlapping release lever. Adjust position of screwed pivot so that it fits freely into bush. Fit clip.

Checking:

Check operation of front doors. Wind window down and close door. Move locking latch to rear. Door will be locked and push-button inoperative. Unlock with key and open with push-button. Close door and open it with inside lever. Note that locking latch on front doors cannot be set locked with door open.

Check operation of rear doors. With window down, move locking latch to rear, and close door. It will be locked and push-button inoperative. Move latch forward. Open door with push-button then close it. Use inside release lever to open it. Set child's safety lever **upwards** and close door. Inside lever will be inoperative. Use outside button to open.

Lubrication:

Do not use grease in key lock cylinders. Smear linkages inside door with grease. Put few drops of thin oil in key slots.

11:5 Bonnet and trunk lid locks

Bonnet lock:

This is a straightforward assembly. Note locknut and slotted end of bonnet lock pin, enabling setting to be altered.

Trunk lid lock:

Refer to **FIG 11:6.** Removal is simple (4 screws). Remove circlip 1 to release lock barrel. Before removing lock catch, mark its position.

When refitting, lever 4 must be horizontal and to the right with key slot at the bottom (see inset). Nut 5 must be tight (first type). Fit washer 2 with slots horizontal. **After refitting, check lock action before closing lid.** Adjust for easy action by moving catch.

11:6 Fitting windscreen glass

If glass is to be removed, take off wiper arms. Prise up end of central finishing strip and pull it out of channel in rubber surround. From inside, press glass at top corner and ease it from rubber channel.

If glass is broken, make sure all particles are removed from demister ducts or occupants may be injured by tiny fragments when blower is switched on. Check that body flange is undamaged.

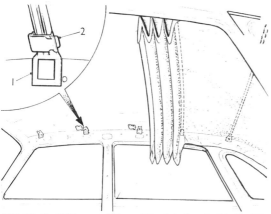

FIG 11:7 Fitting roof liner. Clips 1 in front of hole. Fit extra clips 2 to listing rails 2, 3 and 4

Fit new rubber surround into aperture and lubricate channel for glass with a solution of soap and water. Fit glass in lower channel. Starting at a corner, use a screwdriver with sharp edges removed to lift lip of rubber over glass. Refit finishing strip. When fitting a heated backlight, note that cables are at top and pass through holes in surround. Feed cable passes down righthand side and earth cable down left. Before fitting new surround drill two holes for cables.

11:7 Roof linings

One-piece type:

This is backed by glass-fibre panel that retains it in position. To remove, remove backlight glass (see **Section 11:6**). Remove interior mirror and sun visors. Prise off trim strip at top of windscreen and backlight (spring clips). Remove grab handles and interior light (remove fuse A1-A2). Release rear quarterlight fixings. Remove side trims at top (spring clips). Ease roof liner to rear and

to left to clear front righthand edge of rail. Ease liner from rail and pull forward to clear. Remove through rear aperture.

To refit, slide rear edge and one side into place and enter edges into rail. Slide liner forward and into front rail. Centralize liner to enter opposite rail. Refit remaining parts.

Liner with listing rails:

Refer to **FIG 11:7**. Remove all trim and other parts as in preceding instructions but do not remove the backlight glass. Pull old lining from body. Spring each listing rail out of clips.

Refit clips so that rear edges are aligned with holes in cant rail (see inset). Rails 2, 3 and 4 have an extra clip 2. Fit these to any vehicle without them.

Apply adhesive such as Dunlop S758/MG to cant rails and in a 2 inch (50 mm) strip round edge of lining. Fit listing rails to loops in lining in correct order according to colour marked in centre. Work from front to rear, fitting No. 1 (black) first, followed by No. 2 (red), No. 3 (yellow), No. 4 (blue) and No. 5 (green). Early assemblies had a 'red' rail at No. 3.

Fit listing rails in clips. Starting from rear, tension the lining and stick it to the body rails. Refit trim and other parts.

11:8 Removing instruments

On Austin/Morris:

Disconnect battery. Remove screws securing parcel shelf top (driver's side, second type facia) and lower to clear. Remove locknut from light switch and release clips behind facia to release long finisher on facia. Remove locknuts from wiper switch and washer control and one clip to release short finisher. Withdraw warning light bulbs before removing locknuts.

Withdraw wires from panel light switch. Remove screws securing instrument plate and push forward to clear, with lip downwards. Remove the four securing screws and withdraw instrument assembly.

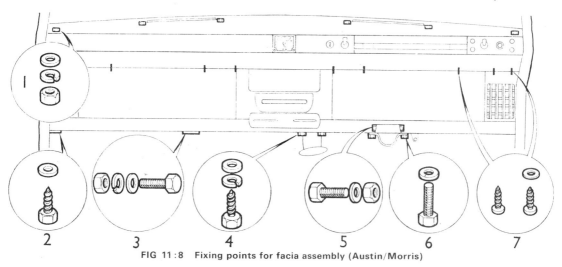

FIG 11:8 Fixing points for facia assembly (Austin/Morris)

Key to Fig 11:8   1 Top cover to panel   2 Parcel rail to 'A' post bracket   3 Support to parcel rail   4 Handbrake bracket
5 Reinforcement bracket to rail   6 Steering column and choke   7 Top cover and vents to panel

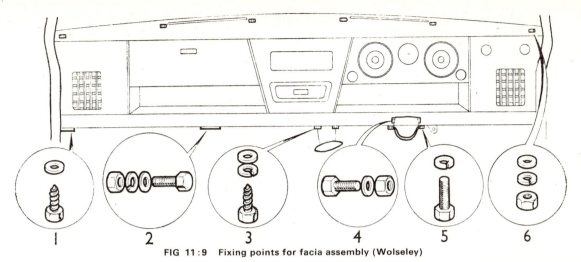

FIG 11:9   Fixing points for facia assembly (Wolseley)

Key to Fig 11:9   1 Parcel rail to 'A' post bracket   2 Support to parcel rail   3 Handbrake bracket
4 Reinforcement bracket to rail   5 Steering column and choke   6 Top cover to panel

On Wolseley:

Disconnect battery. Remove screw at bottom of panel and pull lower edge forward and down to release top pegs. Speedometer and three-in-one instrument are held by clamps and thumbscrews. Clock has bayonet fixing.

11:9 Facia panels

On Austin/Morris:

Refer to **FIG 11:8**. To remove top cover, release instrument panel and pull forward. Withdraw ashtray (first type). Remove nuts 1.

Remove crash pad or lower covering by removing parcel rail finisher (pop rivets—first type). Release control bezel (second type). Remove 5 nuts and pull crash pad from rail.

On Wolseley:

Refer to **FIG 11:9**. To remove facia assembly, disconnect battery. Withdraw front and engine harness plugs from connector panel. Release panel and pass through hole in bulkhead. On Automatic models, remove clevis pin from manual selector rod. Under car, centralize steering and release column-to-pinion clamp bolt.

Release instrument panel and washer switch, column wiring connectors behind parcel shelf, body harness connector, flasher unit and dip switch. Withdraw heater connector (when fitted). Disconnect cable from courtesy light. On Automatic models, remove clevis pin from park control rod. Release handbrake and facia support bracket at parcel rail.

Release steering column from pinion (see **Chapter 8**). Release column bracket from parcel rail. Release facia centre panel from parcel rail (2 screws and nuts). Remove screws 1 and ten crosshead screws securing facia to top panel. Release door finisher adjacent to facia, pull parcel

rail clear of brackets, clear top of panel and disengage hoses from vents. Remove the assembly. Refit in reverse order.

When fitting new facia boards, remove one at a time and fit new ones so that they retain original clearances.

11:10 Removing and refitting heater

Drain cooling system, release heater hoses at bulkhead and apply air line to top hose to clear coolant from matrix. Remove parcel shelf assembly (Austin/Morris). Withdraw facia panel assembly (Wolseley). For these, refer to preceding Section.

Unplug wiring to blower at connector on righthand side of heater case. Release assembly from bulkhead (4 nuts). Tip to rear and withdraw away from steering column. To remove matrix, remove cover (screws round edge of front panel, three across centre and two bolts). Matrix can be slid from casing.

To remove motor, disconnect wiring, remove rear bolts and withdraw motor and bracket.

Refit in reverse order. Ensure that heater duct drain pipes hang outside the front engine mounting and heater pipes. Apart from matrix and coolant, preceding instructions apply to fresh-air unit.

11:11 Seats

Remove front seats by sliding them forward and removing rear screws from runners. Slide seat back and repeat for front screws. Remove nuts securing runners to seat frame and withdraw runners and distance pieces. Seats may be lowered by removing distance pieces and cutting $\frac{1}{2}$ inch (13 mm) from the rear $\frac{5}{16}$ inch UNF studs.

Rear seat may be lifted straight from pan. To remove back squab, remove screw from each lower edge and two screws from centre armrest casing (if fitted). Lift upwards to free clips at top edge.

NOTES

APPENDIX

TECHNICAL DATA

Engine   Fuel system   Ignition system   Cooling system
Clutch   Gearbox transmission   Automatic transmission
Steering (manual)   Steering (power assisted)   Suspension
Drive shafts   Brakes   Electrical equipment   Capacities
Exhaust emission control system   Tyres and dimensions
Torque wrench settings

WIRING DIAGRAMS

HINTS ON MAINTENANCE AND OVERHAUL

GLOSSARY OF TERMS

INDEX

NOTES

TECHNICAL DATA

Inch sizes are given first, followed by metric sizes in brackets

ENGINE

Engine:

Type (Mk 1)	18AMW, 18C, 18WB
Type (Mk 2, Mk 2S and 18/85 with 18H engine)	18H (see also 'Exhaust Emission Control System')
Capacity	109.75 cu in (1798 cc)
Bore	3.160 (80.26)
Stroke	3.50 (88.9)
Compression ratio:	
18AMW and 18C (1964-67)	6.8 to 1, and 8.2 to 1 (up to 18AMW/U/ H101630)
18AMW, 18C and 18WB (1967-68) ...	6.8 to 1, and 8.4 to 1 (from 18AMW/U/ H101631 and 18WB)
18H (1968 on) and Mk 3	8.0 to 1 and 9.0 to 1 (see also 'Exhaust Emission Control System')
18H (Mk 11S, 1968 on)	9.5 to 1
Idling speed, Mk 1	550 rev/min
Mk 2	700 rev/min
'S' type	700 to 800 rev/min (See also 'Exhaust Emission Control')
Firing order	1, 3, 4, 2

Crankshaft:

Type	5 main bearings
Main journal diameter	2.1265 to 2.127 (54.01 to 54.02)
Main bearing regrinds	Minus .010, .020, .030 and .040 (minus .254, .508, .762 and 1.016)
End thrust taken	Thrust washers at centre bearing
End float	.002 to .003 (.051 to .076)
Crankpin journal diameter	1.8759 to 1.8764 (47.648 to 47.661)
Crankpin regrinds	As for main bearings

Main bearings:

Type and material	Steel-backed copper-lead or reticular tin
Diametrical clearance	.001 to .0027 (.025 to .068)

Connecting rods:

For engines 18AMW, 18C and 18WB ...	Angular-split big-end, bushed small-end
For 18H engine	Horizontal-split big-end, solid small-end
Length between centres	6.5 (165.1)
Big-end bearing type and material ...	Steel-backed copper-lead or VP3
Diametrical clearance of big-end ...	.0015 to .0032 (.038 to .081)
End float on crankpin	.008 to .012 (.20 to .30)

Pistons:

Type	Aluminium, solid skirt (oversizes available)
Clearance of skirt in cylinder (top): ...	
18AMW, 18C and 18WB	.0036 to .0045 (.091 to .121)
18H	.0021 to .0033 (.053 to .084)
Clearance of skirt in cylinder (bottom):	
18AMW, 18C and 18WB	.0018 to .0024 (.045 to .061)
18H	.0006 to .0012 (.015 to .030)
Number of rings:	
18AMW, 18C and 18WB	3 compression, one oil control
18H	2 compression, one oil control

Width of ring grooves:
  Compression ... ... .064 to .065 (1.625 to 1.651)
  Oil control ... ... .1578 to .1588 (4.01 to 4.033)
Gudgeon pin bore:
  18AMW, 18C and 18WB ... ... .8128 to .813 (20.610 to 20.617)

Piston rings:
  18AMW, 18C and 18WB:
    Top ... ... Plain, cast iron, molybdenum filled
    Second and third ... ... Tapered, cast iron, molybdenum filled
    Oil control ... ... Slotted scraper
  18H:
    Top ... ... Plain, sintered alloy
    Second ... ... Tapered, sintered alloy (marked 'TOP')
    Oil control ... ... Chrome-faced rings with expander
  Width:
    Compression rings ... ... .0615 to .0625 (1.562 to 1.587)
  Oil control rings:
    18AMW, 18C and 18WB ... ... .1552 to .1562 (3.94 to 3.96)
    18H ... ... .152 to .158 (3.86 to 4.01)
  Fitted Gap:
    Compression rings:
      18AMW, 18C and 18WB ... ... .012 to .017 (.304 to .431)
      18H ... ... .012 to .022 (.30 to .60)
    Oil control rings:
      18AMW, 18C and 18WB ... ... .012 to .017 (.304 to .431)
      18H (rings) ... ... .015 to .045 (.38 to 1.14)

Gudgeon pin:
  Type:
    18AMW, 18C and 18WB ... ... Fully floating
    18H ... ... Press fit in connecting rod
  Diameter (18H) ... ... .8125 to .8127 (20.63 to 20.64)
  Fit in piston ... ... Hand push at 16°C (60°F)
  Fit in small-end (18H) ... ... 12 lb ft (1.7 kg m) minimum, using
                                        18G 1150/C

Camshaft:
  Type ... ... Three-bearing, chain driven
  Bearings ... ... Steel-backed, whitemetal lined
  Journal diameter:
    Front ... ... 1.7887 to 1.7892 (45.424 to 45.437)
    Centre ... ... 1.7287 to 1.7292 (43.910 to 43.923)
    Rear ... ... 1.6227 to 1.6232 (41.218 to 41.230)
  Bearing inside diameter:
    Front ... ... 1.7902 to 1.7907 (45.472 to 45.485)
    Centre ... ... 1.7302 to 1.7307 (43.948 to 43.961)
    Rear ... ... 1.6242 to 1.6247 (41.256 to 41.269)
  Diametrical clearance ... ... .001 to .002 (.0254 to .0508)
  End thrust taken ... ... On locating plate
  End float ... ... .003 to .007 (.076 to .178)
  Driving chain ... ... .375 (9.52) pitch, 52 pitches

Tappets:
  Outside diameter ... ... .8125 (20.64)
  Length ... ... 2.293 to 2.303 (58.25 to 58.5)

Rocker gear:
  Shaft diameter ... ... .624 to .625 (15.85 to 15.87)
  Rocker bush inside diameter ... ... .6255 to .626 (15.8 to 15.9)

Valves:

Seat angle	45½ deg.
Head diameter:	
Inlet (18AMW, 18C and 18WB)	1.562 to 1.567 (39.67 to 39.80)
Inlet (18H)	1.625 to 1.630 (41.27 to 41.40)
Exhaust	.3417 to .3422 (8.66 to 8.692)
Stem diameter:	
Inlet	.3422 to .3427 (8.692 to 8.704)
Exhaust	.3417 to .3422 (8.66 to 8.992)
Stem to guide clearance:	
Inlet	.0015 to .0025 (.0381 to .063)
Exhaust	.002 to .003 (.051 to .076)

Valve guides:

Length:	
Inlet	1.875 (47.63)
Exhaust	2.203 (55.95)
Outside diameter (both)	.5635 to .5640 (14.30 to 14.32)
Bore (both)	.3442 to .3447 (8.743 to 8.755)
Fitted height above head:	
Inlet	.75 (19)
Exhaust	.625 (15.89)
Fit in head (both)	.0005 to .0017 (.012 to .044) inter-ference

Valve springs:

Free length:	
Outer	2.14 (54)
Inner	1.97 (50)
Fitted length:	
Outer	1.5625 (39.7)
Inner	1.4375 (36.5)
Load at fitted length:	
Outer	60.5 lb (24.7 kg)
Inner	30 lb (13.6 kg)

Rocker clearance (cold):

18AMW and 18C; between 18AMW/U/H27523 and H97273, also up to 18AMW/U/H101630 ...	.015 (.38)
Up to 18AMW/U/H27272, L20546; between 18AMW/U/H97274 to H101630, and L97811 to 97850	.018 (.46)
From 18AMW/U/H101631 and 18WB	.015 (.38)
Mk 2 and Mk 2S	.015 (.38). Also with Exhaust Emission Control

Valve timing:

Marks	Dimples on crankshaft and camshaft gears

      Timing is checked with rocker clearance temporarily increased to .020 (.51)

Between 18AMW/U/H27523 to H97273 and L20547 to L97811	Inlet opens TDC, closes 50 deg. ABDC, exhaust opens 35 deg. BBDC and closes 15 deg. ATDC
Up to 18AMW/U/H27272, L20546; and between AMW/U/H97274 to H101630, and L97811 to 97850. Also up to 18WB/SB/U/H3063, A/H3936	Inlet opens 5 deg. BTDC, closes 45 deg. ABDC, exhaust opens 51 deg. BBDC and closes 21 deg. ATDC

From 18AMW/U/H101631, L97851 and 18WB/SB/U/H3064, A/H3937 (camshaft identified by 3 grooves on end of shaft) ... ... Inlet opens 5 deg. BTDC, closes 45 deg. ABDC, exhaust opens 40 deg. BBDC and closes 10 deg. ATDC

For Mk 2S ... ... Inlet opens 16 deg. BTDC, closes 56 deg. ABDC, exhaust opens 51 deg. BBDC and closes 21 deg. ATDC

Lubrication system:

Oil pump	Hobourn Eaton bi-rotor
Oil filter	Tecalemit fullflow, felt element
Pressure:	
Running	50 to 75 lb/sq in (3.5 to 5.0 kg/sq cm)
Idling	15 to 25 lb/sq in (1.0 to 1.8 kg/sq cm)
Pressure relief valve:	
Opens	70 lb/sq in (4.9 kg/sq cm)
Spring free length	3 (76)
Spring fitted length	2.156 (54.77)
Load at fitted length	15.5 to 16.5 lb (7.0 to 7.4 kg)

FUEL SYSTEM

Carburetter:

Type (all models except Mk 2S)	SU HS6 at 30 deg. (see also 'Exhaust Emission control System')
Type (Mk 2S)	Twin SU HS6 at 30 deg.
Piston spring:	
All models except Mk 2S	Yellow
Mk 2S	Red
Needle:	
Mk 1	TW (standard), SW (rich), C1W (weak)
Mk 2 and 18/85 (1968 on), Mk 3	ZH (standard), SA (rich), C1W (weak)
Mk 2S	TZ (standard), C1 (rich), C1W (weak)
Vehicles with exhaust emission control ...	BAJ

Fuel pump:

Type:	
Mk 1	SU electric, AUF 209 or 215
Mk 2, 3 and 2S (also 18/85 with 18H engine)..	SU mechanical, type AUF 704
Delivery rate (minimum):	
SU electric	7 gal/hr (8½ U.S. gal/hr, .32 litre/hr)
Delivery pressure:	
SU electric	2 to 3.8 lb/sq in (.14 to .27 kg/sq cm)
Minimum suction:	
SU mechanical	6 (152) Hg (mercury)
Minimum pressure:	
SU mechanical	3 lb/sq in (.21 kg/sq cm)
Grade of fuel	99 octane (4 star)

IGNITION SYSTEM

Sparking plugs:

Type:	
Mk 1	Champion N5
Mk 2, 3 and 2S, 18/85 (1968 on)	Champion N9Y
Coil:	
Type, all models	Lucas HA12
Distributor:	
Type, all models	Lucas 25D4
Rotation of rotor	Anticlockwise

Dwell angle	60 deg. ±3 deg.
Contact points gap	.014 to .016 (.35 to .40)
Capacitor (condenser) capacity	.18 to .24 mF
Serial No.:	
Mk 1 (1964-67)	40970 (6.8 to 1), 40969 (8.2 to 1)
Mk 1 and 18/85 (1967-68)	40970 (6.8 to 1), 41034 (8.4 to 1)
Mk 2 and 18/85 (1968 on), Mk 3 ...	41035 (8.0 to 1), 41234A (9.0 to 1)
Mk 2S	41238 (see also 'Exhaust Emission Control System')
Firing order	1, 3, 4, 2
Timing marks	Pointers on front cover and groove in crankshaft pulley

Ignition timing, static:

Mk 1 and 18/85	14 deg. BTDC
Mk 2 and 18/85 (from 1968), Mk 3:	
9.0:1 compression ratio (Dist. S/No. 41234) ...	9 deg. BTDC
8.0:1 compression ratio (Dist. S/No. 41035) ...	14 deg. BTDC
6.9:1 compression ratio (Dist. S/No. 41260) ...	12 deg. BTDC
Ignition timing (stroboscopic at 600 rev/min):	
Mk 1 and 18/85 till 1968	16 deg. BTDC
Mk 2, Mk 2S and 18/85 from 1968 on ...	12 deg. BTDC (HC engines)
(Also see 'Exhaust Emission Control System')	17 deg. BTDC (LC engines)
	15 deg. BTDC (LC engines, export)
Mk 3	12 deg. BTDC

COOLING SYSTEM

Type	Pressurized spill return system. Pump and fan. Thermostat control
Cap release pressure	13 lb/sq in (.91 kg/sq cm)

Thermostat setting:

Standard	82°C (180°F)
Hot climate	74°C (165°F)
Cold climate	88°C (190°F)

Fan belt:

	Standard	Power steering	Alternator
Width at 40 deg. angle	.37 (9.5)	.47 (11.9)	.47 (11.9)
Outside, length	36.75 (930)	41.12 (1040)	38.5 (980)
hot climates	35.5 (900)	40 (1010)	40 (1010)
Thickness	.31 (7.9)	.38 (9.7)	.38 (9.7)
Tension	.5 (13) deflection on longest run		

CLUTCH

Type	8 (20.32 cm) single dry plate, diaphragm spring

Facing material:

All models	Wound yarn RY2, WR7, M54 or 2124F
Clutch fluid	Castrol Girling Brake Fluid Amber

GEARBOX TRANSMISSION

Type	Four forward ratios with synchromesh Reverse

Overall ratios (standard):

18AMW, 18C, 18WB:

Top	3.882 to 1
Third	5.371 to 1
Second	8.609 to 1
First	12.779 to 1
Reverse	11.936 to 1

Overall ratios (alternative):
(These were standard ratios up to Engine Nos. 18AMW/U/H27523, 18AMW/U/L20548)
18AMW, 18C, 18WB:

Top	...	...	...	...	...	4.187 to 1
Third	...	...	...	...	...	5.795 to 1
Second	...	...	...	...	...	9.283 to 1
First	...	...	...	...	...	13.784 to 1
Reverse	...	...	...	...	...	12.875 to 1

Overall ratios (Mk 2 and Mk 3 and 18/85 with 18H engine):

Standard second	...	...	...	...	7.99 to 1
Alternative second	...	...	...	...	8.60 to 1

Overall ratios (Mk 2S):

Standard second	...	...	...	...	7.99 to 1
Alternative second	...	...	...	...	8.63 to 1

(Other ratios as for Mk 1)

End float:

Idler gear	...	...	...	...	...	.008 to .010 (.20 to .25)
1st and 3rd speed gear	...	...	...	...	...	.006 to .008 (.15 to .20)
2nd speed gear	...	...	...	...	...	.005 to .008 (.13 to .20)
Laygear	...	...	...	...	...	.002 to .003 (.05 to .08)

Springs:

Synchro hub:

Free length	...	...	...	...	...	.720 (18.3)
Fitted length	...	...	...	...	...	.385 (9.8)
Load at fitted length	...	...	...	...	5.5 to 6 lb (2.5 to 2.7 kg)

Selector fork:

Free length	...	...	...	...	...	1.0625 (30.2)
Fitted length	...	...	...	...	...	.75 (19.0)
Load at fitted length	...	...	...	...	18 to 20 lb (8.2 to 9.1 kg)

Laygear thrust:

Free length	...	...	...	...	...	1.661 (42.2)
Fitted length	...	...	...	...	...	1.161 (29.5)
Load at fitted length	...	...	...	...	9 to 10 lb (4 to 4.5 kg)

Final drive:

Ratio:

Standard	...	...	...	...	...	3.882 to 1 (17/66)
Alternative	...	...	...	...	...	4.187 to 1 (16/67)
Preload on differential bearing	...	...	...	.003 to .005 (.076 to .127)

AUTOMATIC TRANSMISSION

Type	...	...	...	...	...	Threespeed epicyclic, with torque converter. Borg-Warner AS1-35TA
Primary drive	...	...	...	...	...	Sprockets and chain, ratio 1.03 to 1

Ratios:

First	...	...	...	...	...	2.39 to 1
Second	...	...	...	...	...	1.45 to 1
Top	...	...	...	...	...	1.0 to 1
Reverse	...	...	...	...	...	2.09 to 1

Final Drive:

Ratio	...	...	...	...	...	3.83 to 1 (18/69)
Preload on differential bearing	...	...	...	.003 to .005 (.076 to .127)

Overall ratios (converter at 1 to 1):

First	...	...	...	...	...	...	9.417 to 1
Second	...	...	...	...	...	...	5.714 to 1
Top	...	...	...	...	...	...	3.948 to 1
Reverse	...	...	...	...	...	...	8.23 to 1

STEERING (manual)

Type	...	...	...	Rack and pinion
Steering wheel turns (lock to lock)	...	...	4.4 (early), 3.8 (later)
Pinion bearing preload	...	...	...	.001 to .003 (.03 to .08)
Damper spring load (second type) ...	...	...	.001 to .006 (.02 to .15)
Toe-in	...	...	...	.125 (3.2) or 0° 22' (unladen)
Steering angle (inner wheel)	...	...	$21\frac{1}{2} \pm 1\frac{1}{2}$ deg. with outer wheel at 20 deg.

STEERING (power-assisted)

Type	...	...	...	Rack and pinion with integral power assistance
Steering wheel turns (lock to lock) ...	...	...	3.56
Toe-in	...	...	...	.125 (3.2) or 0° 22' (unladen)
Steering angle (inner wheel)	...	...	$21\frac{1}{2} \pm 1\frac{1}{2}$ deg. with outer wheel at 20 deg.
Damper movement ...	...	...	...	.001 to .003 (.03 to .08)

SUSPENSION

Trim height:

First type ... ... 14.625 + .25 (372 + 6)

Second type and automatic transmission ... 14.875 ± .25 (378 ± 6) (unladen— Mk 2)

Fluid pressure (approximate):

First type ... ... 230 lb/sq in (16.2 kg/sq cm)

Second type and automatic transmission ... 245 lb/sq in (17.2 kg/sq cm)

Type (front)... ... ... Independent (unequal arms). Tie rod. Hydrolastic displacers connected to rear

Type (rear) ... ... Independent with trailing arms (anti-roll bar fitted up to A/HS10/32802). Hydraulic displacers

Setting angles (front):

Manual steering:

Swivel hub inclination... ... ... $12 \pm \frac{3}{4}$ deg. (unladen)

Camber angle ... ... $1\frac{1}{2} \pm \frac{3}{4}$ deg. positive (unladen)

Castor angle (Mk 1) ... ... $\frac{1}{4} \pm 1$ deg. positive (unladen)

Castor angle (Mk 2 and Mk 3) ... ... 2 ± 1 deg. positive (unladen). Transverse rib on upper support arms and 'P' on steering arms. Tie rods 11H. 1943 (grey). Also power-assisted

Castor angle (Mk 2 and Mk 3) ... ... 3 deg. negative (unladen). Longitudinal rib on upper support arms and 'M' on steering arms. Tie rods 11H.1942 (black or zincplated, red band at fork end)

Setting angles (front):

Power steering:

Swivel hub inclination... ... ... $11\frac{1}{2} \pm \frac{3}{4}$ deg. (unladen)

Camber angle ... ... $2 \pm \frac{3}{4}$ deg. positive

Castor angle ... ... 2 ± 1 deg. positive (unladen). See 'Manual' for details of Mk 2 arms and tie rods

Setting angles (rear):
Wheel alignment ...   .   Parallel (unladen)
Camber ...   . $\frac{1}{2}$ deg. (unladen)

Wheel bearing end float:
Front ...   .   Zero to .004 (.10)
Rear ...   .   Zero to .002 (.05)

Bearing preload:
Upper support arm (front)   ...   .   Equal to torque of 5 to 10 lb in (.058 to .115 kg m)

Radius arm bearing (rear)   ...   .   Equal to torque of 5 to 10 lb in (.058 to .115 kg m)

Suspension arm bearings (front and rear) ...   ...   Metalastik Slipflex DX (Mk 2 and 18/85 with 18H engine)

DRIVE SHAFTS

Joint:
Wheel end   ...   .   Constant velocity
Inner end:
   First type ...   .   Resilient
   Second type ...   .   Resilient with sliding splines
   Automatic transmission   ...   .   Needle roller with sliding splines and flange

BRAKES

Type   ...   .   Foot hydraulic, disc front, drum rear. Mechanical handbrake. Vacuum-servo assisted. Reducing or limiting valve for rear brakes

Brake fluid ...   .   Castrol Girling Brake Fluid Amber

Diameter:
Disc ...   .   9.28 (236). 9.7 (246) on Mk 2S
Drum 9 (229)

Brake lining material:
Front ...   .   M78 (red/green/red/green/red). Ferodo 2430F on Mk 2S
Rear DON242

Wheel cylinder bore (rear):
Early cars...   ...   .   .75 (19), body stamped '$\frac{3}{4}$'
Later cars...   ...   .   .70 (17.8) body stamped '.7'

Master cylinder:
Type (single) ...   .   Centre valve (CV). .75 (19) bore
Type (tandem) ...   .   Tipping valve (CV/TV). .812 (20.6) bore

Servo:
First type ...   .   Girling Powerstop Mk 2
Second type ...   .   Girling Powerstop Mk 2B
Later type (lefthand drive)   ...   ...   Girling Super Vac (direct-acting with single or tandem master cylinder)

'G' valves:
Mounting angle:
   Reducing valve (up to A17S.15245A)   ...   17 deg. (bracket unstamped)
   Reducing valve (later)...   ...   ...   13 deg. (bracket stamped '13')
   Limiting valve ...   .   25 deg.

ELECTRICAL EQUIPMENT

Battery:

11-plate, 12-volt	Lucas D11/13 (50 A/hr at 20 hr rate)
13-plate, 12-volt	Lucas D13 (57 A/hr at 20 hr rate)
Battery earth	Positive, Mk 1 and 2(S). Negative, all Mk 3

Generator (dynamo):

Type	Lucas C40/1 or C40/PS
Maximum output...	22 ± 1 amp
Cut-in speed	1585 rev/min at 13.5-volt
Field resistance	6.0 ohm at 20°C (68°F)
Brush minimum length	.25 (6.5)
Brush spring tension	20 to 34 oz (567 to 964 gm)

Alternator:

Type	Lucas 11 AC
Maximum output (normal)	43 amp
Rotor windings:	
Resistance	3.8 ± .2 ohm at 20°C (68°F)
Current	3.2 amp
Brush minimum length	.156 (4)
Pulley ratio	2 to 1

Regulator (generator):

Type	Lucas RB340
Setting at 20°C (68°F)	14.5 to 15.5 (Mk 1 and 2). Generator at 3000 rev/min
Setting at 20°C (68°F)	14.5 to 15.5 (Mk 2S). Generator at 2250 rev/min
Cut-in voltage	12.7 to 13.3-volt
Drop-off voltage	9.5 to 11.0-volt

Regulator (alternator):

Type	Lucas 4TR
Setting at 20°C (68°F)	13.9 to 14.3-volt. Alternator at 3000 rev/min
Maximum circuit resistance	.1 ohm

Starter:

Type	Lucas M418G
Lock current draw:	
Inertia-type pinion	430 to 450 amp at 7.0 to 7.4-volt
Pre-engaged pinion	465 at 7.0 to 7.4-volt
Brush minimum length	.3125 (7.9)
Brush spring tension	30 to 40 oz (850 to 1130 gm)
Field isolating relay (alternator)	Lucas 6RA
Warning light control (alternator)	Lucas 3AW

Wiper motor (single speed):

Type	Lucas 6WA
Wiper speed	44 to 48 cycles per minute (after 60 seconds)
Running current	2.6 to 3.4 amp
Armature end float	.008 to .012 (.20 to .30)

Wiper motor (two speed):

Type	Lucas 14WA
Current (rack disconnected)	1.5 amp (low), 2 amp (high)
Wipe speed after 60 seconds	46 to 52 cycles (low), 60 to 70 cycles (high)
Armature end float	.002 to .008 (.05 to .20)
Pull to move rack in tube	6 lb (2.7 kg) maximum
Minimum brush length	.18 (4.7)

Horns:

Type	Lucas 9H (or 9H modified), Clear Hooters F725/N
Current consumption	3½ amp (maximum). 4 amp (modified 9H with connectors wide apart)

CAPACITIES

Fuel tank	10½ gal. (12½ U.S. gal., 47.5 litres)

Cooling system:

With heater	9½ pints (11½ U.S. pints, 5.4 litres)
Without heater	8½ pints (10¼ U.S. pints, 4.8 litres)

Manual transmission (from 18AMW/U/H71232, L42259, 18WB):

Refill, with new filter	10¼ pints (12¼ U.S. pints, 5.8 litres)
Refill without filter change	9 pints (10¾ U.S. pints, 5.1 litres)
Primary drive case	1½ pints (1¾ U.S. pints, .8 litre)
Total from dry	12½ pints (15 U.S. pints, 7.1 litres) (all these with 18(457) dipstick blade and strainer with suction pipe)

Manual transmission (from 18AMW/U/H101, L101):

Refill, with new filter	12¾ pints (15¼ U.S. pints, 7.25 litre)
Refill without filter change	11½ pints (13¾ U.S. pints, 6.5 litres)
Primary drive case	1½ pints (1¾ U.S. pints, .8 litre)
Total from dry	15 pints (18 U.S. pints, 8.5 litres)

Automatic transmission:

Engine sump	6½ pints (7¾ U.S. pints, 3.7 litres)
Engine filter	1¼ pints (1½ U.S. pints, .7 litre)
Transmission fluid	13 pints (15½ U.S. pints, 7.4 litres) which includes up to 5 pints (6 U.S. pints, 2.7 litres) in torque converter
Steering rack (manual)	⅓ pint (½ U.S. pint, .2 litre)

Power steering:

Rack	⅓ pint (½ U.S. pint, .2 litre)
Pump	2 pints (2½ U.S. pints, 1.1 litres)

EXHAUST EMISSION CONTROL SYSTEM

Engine type	18H359B, 18H360B, 18H361B, 18H362B, 18H363B and 18H364B
Compression ratio	9.0 to 1
Idling speed...	800 rev/min
Fast idle speed	1100 to 1200 rev/min
Stroboscopic ignition timing	14 deg. BTDC at 1000 rev/min with vacuum pipe disconnected
Distributor serial number	41234
Carburetter(s)	HS6/AUD 314 (manual), AUD 315 (automatic)

Exhaust gas analyser reading:

At engine idling speed	3% CO (maximum)
Air pump test speed	1000 rev/min (engine)

TYRES AND DIMENSIONS

Tyres:

Mk 1	175–13
Mk 2, Mk 2S and Mk 3	165-14

Normal tyre pressures:

Front (Mk 1)	28 lb/sq in (1.97 kg/sq cm)
Front (Mk 2, Mk 2S and Mk 3)	30 lb/sq in (2.1 kg/sq cm)
Rear (Mk 1)	22 lb/sq in (1.55 kg/sq cm)
Rear (Mk 2, Mk 2S and Mk 3)	24 lb/sq in (1.7 kg/sq cm)

Dimensions:

Wheelbase (unladen):

Mk 1	106.125 (2694)
Mk 2 1800 and Mk 2S (manual steering) ...	106.16 (2696)
Mk 2 1800 and 18/85 and Mk 2S (power steering)	106.4 (2703)
Mk 3	105.88 (2689)

Overall length:

Mk 1 Austin/Morris	164.2 (4170)
Mk 1 Wolseley	166.1 (4217)
Mk 2 and Mk 2S	166.67 (4233)
18/85 Mk 2	166.93 (4240)
Mk 3	166.21 (4221)

Overall width:

Mk 1 Austin/Morris	66.75 (1695)
Mk 1 Wolseley	67 (1700)
Mk 2 and 3	66.87 (1699)
Mk 2S	66.68 (1694)

Overall height (unladen):

Mk 1 Austin/Morris	56.25 (1429)
Mk 1 Wolseley	55.5 (1420)
Mk 2 and Mk 2S	56.5 (1435)
Mk 3	56.17 (1427)

Ground clearance (unladen)	6.5 (165)

Track (unladen):

Front	56 (1422)
Rear	55.5 (1410)

TORQUE WRENCH SETTINGS

Dimensions are in lb ft—dimensions in parenthesis are kg m

Engine:

Main bearing nuts	70 (9.7)
Flywheel bolts	40 (5.5)
Big-end bolts	35 (4.8)
Big-end nuts (12-sided)	33 ± 2 (4.5 ± .3). Oil thread
Cylinder head nuts (up to 18AMW/U/H95775, L94704)	40 (5.5)
Cylinder head nuts	45 to 50 (6.2 to 6.9)
Rocker bracket nuts	25 (3.4)
Oil pump to crankcase	14 (1.9)
Transmission case to crankcase	25 (3.4)
Side cover bolts (early)	2 (.3)
Side cover bolts (from 18AMW/U/H37052, L20578)	5 (.7)
Timing cover ($\frac{1}{4}$ inch bolts)	6 (.8)
Timing cover ($\frac{5}{16}$ inch bolts)	14 (1.9)
Crankshaft pulley nut	70 (9.6)
Front plate ($\frac{5}{16}$ inch bolts)	20 (2.8)
Water pump to crankcase	17 (2.3)
Water outlet nuts	8 (1.1)
Rocker cover nuts	4 (.56)
Manifold nuts	15 (2.1)
Oil filter centre bolt	15 (2.1)
Clutch to flywheel	25 to 30 (3.4 to 4.1)
Carburetter flange nuts	15 (2.1)
Float chamber bolt	7.5 (1.0)
Distributor clamp nut	2.5 (.35)
Sparking plugs	30 (4.1)

Manual transmission:

Drain plug	40 to 50 (5.5 to 6.9)
Casing nuts ($\frac{7}{16}$ UNF)	40 to 45 (5.5 to 6.2)
Casing nuts ($\frac{3}{8}$ UNF)	25 (3.46)
Casing nuts ($\frac{5}{16}$ UNF)	18 to 20 (2.5 to 2.7)
Adaptor plate to crankcase ($\frac{5}{16}$ UNF)	18 to 20 (2.5 to 2.7)
Clutch shaft bearing retainer	18 to 20 (2.5 to 2.7)
Adaptor plate to crankcase ($\frac{3}{8}$ UNF)	33 to 35 (4.5 to 4.8)
Flywheel housing to adaptor plate $\frac{5}{16}$ UNF)	33 to 35 (4.5 to 4.8)
Clutch slave cylinder	33 to 35 (4.5 to 4.8)
Flywheel housing to adaptor plate ($\frac{5}{16}$ UNF)	23 to 25 (3.2 to 3.4)
Clutch lever fulcrum shaft	12 to 14 (1.7 to 1.9)
Clutch shaft nut	60 (8.3) minimum
First motion shaft nut (inner and outer)	120 (16.6)
Third motion shaft nut ($\frac{15}{16}$ UNS)	40 (5.5) minimum
Third motion shaft nut (1 inch UNS)	150 to 170 (20.7 to 23.5)
Retaining plate (changespeed cables)	13 to 15 (1.8 to 2.1)
Retaining plate (control box)	10 to 12 (1.4 to 1.7)
Nut for control box rubber mounting	10 to 12 (1.4 to 1.7)
Locknut (cable to jaws)	8 to 10 (1.1 to 1.4)
Mounting bracket to control box	8 to 10 (1.1 to 1.4)

Automatic transmission

Chain cover to converter housing	5 to 9 (.7 to 1.2)
Converter housing to main case	8 to 13 (1.1 to 1.8)
Adaptor plate to converter housing	8 to 13 (1.1 to 1.8)
Drive plate to converter	25 to 30 (3.5 to 4.1)

Final drive:
Driven gear to differential cage ... ... 55 to 60 (7.6 to 8.3)
End cover bolts ... ... 8 to 13 (1.1 to 1.8)
Drive flange nuts ... ... 28 (3.9). New nuts must be used

Steering:
Steering wheel nut ... ... 32 to 37 (4.4 to 5.1)
Coupling flange and power-steering column pinch bolt ... 12 to 15 (1.7 to 2.1)
Tie rod to ball housing locknut ... ... 38 to 43 (5.2 to 5.9)
Nut for steering lever ball joint 35 (4.8)
Steering lever ballpin housing 70 (9.6)
Steering lever to hub nut ... ... 85 (11.7) minimum. Copper-plated key

Suspension:
Front upper arm pivot pin nut 60 (8.3)
Rear radius arm pivot nut 60 (8.3)
Front lower arm pivot pin 45 (6.2)
Swivel axle ballpin nuts 45 (6.2)
Front tie rod to bracket Nylon nut ... ... 45 to 50 (6.2 to 6.9)
Ballpin housing ... ... 70 ± 5 (9.6 ± .7)
Front hub nut 150 (20.7)
Rear hub stub axle nut 40 (5.5)
Drive flange-to-disc bolts ... ... 40 to 45 (5.5 to 6.2)
Brake caliper to swivel hub ... ... 45 to 50 (6.2 to 6.9)
Rear brake adjuster securing nuts ... ... 4 to 5 (.55 to .69)

Brakes
Master cylinder to servo 17 (2.3)
Reservoir to single cylinder ... ... 20 to 25 (2.7 to 3.4)
Tipping valve nut ... ... 35 to 45 (4.8 to 6.2)
Inlet and end plugs ('G' valves) ... ... 25 to 35 (3.4 to 4.8)
Bleed screws ... ... 4 to 6 (.5 to .8)

Road wheels:
Nuts 60 (8.3)

Alternator:
Through-bolts ... ... 45 to 60 lb in (.52 to .58)
Diode heat sink fixings ... ... 25 lb in (.28)
Brush box screws ... ... 10 lb in (.12)

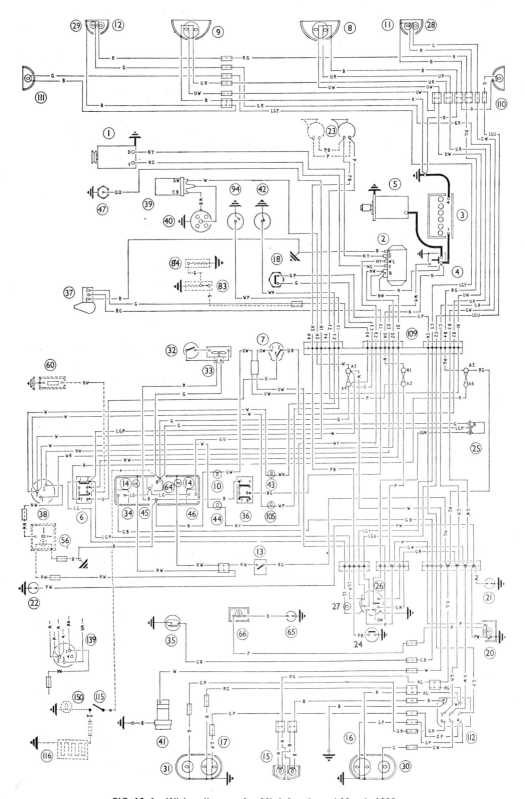

FIG 12:1   Wiring diagram for Mk 1 Austin and Morris 1800

Key to Fig 12:1   1 Generator   2 Control box   3 Battery   4 Starter solenoid   5 Starter motor   6 Lighting switch
7 Headlight dip switch   8 RH headlamp   9 LH headlamp   10 Main-beam warning light   11 RH sidelamp   12 LH sidelamp
13 Panel light switch   14 Panel lights   15 Number-plate lamp   16 RH stop and tail lamp   17 LH stop and tail lamp
18 Stop light switch   19 Fuses   20 Interior lamp   21 RH door switch   22 LH door switch   23 Horn (twin horns when fitted)
24 Horn-push   25 Flasher unit   26 Direction indicator switch with headlamp flasher   27 Direction indicator warning light
28 RH front flasher   29 LH front flasher   30 RH rear flasher   31 LH rear flasher   32 Heater or fresh-air motor switch
33 Heater or fresh-air motor   34 Fuel gauge   35 Fuel gauge tank unit   36 Windscreen wiper switch   37 Windscreen wiper
38 Starter and ignition switch   39 Ignition coil   40 Distributor   41 Fuel pump   42 Oil pressure switch
43 Oil pressure warning light   44 Ignition warning light   45 Speedometer   46 Coolant temperature gauge
47 Coolant temperature transmitter   56 Clock*   60 Radio*   64 Bi-metal instrument voltage stabilizer
65 Luggage compartment lamp switch   66 Luggage compartment lamp   83 Induction heater and thermostat†
84 Suction chamber heater†   94 Oil filter switch   105 Lubrication warning light   109 Multi-connector board with three
35 amp fuses   110 RH repeater flasher   111 LH repeater flasher   112 Day/night direction indicator and stop lamp relay
115 Switch*   116 Demist unit*   139 Ignition-starter switch—4 position alternative (early models)   150 Warning light—
backlight demist*

*Optional extra or accessory   †Special market fitment

Cable Colour Code   **N** Brown   **U** Blue   **R** Red   **P** Purple   **G** Green   **LG** Light Green   **W** White   **Y** Yellow   **B** Black
When a cable has two colour code letters the first denotes the main colour and the second denotes the tracer colour

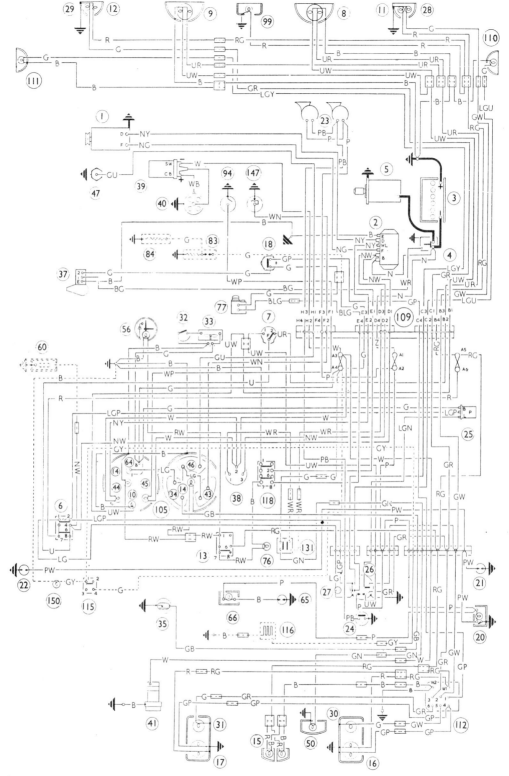

FIG 12:2   Wiring diagram for Mk 1 Wolseley 18/85

Key to Fig 12:2   1 Generator   2 Control box   3 Battery   4 Starter solenoid   5 Starter motor   6 Lighting switch
7 Headlight dip switch   8 RH headlamp   9 LH headlamp   10 Main-beam warning light   11 RH sidelamp   12 LH sidelamp
13 Panel lights switch   14 Panel lights   15 Number-plate lamp   16 RH stop and tail lamp   17 LH stop and tail lamp
18 Stoplight switch   20 Interior lamp   21 RH door switch   22 LH door switch   23 Horns   24 Horn-push   25 Flasher unit
26 Direction indicator switch with headlamp flasher   27 Direction indicator warning light   28 RH front flasher
29 LH front flasher   30 RH rear flasher   31 LH rear flasher   32 Heater or fresh-air motor switch   33 Heater or fresh-air motor
34 Fuel gauge   35 Fuel gauge tank unit   37 Windscreen wiper   38 Starter and ignition switch   39 Ignition coil   40 Distributor
41 Fuel pump   43 Oil pressure gauge   44 Ignition warning light   45 Speedometer   46 Coolant temperature gauge
47 Coolant temperature transmitter   50 Reverse lamp   56 Clock*   60 Radio*   64 Bi-metal instrument voltage stabilizer
65 Luggage compartment lamp switch   66 Luggage compartment lamp   76 Indicator lamp—automatic transmission*
77 Electric windscreen washer   83 Induction heater and thermostat†   84 Suction chamber heater†   94 Oil filter switch
99 Radiator badge lamp   105 Oil filter warning light   109 Multi-connector board with three 35 amp fuses   110 RH repeater flasher
111 LH repeater flasher   112 Day/night direction indicator and stop lamp relay   115 Demist switch*   116 Demist unit*
118 Combined windscreen wiper and washer switch   131 Reverse and automatic transmission safety switches   147 Oil pressure
transmitter   150 Warning light—rear window demist*
                    *Accessory or optional extra   †Special market fitment

Cable Colour Code   **B** Black   **U** Blue   **N** Brown   **G** Green   **LG** Green   **P** Purple   **R** Red   **W** White   **Y** Yellow
          When a cable has two colour code letters the first denotes the main colour and the second denotes the tracer colour

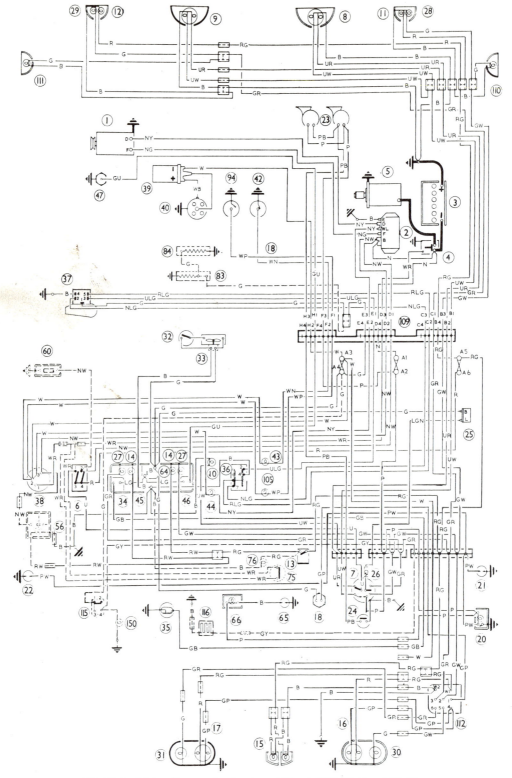

FIG 12:3   Wiring diagram for Austin and Morris 1800 Mk 2 and Mk 2S

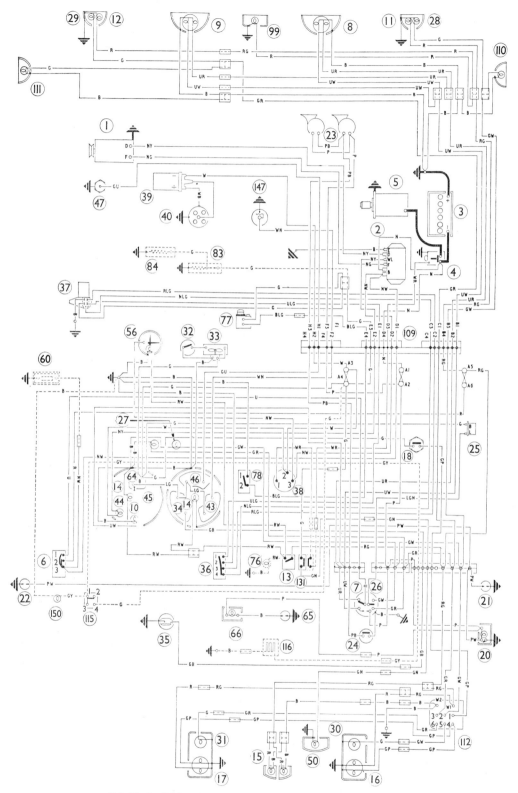

FIG 12:4   Wiring diagram for Wolseley 18/85 Mk 2 and Mk 2S

Key to Fig 12 : 4   1 Generator   2 Regulator   3 Battery   4 Starter solenoid (inertia-type)   5 Starter motor (inertia-type)
6 Lighting switch   7 Headlight dip switch   8 RH headlamp   9 LH headlamp   10 Main-beam warning light   11 RH sidelamp
12 LH sidelamp   13 Panel lights switch   14 Panel lights   15 Number-plate lamp   16 RH stop and tail lamp
17 LH stop and tail lamp   .   18 Stop light switch   20 Interior lamp   21 RH door switch   22 LH door switch
23 Horn (twin horns when fitted)   24 Horn-push   25 Flasher unit   26 Combined direction indicator/headlamp flasher/headlamp
high-low beam/horn-push switch   27 Direction indicator warning light   28 RH front flasher   29 LH front flasher
30 RH rear flasher   31 LH rear flasher   32 Heater or fresh-air motor switch   33 Heater or fresh-air motor   34 Fuel gauge
35 Fuel gauge tank unit   36 Windscreen wiper   37 Windscreen wiper motor   38 Ignition/starter switch   39 Ignition coil
40 Distributor   43 Oil pressure gauge   44 Ignition warning light   45 Speedometer   46 Coolant temperature gauge
47 Coolant temperature transmitter   50 Reverse lamp   56 Clock   60 Radio*   64 Bi-metal instrument voltage stabilizer
65 Luggage compartment lamp switch   66 Luggage compartment lamp   76 Indicator lamp—automatic transmission*
77 Electric windscreen washer   78 Electric windscreen washer switch   83 Induction heater and thermostat†
84 Suction chamber heater†   99 Radiator badge lamp   109 Multi-connector board with three 17 amp fuses
110 RH repeater flasher   111 LH repeater flasher   112 Day/night direction indicator and stop lamp relay   115 Demist switch*
116 Demist unit*   131 Reverse and automatic transmission safety switches   147 Oil pressure transmitter   150 Warning light—
rear window demist*

*Accessory or optional extra   †Special market fitment

Cable Colour Code   **N** Brown   **U** Blue   **R** Red   **P** Purple   **G** Green   **LG** Light Green   **W** White   **Y** Yellow   **B** Black
When a cable has two colour code letters the first denotes the main colour and the second denotes the tracer colour

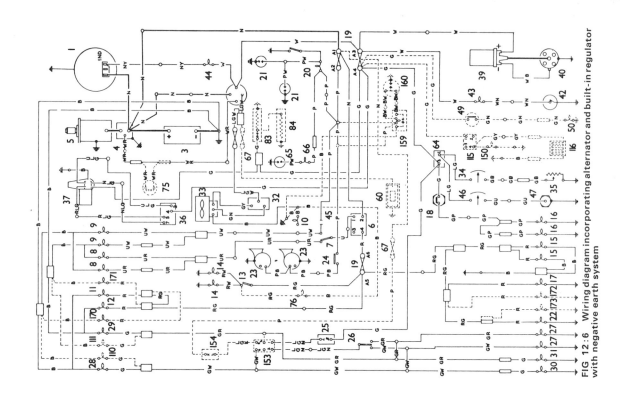

FIG 12 : 6   Wiring diagram incorporating alternator and built-in regulator with negative earth system

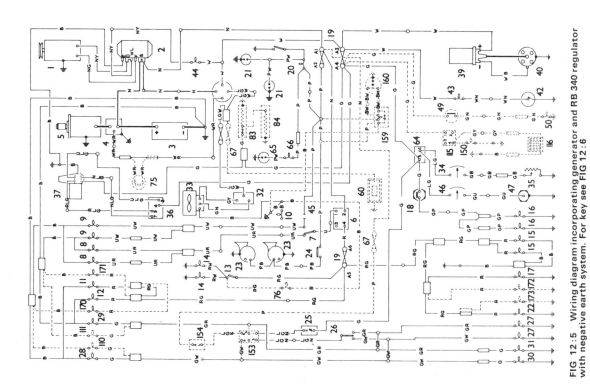

FIG 12 : 5   Wiring diagram incorporating generator and RB 340 regulator with negative earth system. For key see FIG 12 : 6

168

Key to FIGS 12:5 and 12:6

1 Dynamo or alternator
2 Control box—RB340
3 Battery—12 volt
4 Starter solenoid
5 Starter motor
6 Lighting switch
7 Dip switch
8 Headlamp high beam
9 Headlamp low beam
10 Main beam warning lamp
11 R.H. sidelamp
12 L.H. sidelamp
13 Panel lamp switch
14 Panel lamps
15 Number-plate lamps
16 Stop lamps
17 R.H. tail lamp
18 Stop lamp switch
19 Fuse unit: 35 amps
20 Interior light
21 Door switch
22 L.H. tail lamp
23 Horns
24 Horn-push
25 Flasher unit
26 Direction indicator switch
27 Direction indicator warning light
28 R.H. front flasher
29 L.H. front flasher
30 R.H. rear flasher
31 L.H. rear flasher
32 Heater switch
33 Heater motor
34 Fuel gauge tank unit
35 Fuel gauge
36 Wiper switch
37 Wiper motor
38 Ignition switch
39 Ignition coil
40 Distributor
42 Oil pressure switch
43 Oil pressure warning light
44 Ignition warning light
45 Headlamp flasher switch
46 Water temperature gauge
47 Water temperature transmitter
49 Reverse lamp switch*
50 Reverse lamp*
60 Radio
64 Voltage stabilizer
65 Luggage compartment light switch
66 Luggage compartment lamp
67 Line fuse
75 Automatic gearbox safety switch*
76 Automatic gearbox quadrant lamp*
83 Induction heater and thermostat*
84 Suction chamber heater*
110 R.H. repeater flasher
111 L.H. repeater flasher
115 Heated rear window switch*
116 Heated rear window unit*
150 Heated rear window
153 Hazard warning switch*
154 Hazard warning flasher unit*
159 Brake pressure warning lamp and lamp test-push*
160 Brake pressure failure switch*
164 Ballast resistance or cable*
168 Ignition key audible warning buzzer*
169 Ignition key audible warning door switch*
170 R.H. front side-marker lamp*
171 L.H. front side-marker lamp*
172 R.H. rear side-marker lamp*
173 L.H. rear side-marker lamp*

* Optional or special market fitment, circuits shown dotted

Cable Colour Code   N Brown   U Blue   W White   R Red   P Purple   G Green   LG Light Green   O Orange   Y Yellow   K Pink   B Black

When a cable has two colour code letters the first denotes the main colour and the second denotes the tracer colour

Inches		Decimals	Milli-metres	Inches to Millimetres		Millimetres to Inches	
				Inches	mm	mm	Inches
	1/64	.015625	.3969	.001	.0254	.01	.00039
1/32		.03125	.7937	.002	.0508	.02	.00079
	3/64	.046875	1.1906	.003	.0762	.03	.00118
1/16		.0625	1.5875	.004	.1016	.04	.00157
	5/64	.078125	1.9844	.005	.1270	.05	.00197
3/32		.09375	2.3812	.006	.1524	.06	.00236
	7/64	.109375	2.7781	.007	.1778	.07	.00276
1/8		.125	3.1750	.008	.2032	.08	.00315
	9/64	.140625	3.5719	.009	.2286	.09	.00354
5/32		.15625	3.9687	.01	.254	.1	.00394
	11/64	.171875	4.3656	.02	.508	.2	.00787
3/16		.1875	4.7625	.03	.762	.3	.01181
	13/64	.203125	5·1594	.04	1.016	.4	.01575
7/32		.21875	5.5562	.05	1.270	.5	.01969
	15/64	.234375	5.9531	.06	1.524	.6	.02362
1/4		.25	6.3500	.07	1.778	.7	.02756
	17/64	.265625	6.7469	.08	2.032	.8	.03150
9/32		.28125	7.1437	.09	2.286	.9	.03543
	19/64	.296875	7.5406	.1	2.54	1	.03937
5/16		.3125	7.9375	.2	5.08	2	.07874
	21/64	.328125	8.3344	.3	7.62	3	.11811
11/32		.34375	8.7312	.4	10.16	4	.15748
	23/64	.359375	9.1281	.5	12.70	5	.19685
3/8		.375	9.5250	.6	15.24	6	.23622
	25/64	.390625	9.9219	.7	17.78	7	.27559
13/32		.40625	10.3187	.8	20.32	8	.31496
	27/64	.421875	10.7156	.9	22.86	9	.35433
7/16		.4375	11.1125	1	25.4	10	.39370
	29/64	.453125	11.5094	2	50.8	11	.43307
15/32		.46875	11.9062	3	76.2	12	.47244
	31/64	.484375	12.3031	4	101.6	13	.51181
1/2		.5	12.7000	5	127.0	14	.55118
	33/64	.515625	13.0969	6	152.4	15	.59055
17/32		.53125	13.4937	7	177.8	16	.62992
	35/64	.546875	13.8906	8	203.2	17	.66929
9/16		.5625	14.2875	9	228.6	18	.70866
	37/64	.578125	14.6844	10	254.0	19	.74803
19/32		.59375	15.0812	11	279.4	20	.78740
	39/64	.609375	15.4781	12	304.8	21	.82677
5/8		.625	15.8750	13	330.2	22	.86614
	41/64	.640625	16.2719	14	355.6	23	.90551
21/32		.65625	16.6687	15	381.0	24	.94488
	43/64	.671875	17.0656	16	406.4	25	.98425
11/16		.6875	17.4625	17	431.8	26	1.02362
	45/64	.703125	17.8594	18	457.2	27	1.06299
23/32		.71875	18.2562	19	482.6	28	1.10236
	47/64	.734375	18.6531	20	508.0	29	1.14173
3/4		.75	19.0500	21	533.4	30	1.18110
	49/64	.765625	19.4469	22	558.8	31	1.22047
25/32		.78125	19.8437	23	584.2	32	1.25984
	51/64	.796875	20.2406	24	609.6	33	1.29921
13/16		.8125	20.6375	25	635.0	34	1.33858
	53/64	.828125	21.0344	26	660.4	35	1.37795
27/32		.84375	21.4312	27	685.8	36	1.41732
	55/64	.859375	21.8281	28	711.2	37	1.4567
7/8		.875	22.2250	29	736.6	38	1.4961
	57/64	.890625	22.6219	30	762.0	39	1.5354
29/32		.90625	23.0187	31	787.4	40	1.5748
	59/64	.921875	23.4156	32	812.8	41	1.6142
15/16		.9375	23.8125	33	838.2	42	1.6535
	61/64	.953125	24.2094	34	863.6	43	1.6929
31/32		.96875	24.6062	35	889.0	44	1.7323
	63/64	.984375	25.0031	36	914.4	45	1.7717

UNITS	Pints to Litres	Gallons to Litres	Litres to Pints	Litres to Gallons	Miles to Kilometres	Kilometres to Miles	Lbs. per sq. In. to Kg. per sq. Cm.	Kg. per sq. Cm. to Lbs. per sq. In.
1	.57	4.55	1.76	.22	1.61	.62	.07	14.22
2	1.14	9.09	3.52	.44	3.22	1.24	.14	28.50
3	1.70	13.64	5.28	.66	4.83	1.86	.21	42.67
4	2.27	18.18	7.04	.88	6.44	2.49	.28	56.89
5	2.84	22.73	8.80	1.10	8.05	3.11	.35	71.12
6	3.41	27.28	10.56	1.32	9.66	3.73	.42	85.34
7	3.98	31.82	12.32	1.54	11.27	4.35	.49	99.56
8	4.55	36.37	14.08	1.76	12.88	4.97	.56	113.79
9		40.91	15.84	1.98	14.48	5.59	.63	128.00
10		45.46	17.60	2.20	16.09	6.21	.70	142.23
20				4.40	32.19	12.43	1.41	284.47
30				6.60	48.28	18.64	2.11	426.70
40				8.80	64.37	24.85		
50					80.47	31.07		
60					96.56	37.28		
70					112.65	43:50		
80					128.75	49.71		
90					144.84	55.92		
100					160.93	62.14		

UNITS	Lb ft to kgm	Kgm to lb ft	UNITS	Lb ft to kgm	Kgm to lb ft
1	.138	7.233	7	.967	50.631
2	.276	14.466	8	1.106	57.864
3	.414	21.699	9	1.244	65.097
4	.553	28.932	10	1.382	72.330
5	.691	36.165	20	2.765	144.660
6	.829	43.398	30	4.147	216.990

HINTS ON MAINTENANCE AND OVERHAUL

There are few things more rewarding than the restoration of a vehicle's original peak of efficiency and smooth performance.

The following notes are intended to help the owner to reach that state of perfection. Providing that he possesses the basic manual skills he should have no difficulty in performing most of the operations detailed in this manual. It must be stressed, however, that where recommended in the manual, highly-skilled operations ought to be entrusted to experts, who have the necessary equipment, to carry out the work satisfactorily.

Quality of workmanship:

The hazardous driving conditions on the roads to-day demand that vehicles should be as nearly perfect, mechanically, as possible. It is therefore most important that amateur work be carried out with care, bearing in mind the often inadequate working conditions, and also the inferior tools which may have to be used. It is easy to counsel perfection in all things, and we recognize that it may be setting an impossibly high standard. We do, however, suggest that every care should be taken to ensure that a vehicle is as safe to take on the road as it is humanly possible to make it.

Safe working conditions:

Even though a vehicle may be stationary, it is still potentially dangerous if certain sensible precautions are not taken when working on it while it is supported on jacks or blocks. It is indeed preferable not to use jacks alone, but to supplement them with carefully placed blocks, so that there will be plenty of support if the car rolls off the jacks during a strenuous manoeuvre. Axle stands are an excellent way of providing a rigid base which is not readily disturbed. Piles of bricks are a dangerous substitute. Be careful not to get under heavy loads on lifting tackle, the load could fall. It is preferable not to work alone when lifting an engine, or when working underneath a vehicle which is supported well off the ground. To be trapped, particularly under the vehicle, may have unpleasant results if help is not quickly forthcoming. Make some provision, however humble, to deal with fires. Always disconnect a battery if there is a likelihood of electrical shorts. These may start a fire if there is leaking fuel about. This applies particularly to leads which can carry a heavy current, like those in the starter circuit. While on the subject of electricity, we must also stress the danger of using equipment which is run off the mains and which has no earth or has faulty wiring or connections. So many workshops have damp floors, and electrical shocks are of such a nature that it is sometimes impossible to let go of a live lead or piece of equipment due to the muscular spasms which take place.

Work demanding special care:

This involves the servicing of braking, steering and suspension systems. On the road, failure of the braking system may be disastrous. Make quite sure that there can be no possibility of failure through the bursting of rusty brake pipes or rotten hoses, nor to a sudden loss of pressure due to defective seals or valves.

Problems:

The chief problems which may face an operator are:
1 External dirt.
2 Difficulty in undoing tight fixings
3 Dismantling unfamiliar mechanisms.
4 Deciding in what respect parts are defective.
5 Confusion about the correct order for reassembly.
6 Adjusting running clearances.
7 Road testing.
8 Final tuning.

Practical suggestion to solve the problems:

1 Preliminary cleaning of large parts—engines, transmissions, steering, suspensions, etc.—should be carried out before removal from the car. Where road dirt and mud alone are present, wash clean with a high-pressure water jet, brushing to remove stubborn adhesions, and allow to drain and dry. Where oil or grease is also present, wash down with a proprietary compound (Gunk, Teepol etc.,) applying with a stiff brush—an old paint brush is suitable—into all crevices. Cover the distributor and ignition coils with a polythene bag and then apply a strong water jet to clear the loosened deposits. Allow to drain and dry. The assemblies will then be sufficiently clean to remove and transfer to the bench for the next stage.

On the bench, further cleaning can be carried out, first wiping the parts as free as possible from grease with old newspaper. Avoid using rag or cotton waste which can leave clogging fibres behind. Any remaining grease can be removed with a brush dipped in paraffin. If necessary, traces of paraffin can be removed by carbon tetrachloride. Avoid using paraffin or petrol in large quantities for cleaning in enclosed areas, such as garages on account of the high fire risk.

When all exteriors have been cleaned, and not before, dismantling can be commenced. This ensures that dirt will not enter into interiors and orifices revealed by dismantling. In the next phases, where components have to be cleaned, use carbon tetrachloride in preference to petrol and keep the containers covered except when in use. After the components have been cleaned, plug small holes with tapered hard wood plugs cut to size and blank off larger orifices with grease-proof paper and masking tape. Do not use soft wood plugs or matchsticks as they may break.

2 It is not advisable to hammer on the end of a screw thread, but if it must be done, first screw on a nut to protect the thread, and use a lead hammer. This applies particularly to the removal of tapered cotters. Nuts and bolts seem to 'grow' together, especially in exhaust systems. If penetrating oil does not work, try the judicious application of heat, but be careful of starting a fire. Asbestos sheet or cloth is useful to isolate heat.

Tight bushes or pieces of tail-pipe rusted into a silencer can be removed by splitting them with an open-ended hacksaw. Tight screws can sometimes be started by a tap from a hammer on the end of a suitable screwdriver. Many tight fittings will yield to the judicious use of a hammer, but it must be a soft-faced hammer if damage is to be avoided, use a heavy block on the opposite side to absorb shock. Any parts of the steering system which have been damaged should be renewed, as attempts to repair them may lead to cracking and subsequent failure, and steering ball joints should be disconnected using a recommended tool to prevent damage.

3 If often happens that an owner is baffled when trying to dismantle an unfamiliar piece of equipment. So many modern devices are pressed together or assembled by spinning-over flanges, that they must be sawn apart. The intention is that the whole assembly must be renewed. However, parts which appear to be in one piece to the naked eye, may reveal close-fitting joint lines when inspected with a magnifying glass, and, this may provide the necessary clue to dismantling. Left-handed screw threads are used where rotational forces would tend to unscrew a right-handed screw thread.

Be very careful when dismantling mechanisms which may come apart suddenly. Work in an enclosed space where the parts will be contained, and drape a piece of cloth over the device if springs are likely to fly in all directions. Mark everything which might be reassembled in the wrong position, scratched symbols may be used on unstressed parts, or a sequence of tiny dots from a centre punch can be useful. Stressed parts should never be scratched or centre-popped as this may lead to cracking under working conditions. Store parts which look alike in the correct order for reassembly. Never rely upon memory to assist in the assembly of complicated mechanisms, especially when they will be dismantled for a long time, but make notes, and drawings to supplement the diagrams in the manual, and put labels on detached wires. Rust stains may indicate unlubricated wear. This can sometimes be seen round the outside edge of a bearing cup in a universal joint. Look for bright rubbing marks on parts which normally should not make heavy contact. These might prove that something is bent or running out of truth. For example, there might be bright marks on one side of a piston, at the top near the ring grooves, and others at the bottom of the skirt on the other side. This could well be the clue to a bent connecting rod. Suspected cracks can be proved by heating the component in a light oil to approximately 100°C, removing, drying off, and dusting with french chalk, if a crack is present the oil retained in the crack will stain the french chalk.

4 In determining wear, and the degree, against the permissible limits set in the manual, accurate measurement can only be achieved by the use of a micrometer. In many cases, the wear is given to the fourth place of decimals; that is in ten-thousandths of an inch. This can be read by the vernier scale on the barrel of a good micrometer. Bore diameters are more difficult to determine. If, however, the matching shaft is accurately measured, the degree of play in the bore can be felt as a guide to its suitability. In other cases, the shank of a twist drill of known diameter is a handy check.

Many methods have been devised for determining the clearance between bearing surfaces. To-day the best and simplest is by the use of Plastigage, obtainable from most garages. A thin plastic thread is laid between the two surfaces and the bearing is tightened, flattening the thread. On removal, the width of the thread is compared with a scale supplied with the thread and the clearance is read off directly. Sometimes joint faces leak persistently, even after gasket renewal. The fault will then be traceable to distortion, dirt or burrs. Studs which are screwed into soft metal frequently raise burrs at the point of entry. A quick cure for this is to chamfer the edge of the hole in the part which fits over the stud.

5 **Always check a replacement part with the original one before it is fitted.**

If parts are not marked, and the order for reassembly is not known, a little detective work will help. Look for marks which are due to wear to see if they can be mated. Joint faces may not be identical due to manufacturing errors, and parts which overlap may be stained, giving a clue to the correct position. Most fixings leave identifying marks especially if they were painted over on assembly. It is then easier to decide whether a nut, for instance, has a plain, a spring, or a shakeproof washer under it. All running surfaces become 'bedded' together after long spells of work and tiny imperfections on one part will be found to have left corresponding marks on the other. This is particularly true of shafts and bearings and even a score on a cylinder wall will show on the piston.

6 Checking end float or rocker clearances by feeler gauge may not always give accurate results because of wear. For instance, the rocker tip which bears on a valve stem may be deeply pitted, in which case the feeler will simply be bridging a depression. Thrust washers may also wear depressions in opposing faces to make accurate measurement difficult. End float is then easier to check by using a dial gauge. It is common practice to adjust end play in bearing assemblies, like front hubs with taper rollers, by doing up the axle nut until the hub becomes stiff to turn and then backing it off a little. Do not use this method with ballbearing hubs as the assembly is often preloaded by tightening the axle nut to its fullest extent. If the splitpin hole will not line up, file the base of the nut a little.

Steering assemblies often wear in the straight-ahead position. If any part is adjusted, make sure that it remains free when moved from lock to lock. Do not be surprised if an assembly like a steering gearbox, which is known to be carefully adjusted outside the car, becomes stiff when it is bolted in place. This will be due to distortion of the case by the pull of the mounting bolts, particularly if the mounting points are not all touching together. This problem may be met in other equipment and is cured by careful attention to the alignment of mounting points.

When a spanner is stamped with a size and A/F it means that the dimension is the width between the jaws and has no connection with ANF, which is the designation for the American National Fine thread. Coarse threads like Whitworth are rarely used on cars to-day except for studs which screw into soft aluminium or cast iron. For this reason it might be found that the top end of a cylinder head stud has a fine thread and the lower end a coarse thread to screw into the cylinder block. If the car has mainly UNF threads then it is likely that any coarse threads will be UNC, which are not the same as Whitworth. Small sizes have the same number of threads in Whitworth and UNC, but in the $\frac{1}{2}$ inch size for example, there are twelve threads to the inch in the former and thirteen in the latter.

7 After a major overhaul, particularly if a great deal of work has been done on the braking, steering and suspension systems, it is advisable to approach the problem of testing with care. If the braking system has been overhauled, apply heavy pressure to the brake pedal and get a second operator to check every possible source of leakage. The brakes may work extremely well, but a leak could cause complete failure after a few miles.

Do not fit the hub caps until every wheel nut has been checked for tightness, and make sure the tyre pressures are correct. Check the levels of coolant, lubricants and hydraulic fluids. Being satisfied that all is well, take the car on the road and test the brakes at once. Check the steering and the action of the handbrake. Do all this at moderate speeds on quiet roads, and make sure there is no other vehicle behind you when you try a rapid stop.

Finally, remember that many parts settle down after a time, so check for tightness of all fixings after the car has been on the road for a hundred miles or so.

8 It is useless to tune an engine which has not reached its normal running temperature. In the same way, the tune of an engine which is stiff after a rebore will be different when the engine is again running free. Remember too, that rocker clearances on pushrod operated valve gear will change when the cylinder head nuts are tightened after an initial period of running with a new head gasket.

Trouble may not always be due to what seems the obvious cause. Ignition, carburation and mechanical condition are interdependent and spitting back through the carburetter, which might be attributed to a weak mixture, can be caused by a sticking inlet valve.

For one final hint on tuning, never adjust more than one thing at a time or it will be impossible to tell which adjustment produced the desired result.

NOTES

GLOSSARY OF TERMS

Allen key — Cranked wrench of hexagonal section for use with socket head screws.

Alternator — Electrical generator producing alternating current. Rectified to direct current for battery charging.

Ambient temperature — Surrounding atmospheric temperature.

Annulus — Used in engineering to indicate the outer ring gear of an epicyclic gear train.

Armature — The shaft carrying the windings, which rotates in the magnetic field of a generator or starter motor. That part of a solenoid or relay which is activated by the magnetic field.

Axial — In line with, or pertaining to, an axis.

Backlash — Play in meshing gears.

Balance lever — A bar where force applied at the centre is equally divided between connections at the ends.

Banjo axle — Axle casing with large diameter housing for the crownwheel and differential.

Bendix pinion — A self-engaging and self-disengaging drive on a starter motor shaft.

Bevel pinion — A conical shaped gearwheel, designed to mesh with a similar gear with an axis usually at 90 deg. to its own.

bhp — Brake horse power, measured on a dynamometer.

bmep — Brake mean effective pressure. Average pressure on a piston during the working stroke.

Brake cylinder — Cylinder with hydraulically operated piston(s) acting on brake shoes or pad(s).

Brake regulator — Control valve fitted in hydraulic braking system which limits brake pressure to rear brakes during heavy braking to prevent rear wheel locking.

Camber — Angle at which a wheel is tilted from the vertical.

Capacitor — Modern term for an electrical condenser. Part of distributor assembly, connected across contact breaker points, acts as an interference suppressor.

Castellated — Top face of a nut, slotted across the flats, to take a locking splitpin.

Castor — Angle at which the kingpin or swivel pin is tilted when viewed from the side.

cc — Cubic centimetres. Engine capacity is arrived at by multiplying the area of the bore in sq cm by the stroke in cm by the number of cylinders.

Clevis — U-shaped forked connector used with a clevis pin, usually at handbrake connections.

Collet — A type of collar, usually split and located in a groove in a shaft, and held in place by a retainer. The arrangement used to retain the spring(s) on a valve stem in most cases.

Commutator — Rotating segmented current distributor between armature windings and brushes in generator or motor.

Compression ratio — The ratio, or quantitative relation, of the total volume (piston at bottom of stroke) to the unswept volume (piston at top of stroke) in an engine cylinder.

Condenser — See capacitor.

Core plug — Plug for blanking off a manufacturing hole in a casting.

Crownwheel — Large bevel gear in rear axle, driven by a bevel pinion attached to the propeller shaft. Sometimes called a 'ring gear'.

'C'-spanner — Like a 'C' with a handle. For use on screwed collars without flats, but with slots or holes.

Damper — Modern term for shock-absorber, used in vehicle suspension systems to damp out spring oscillations.

Depression — The lowering of atmospheric pressure as in the inlet manifold and carburetter.

Dowel — Close tolerance pin, peg, tube, or bolt, which accurately locates mating parts.

Drag link — Rod connecting steering box drop arm (pitman arm) to nearest front wheel steering arm in certain types of steering systems.

Dry liner — Thinwall tube pressed into cylinder bore

Dry sump — Lubrication system where all oil is scavenged from the sump, and returned to a separate tank.

Dynamo — See Generator.

Electrode — Terminal, part of an electrical component, such as the points or 'Electrodes' of a sparking plug.

Electrolyte — In lead-acid car batteries a solution of sulphuric acid and distilled water.

End float — The axial movement between associated parts, end play.

EP — Extreme pressure. In lubricants, special grades for heavily loaded bearing surfaces, such as gear teeth in a gearbox, or crownwheel and pinion in a rear axle.

Fade	Of brakes. Reduced efficiency due to overheating.
Field coils	Windings on the polepieces of motors and generators.
Fillets	Narrow finishing strips usually applied to interior bodywork.
First motion shaft	Input shaft from clutch to gearbox.
Fullflow filter	Filters in which all the oil is pumped to the engine. If the element becomes clogged, a bypass valve operates to pass unfiltered oil to the engine.
FWD	Front wheel drive.
Gear pump	Two meshing gears in a close fitting casing. Oil is carried from the inlet round the outside of both gears in the spaces between the gear teeth and casing to the outlet, the meshing gear teeth prevent oil passing back to the inlet, and the oil is forced through the outlet port.
Generator	Modern term for 'Dynamo'. When rotated produces electrical current.
Grommet	A ring of protective or sealing material. Can be used to protect pipes or leads passing through bulkheads.
Grubscrew	Fully threaded headless screw with screwdriver slot. Used for locking, or alignment purposes.
Gudgeon pin	Shaft which connects a piston to its connecting rod. Sometimes called 'wrist pin', or 'piston pin'.
Halfshaft	One of a pair transmitting drive from the differential.
Helical	In spiral form. The teeth of helical gears are cut at a spiral angle to the side faces of the gearwheel.
Hot spot	Hot area that assists vapourisation of fuel on its way to cylinders. Often provided by close contact between inlet and exhaust manifolds.
HT	High Tension. Applied to electrical current produced by the ignition coil for the sparking plugs.
Hydrometer	A device for checking specific gravity of liquids. Used to check specific gravity of electrolyte.
Hypoid bevel gears	A form of bevel gear used in the rear axle drive gears. The bevel pinion meshes below the centre line of the crownwheel, giving a lower propeller shaft line.
Idler	A device for passing on movement. A free running gear between driving and driven gears. A lever transmitting track rod movement to a side rod in steering gear.
Impeller	A centrifugal pumping element. Used in water pumps to stimulate flow.
Journals	Those parts of a shaft that are in contact with the bearings.
Kingpin	The main vertical pin which carries the front wheel spindle, and permits steering movement. May be called 'steering pin' or 'swivel pin'.
Layshaft	The shaft which carries the laygear in the gearbox. The laygear is driven by the first motion shaft and drives the third motion shaft according to the gear selected. Sometimes called the 'countershaft' or 'second motion shaft.'
lb ft	A measure of twist or torque. A pull of 10 lb at a radius of 1 ft is a torque of 10 lb ft.
lb/sq in	Pounds per square inch.
Little-end	The small, or piston end of a connecting rod. Sometimes called the 'small-end'.
LT	Low Tension. The current output from the battery.
Mandrel	Accurately manufactured bar or rod used for test or centring purposes.
Manifold	A pipe, duct, or chamber, with several branches.
Needle rollers	Bearing rollers with a length many times their diameter.
Oil bath	Reservoir which lubricates parts by immersion. In air filters, a separate oil supply for wetting a wire mesh element to hold the dust.
Oil wetted	In air filters, a wire mesh element lightly oiled to trap and hold airborne dust.
Overlap	Period during which inlet and exhaust valves are open together.
Panhard rod	Bar connected between fixed point on chassis and another on axle to control sideways movement.
Pawl	Pivoted catch which engages in the teeth of a ratchet to permit movement in one direction only.
Peg spanner	Tool with pegs, or pins, to engage in holes or slots in the part to be turned.
Pendant pedals	Pedals with levers that are pivoted at the top end.
Phillips screwdriver	A cross-point screwdriver for use with the cross-slotted heads of Phillips screws.
Pinion	A small gear, usually in relation to another gear.
Piston-type damper	Shock absorber in which damping is controlled by a piston working in a closed oil-filled cylinder.
Preloading	Preset static pressure on ball or roller bearings not due to working loads.
Radial	Radiating from a centre, like the spokes of a wheel.

Radius rod	Pivoted arm confining movement of a part to an arc of fixed radius.
Ratchet	Toothed wheel or rack which can move in one direction only, movement in the other being prevented by a pawl.
Ring gear	A gear tooth ring attached to outer periphery of flywheel. Starter pinion engages with it during starting.
Runout	Amount by which rotating part is out of true.
Semi-floating axle	Outer end of rear axle halfshaft is carried on bearing inside axle casing. Wheel hub is secured to end of shaft.
Servo	A hydraulic or pneumatic system for assisting, or, augmenting a physical effort. See 'Vacuum Servo'.
Setscrew	One which is threaded for the full length of the shank.
Shackle	A coupling link, used in the form of two parallel pins connected by side plates to secure the end of the master suspension spring and absorb the effects of deflection.
Shell bearing	Thinwalled steel shell lined with anti-friction metal. Usually semi-circular and used in pairs for main and big-end bearings.
Shock absorber	See 'Damper'.
Silentbloc	Rubber bush bonded to inner and outer metal sleeves.
Socket-head screw	Screw with hexagonal socket for an Allen key.
Solenoid	A coil of wire creating a magnetic field when electric current passes through it. Used with a soft iron core to operate contacts or a mechanical device.
Spur gear	A gear with teeth cut axially across the periphery.
Stub axle	Short axle fixed at one end only.
Tachometer	An instrument for accurate measurement of rotating speed. Usually indicates in revolutions per minute.

TDC	Top Dead Centre. The highest point reached by a piston in a cylinder, with the crank and connecting rod in line.
Thermostat	Automatic device for regulating temperature. Used in vehicle coolant systems to open a valve which restricts circulation at low temperature.
Third motion shaft	Output shaft of gearbox.
Threequarter floating axle	Outer end of rear axle halfshaft flanged and bolted to wheel hub, which runs on bearing mounted on outside of axle casing. Vehicle weight is not carried by the axle shaft.
Thrust bearing or washer	Used to reduce friction in rotating parts subject to axial loads.
Torque	Turning or twisting effort. See 'lb ft'.
Track rod	The bar(s) across the vehicle which connect the steering arms and maintain the front wheels in their correct alignment.
UJ	Universal joint. A coupling between shafts which permits angular movement.
UNF	Unified National Fine screw thread.
Vacuum servo	Device used in brake system, using difference between atmospheric pressure and inlet manifold depression to operate a piston which acts to augment brake pressure as required. See 'Servo'.
Venturi	A restriction or 'choke' in a tube, as in a carburetter, used to increase velocity to obtain a reduction in pressure.
Vernier	A sliding scale for obtaining fractional readings of the graduations of an adjacent scale.
Welch plug	A domed thin metal disc which is partially flattened to lock in a recess. Used to plug core holes in castings.
Wet liner	Removable cylinder barrel, sealed against coolant leakage, where the coolant is in direct contact with the outer surface.
Wet sump	A reservoir attached to the crankcase to hold the lubricating oil.

NOTES

INDEX

NOTES

Alfa Romeo Giulia 1600,
1750, 2000 1962 on
Aston Martin 1921-58
Auto Union Audi 70, 80,
Super 90, 1966-72
Audi 100 1969 on
Austin, Morris etc.
1100 Mk. 1 1962-67
Austin, Morris etc. 1100
Mk. 2, 3, 1300 Mk. 1, 2, 3
America 1968 on
Austin A30, A35, A40
Farina 1951-67
Austin A55 Mk. 2, A60
1958-69
Austin A99, A110 1959-68
Austin J4 1960 on
Austin Maxi 1969 on
Austin, Morris 1800
1964 on
Austin, Morris 2200 1972 on
Austin Kimberley, Tasman
1970 on
Austin, Morris 1300, 1500
Nomad 1969 on
BMC 3 (Austin A50, A55
Mk. 1, Morris Oxford
2, 3 1954-59)
Austin Healey 100/6,
3000 1956-68
Austin Healey, MG
Sprite, Midget 1958 on
Bedford CA Mk2 1964-69
Bedford CF Vans 1969 on
Bedford Beagle HA Vans
1964 on
BMW 1600 1966 on
BMW 1800 1964-71
BMW 2000, 2002 1966 on

Chevrolet Corvair 1960-69
Chevrolet Corvette V8
1957-65
Chevrolet Corvette V8
1965 on
Chevrolet Vega 2300
1970 on
Chrysler Valiant V8
1965 on
Chrysler Valiant Straight
Six 1966-70
Citroen DS 19, ID 19
1955-66
Citroen ID 19, DS 19, 20,
21 1966 on
Citroen Dyane Ami 1964 on

Daf 31, 32, 33, 44, 55
1961 on
Datsun 1000, 1200 1968 on
Datsun 1300, 1400, 1600
1968 on
Datsun 240C 1971 on
Datsun 240Z Sport 1970 on

Fiat 124 1966 on
Fiat 124 Sport 1966 on
Fiat 125 1967-72
Fiat 127 1971 on
Fiat 128 1969 on
Fiat 500 1957 on
Fiat 600, 600D 1955-69
Fiat 850 1964 on
Fiat 1100 1957-69

Fiat 1300, 1500 1961-67
Ford Anglia Prefect 100E
1953-62
Ford Anglia 105E, Prefect
107E 1959-67
Ford Capri 1300, 1600 OHV
1968 on
Ford Capri 1300, 1600,
2000 OHC 1972 on
Ford Capri 2000 V4, 3000 V6
1969 on
Ford Classic, Capri
1961-64
Ford Consul, Zephyr,
Zodiac, 1, 2 1950-62
Ford Corsair Straight
Four 1963-65
Ford Corsair V4 1965-68
Ford Corsair V4 2000
1969-70
Ford Cortina 1962-66
Ford Cortina 1967-68
Ford Cortina 1969-70
Ford Cortina Mk. 3
1970 on
Ford Escort 1967 on
Ford Falcon 6 1964-70
Ford Falcon XK, XL
1960-63
Ford Falcon 6 XR/XA
1966 on
Ford Falcon V8 (U.S.A.)
1965-71
Ford Falcon V8 (Aust.)
1966 on
Ford Pinto 1970 on
Ford Maverick 6 1969 on
Ford Maverick V8 1970 on
Ford Mustang 6 1965 on
Ford Mustang V8 1965 on
Ford Thames 10, 12,
15 cwt 1957-65
Ford Transit V4 1965 on
Ford Zephyr Zodiac Mk. 3
1962-66
Ford Zephyr Zodiac V4,
V6, Mk. 4 1966-72
Ford Consul, Granada
1972 on

Hillman Avenger 1970 on
Hillman Hunter 1966 on
Hillman Imp 1963-68
Hillman Imp 1969 on
Hillman Minx 1 to 5
1956-65
Hillman Minx 1965-67
Hillman Minx 1966-70
Hillman Super Minx
1961-65
Holden V8 1968 on
Holden Straight Six
1948-66
**Holden Straight Six
1966 on**
Holden Torana 4 Series
HB 1967-69

Jaguar XK120, 140, 150,
Mk. 7, 8, 9 1948-61
Jaguar 2.4, 3.4, 3.8 Mk.
1, 2 1955-69
Jaguar 'E' Type 1961-72

Jaguar 'S' Type 420
1963-68
Jaguar XJ6 1968 on
Jowett Javelin Jupiter
1947-53
Landrover 1, 2 1948-61
Landrover 2, 2a, 3 1959 on
Mazda 616 1970 on
Mazda 808, 818 1972 on
Mazda 1200, 1300 1969 on
Mazda 1500, 1800 1967 on
Mercedes-Benz 190b,
190c, 200 1959-68
Mercedes-Benz 220
1959-65
Mercedes-Benz 220/8
1968 on
Mercedes-Benz 230
1963-68
Mercedes-Benz 250
1965-67
Mercedes-Benz 250
1968 on
Mercedes-Benz 280
1968 on
MG TA to TF 1936-55
MGA MGB 1955-68
MGB 1969 on
Mini 1959 on
Mini Cooper 1961-72
Morgan Four 1936-72
Morris Marina 1971 on
Morris (Aust) Marina
1972 on
Morris Minor 2, 1000
1952-71
Morris Oxford 5, 6 1959-71
NSU 1000 1963-72
NSU Prinz 1 to 4 1957-72
Opel Ascona, Manta
1970 on
Opel GT 1900 1968 on
Opel Kadett, Olympia 993cc
1078cc 1962 on
Opel Kadett, Olympia 1492,
1698, 1897cc 1967 on
Opel Rekord C 1966-72
Peugeot 204 1965 on
Peugeot 304 1970 on
Peugeot 404 1960 on
Peugeot 504 1968 on
Porsche 356A, B, C 1957-65
Porsche 911 1964-69
Porsche 912 1965-69
Porsche 914S 1969 on
Reliant Regal 1952-73
Renault R4, R4L, 4 1961 on
Renault 6 1968 on
Renault 8, 10, 1100 1962-71
Renault 12, 1969 on
Renault R16 1965 on
Renault Dauphine
Floride 1957-67
Renault Caravelle 1962-68
Rover 60 to 110 1953-64
Rover 2000 1963-73
Rover 3 Litre 1958-67
Rover 3500, 3500S 1968 on
Saab 95, 96, Sport
1960-68
Saab 99 1969 on
Saab V4 1966 on

Simca 1000 1961 on
Simca 1100 1967 on
Simca 1300, 1301, 1500,
1501 1963 on
Skoda One (440, 445, 450)
1955-70
Sunbeam Rapier Alpine
1955-65
Toyota Carina, Celica
1971 on
Toyota Corolla 1100,
1200 1967 on
Toyota Corona 1500 Mk. 1
1965-70
Toyota Corona Mk. 2
1969 on
Triumph TR2, TR3, TR3A
1952-62
Triumph TR4, TR4A
1961-67
Triumph TR5, TR250,
TR6 1967 on
Triumph 1300, 1500
1965-73
Triumph 2000 Mk. 1, 2.5 PI
Mk. 1 1963-69
Triumph 2000 Mk. 2, 2.5 PI
Mk. 2 1969 on
Triumph Dolomite 1972 on
Triumph Herald 1959-68
Triumph Herald 1969-71
Triumph Spitfire, Vitesse
1962-68
Triumph Spitfire Mk. 3, 4
1969 on
Triumph GT6, Vitesse
2 Litre 1969 on
Triumph Toledo 1970 on
Vauxhall Velox, Cresta
1957-72
Vauxhall Victor 1, 2, FB
1957-64
Vauxhall Victor 101
1964-67
Vauxhall Victor FD 1600,
2000 1967-72
Vauxhall Victor 3300,
Ventora 1968-72
Vauxhall Victor FE
Ventora 1972 on
Vauxhall Viva HA 1963-66
Vauxhall Viva HB 1966-70
Vauxhall Viva, HC Firenza
1971 on
Volkswagen Beetle 1954-67
Volkswagen Beetle 1968 on
Volkswagen 1500 1961-66
Volkswagen 1600 Fastback
1965-73
Volkswagen Transporter
1954-67
Volkswagen Transporter
1968 on
Volkswagen 411 1968-72
Volvo 120 series 1961-70
Volvo 140 series 1966 on
Volvo 160 series 1968 on
Volvo 1800 1960-73

NOTES